SNOWFALL AND SECOND CHANCES

Is it ever too late for a second chance?

Jeremy Lewis left Thistle Bay two decades ago to join the Marines. But five years ago, his one-night stand with childhood sweetheart Rebecca resulted in their twin boys. Now Jeremy is leaving the Marines and is determined to reclaim his family – including Rebecca.

Rebecca Knight is used to doing everything for everyone. She puts herself second, always. Being a single mother and working in her family's business full-time has been tough for her. With Jeremy moving back to town, Rebecca had thought it was finally time for their second chance. But with big changes at work, she doesn't have the time needed to make a relationship work.

While Jeremy focuses on building his new business, Rebecca finds herself torn between her career and love.

Can a relationship that's been neglected for so long still have a chance?

Snowfall and Second Chances is part of the Thistle Bay series. It can be read as a standalone novel, but it contains a spoiler if you haven't read *Sunrise in Thistle Bay*.

SNOWFALL AND SECOND CHANCES

CLAIRE ANDERS

Copyright © 2023 by Claire Anders

Claire Anders has asserted her right to be identified as the author of this work in accordance with the Copyright, Designs and Patents Act 1988.

This novel is a work of fiction. Names and characters are the product of the author's imagination and any resemblance to actual persons, living or dead, is entirely coincidental.

All rights reserved. No part of this book may be reproduced or transmitted in any form or by any means, mechanical or electronic, including photocopying or recording, or by any information storage and retrieval system, or transmitted by email without the written permission of the publisher, except for the use of brief quotations.

A CIP catalogue record for this book is available from the British Library.

Published by TLC Publications Ltd

Cover Design by MiblArt

ISBN 978-1-7395389-1-0 (ebook)

ISBN 978-1-7395389-0-3 (print)

SNOWFALL AND SECOND CHANCES

CLAIRE ANDERS

Copyright © 2023 by Claire Anders

Claire Anders has asserted her right to be identified as the author of this work in accordance with the Copyright, Designs and Patents Act 1988.

This novel is a work of fiction. Names and characters are the product of the author's imagination and any resemblance to actual persons, living or dead, is entirely coincidental.

All rights reserved. No part of this book may be reproduced or transmitted in any form or by any means, mechanical or electronic, including photocopying or recording, or by any information storage and retrieval system, or transmitted by email without the written permission of the publisher, except for the use of brief quotations.

A CIP catalogue record for this book is available from the British Library.

Published by TLC Publications Ltd

Cover Design by MiblArt

ISBN 978-1-7395389-1-0 (ebook)

ISBN 978-1-7395389-0-3 (print)

For my mum and dad, who know how to make Christmas merry and bright

1

Rebecca Knight had a habit of lying. She'd been doing it since she was a teenager. Only she didn't consider it lying. Lying was an unkind act that she was teaching her five-year-old twins not to do. What she did was different.

Rebecca told people what they needed to hear. And on most days, that felt like the kindest thing. So when she'd told her boys that their father was coming home tomorrow morning, it wasn't a lie. It was what they needed to hear to get a full night's sleep. Telling Jeremy he couldn't come over tonight was harsh after not having seen his children for three months, but it was best for everyone. The boys would enjoy a morning with their dad rather than a crotchety hour before bed; Jeremy would see his children as their most adorable selves rather than grumpy little gremlins; and daylight would stop Rebecca from doing something with Jeremy that she really didn't want to do.

Jeremy had been clear that he wasn't just here for the boys. He was here for her. But they hadn't been a couple since they were teenagers. Sure, they'd done some very couple-like stuff in the intervening years, including the night in London that had resulted in her pregnancy, but they had two five-year-olds to consider now and that meant being careful, didn't it? If she and Jeremy couldn't make it work as a couple, then they would shield their children from that. And the only way Rebecca knew how was to take things slowly so they could get out without either of them getting too hurt if they had to go their separate ways.

Not that she planned to fail. She was just realistic. Relationships have a high rate of failure, and she and Jeremy had already failed at their relationship once before. When Jeremy had joined the Royal Marines and Rebecca had gone to university, their relationship had ended. Their focus needed to be elsewhere.

But circumstances were different now. After floundering for the last few years trying to balance motherhood and supporting her father with running their family business, life was stable. The boys were in their first year of school and that had made it easier to create a schedule that Rebecca could control. And Jeremy had retired from the Royal Marines. He wasn't just on leave. He was coming home. Now was finally the right time for her and Jeremy. If they had a future together, it started tomorrow, and she would not risk ruining it by moving too fast.

She glanced at the time. After-school club closed in half an hour. Rebecca scooped up her phone, a mug of what was now lukewarm coffee, and her paper diary. Gone were the days when her to-do list existed only in her head. These days she had a physical diary, an online calendar synced across all of her devices, and a weekly planner on the wall in the kitchen to keep track of Oliver and Liam's activities.

Her stiletto heels clacked on the floor as she strode to the compact office Ryan had chosen in their Thistle Bay headquarters. The scent of chocolate filled the corridors, a sweet and inviting aroma from the factory floor. Ryan's door was ajar, but inside, his office still had the musty odour of a windowless room. From her own office she could see the full length of Main Street stretching down to the sandy beach and the North Sea, but she almost never looked long enough to admire the beauty of her town. Rebecca dropped into one of the chairs in front of Ryan's desk and flipped open her diary. 'Shall we compare notes for next week?'

Ryan ran a hand through his messy blond hair, unlocked his phone, and pressed a few buttons. The business had expanded rapidly over the last couple of years, forcing Rebecca and her brother, Ryan, to work closely, but they had each found their place and had settled into a rhythm that worked. 'I'm in Edinburgh most of the week. We've got the first full production run on the hazelnut swirls on Monday. Wednesday is the next meeting with the conference space provider. Dial-in thankfully.'

Rebecca sighed and took a swig of her tepid coffee. 'I've never had so many face-to-face meetings about one contract. Harry Mitchell is now just nit-picking over words that don't matter.'

'Jane wants the contract as much as we do. It's just the quirk of dealing with family businesses. You know it's bad when even his own daughter is fed up with him. She told me he's just old-fashioned, but she thinks we're close to signing. Apparently, he likes to look people in the eye when doing business. I can go alone if you have somewhere else you'd rather be.'

'No, sorry, I'll be there. Cat won't be. She's still not keen to get involved.'

Cat Radcliffe had given them the idea to partner with a conference centre provider. Thistle Bay Chocolate Company would supply chocolates with branding bespoke to the companies using the event space. It gave the business another way to diversify their income while still focusing on their core product – chocolate. Rebecca had hoped it would help the strain in their relationship if she and Cat could spend a bit more time together.

'How's it going with you two?'

Rebecca sank back in the chair. 'Better,' she said with a confidence she didn't feel. She caught a glimpse of Ryan's doubt. 'Really,' she added, sticking with her lie for Ryan's sake. Not telling Cat about her biological link to the Knight family when she'd first arrived in town had been a mistake. The plan had been to tell her she was a Knight, that Alan and Catherine were her biological parents, as soon as she'd arrived in town. Alan had planned to explain everything: Catherine's breakdown, the mix-up at the hospital, the decisions he had made when he'd first found Cat, and then losing track of her in the foster care system after her adoptive parents had died. Rebecca, Ryan, and their other two sisters had known it wouldn't be easy. But none of them had expected their father's reaction.

The heartbreak he'd suffered thirty years before had resurfaced, and it had been painful to watch. Rebecca had insisted they give him time to process everything before any of them told Cat the truth. On this occasion, she'd made the wrong call. She would have to keep trying to make amends for that and build a relationship with Cat. Ryan didn't need to know how challenging that was proving to be. She didn't want him worrying that the tension was going to drive Cat away now that they'd finally found her again.

Rebecca looked back at her diary. 'I need to leave Edinburgh before noon on Wednesday. There's a Christmas fundraising fair at the boys' school and I'm on the tombola stall.' Ryan laughed and Rebecca waved her hand towards him. 'I know, I know. My first instinct was to write a cheque, but the boys begged me to come along.'

'How did going along turn into you handing out bottles of bubble bath and booze?'

'Joanne Ferrier is on the organising committee and I made the mistake of telling her I was going.'

Ryan laughed and shook his head. 'I can't quite see you folding raffle tickets into little squares. This is payback because you two didn't like each other in high school.'

'We liked each other,' Rebecca insisted. Ryan raised an eyebrow. 'Maybe we weren't best friends, but she's assured me everything is ready. I just need to turn up, take the cash, and help people to find their prizes. And it could have been worse. I could have been on the cake stand serving sticky kids hyped up on sugar.'

'That's true.' Ryan locked his phone and tossed it onto the table in front of him. 'I'm going to crash at Dad's tonight, so I'll work from here tomorrow morning. I haven't decided if I'll stay for the weekend or not.'

'Yeah, thanks for accommodating the date change for the marketing meeting. I had to reschedule a few things and the original slot was just too much of a squeeze.'

'No problem. What time are you heading off to collect Jeremy?'

Rebecca kept her gaze down and flicked forwards a few pages in her diary. 'Arthur's collecting Jeremy.'

'Why?'

'I had the marketing meeting this afternoon.'

'Oh, how inconvenient for you.' The sarcasm in her brother's tone was as subtle as their office fire alarm.

Arthur was the company's driver. It was literally his job to drive people around. Collecting the father of her children at the airport wasn't strictly a business-related activity, but she couldn't collect him herself because she had work to do. Rebecca flicked to next week in her diary. She really didn't have time for the meeting in that week. She could have pushed it into the following week, but that week was already looking just as busy. 'Besides, Jeremy isn't back until the kids' bedtime, assuming his flight is on time. He's coming over first thing tomorrow morning.'

'Over where?'

'My house.'

'Your house? Isn't he staying with you guys?'

'Why would he?'

'I can think of a couple of reasons. Not to mention he stays with you every time he's home.'

Jeremy crashing at her house had been their pattern since the boys had been born. They didn't want to waste any of Jeremy's precious time with his sons. When Jeremy stayed, everyone was clear it was only for a few days, a few weeks at most. Explaining to Oliver and Liam why their dad was leaving had been easy. Those days were gone, as was the *Daddy has to go back to work* explanation. 'It would be confusing for the boys when Jeremy left again. He reckons he'll have the farmhouse at least habitable by February. His camping cabins get installed in a couple of weeks, and he wants to stay in one of those until the house is ready.'

'Rebecca,' Ryan started. Her stomach lurched; she knew what her younger brother was going to say. 'He's not just coming home for the kids, and you know it. He's building a business here and making a new life for himself. You'll see him every day. That changes everything, whether you want it to or not.'

Rebecca smoothed down her heavy fringe, closed her diary, and placed it on the edge of Ryan's desk. She wanted change. She wanted Jeremy at home with her every night.

But she also wanted a relationship that couldn't lead to pain for her children. If things didn't work out, she couldn't just step away and leave the heartbreak behind her.

Rebecca's sister Elizabeth had been the same age as Oliver and Liam were now when their parents' marriage had broken down. Rebecca had been ten and still remembered watching her little sister trying to comprehend what had happened to her mum and dad. Her boys would not experience that trauma. Relationships were unpredictable and emotional in both the best and the worst of ways, and when kids were involved, they needed careful management.

'We're taking it slowly. Between the business and the boys, it all works. Adding something else too quickly risks unravelling everything.'

Ryan leaned across the desk and placed his hand on top of her diary. 'Or it could make everything so much better.'

Someone rapped on the door, and Rebecca turned to see her father standing tall in the doorway. Rebecca took after her father in terms of height and colouring, but Alan's thick, dark hair was now a shimmering silver. 'Do you kids have a minute?' Alan asked.

'Of course, come in.' He may have been the chief executive of the company and their boss, but when there was no one else around, he always defaulted to being their dad. Rebecca dragged the empty chair back from Ryan's desk and Alan Knight sat down.

He gestured to Rebecca's diary on the desk. 'Don't let me interrupt you. Finish, please.'

'We were done,' said Ryan. 'We were just chatting about Jeremy coming home.'

Rebecca's head snapped around and she glared at her brother.

'That's right,' said Alan, seemingly choosing to ignore

the sudden chill in the atmosphere. 'I saw his mother the other day. She told me he's staying at Gloria's. She's delighted to have her boy back safe and sound after all these years, but it surprised me to hear he's not staying with you and the children.'

Her father was fishing for information. He had always been one of those parents who believed it was important his children had the freedom to make their own way in life. He had never tried to dictate friends, degree subjects, or career choices. Despite building a business he always planned to hand down to his family, he hadn't even insisted on any of them joining the company, although three of them had. The one area of life where personal freedom should have been the most important facet, relationships, was the one area he couldn't help meddling in.

Rebecca sighed. 'Dad, you know we're not together.' It was the statement she had used to dodge questions about her future with Jeremy since her surprise pregnancy.

'I know that. I just don't know why.'

'It's complicated.'

'We make matters of the heart more complicated than they really are. The heart always knows what it wants.' Rebecca felt a prickle of irritation and opened her mouth to defend her decision, but Alan silenced her with just the raise of his hand. 'But I didn't come here to talk about Jeremy. I wanted to talk to you both about my retirement, and announcing the new chief executive officer and transitional arrangements in the New Year.'

'The New Year?' asked Rebecca. 'As in, four weeks away?' She looked at Ryan and could tell from the sideways glance he gave her that the proposed timing of their dad's announcement was just as big a surprise to him. Alan's plan to retire wasn't unexpected – they were celebrating his sixty-fourth birthday next weekend – but Rebecca had planned for at least another year of their father at the helm of the business he had built, then another couple of years of him talking about winding down before he actually did it.

Alan nodded. 'Business is better than it's ever been and you kids have been instrumental in that. You're ready.'

'You're not ready, though.' Rebecca's words shot out with more force than she had intended.

Her father smiled, picked up her hand and held it in his. 'I am.'

Rebecca had thought of this day many times. She'd been prepared for the mix of emotions that would accompany it, a confusing combination of sadness that her father was stepping down and personal pride that he considered her and Ryan ready to take over. She had even prepared herself to experience the weight of responsibility that came with taking charge of the business that financially supported her entire family. What she hadn't expected was this sinking feeling in her gut. She touched the back of her hand to her suddenly damp forehead.

Alan cleared his throat and brought her attention back into the room. 'Are you OK, Rebecca? You've gone pale.'

The prawns she'd had for lunch made a reappearance and lingered at the back of her throat. There was no way she could handle the demands of the CEO role and her feelings for Jeremy. It was too much too soon. Examples of people trying to have it all and not succeeding were strewn around her like litter along the side of the motorway. Her mother, Catherine, had given up her career when her second child had been born. Her father had given up his corporate career when Catherine had become ill, and he'd sacrificed time with his children to build the business. Her mother's best friend, Gloria, had given up the chance to have her own family when she'd stepped in to help raise Rebecca and her siblings.

This wasn't the eighties. Time had moved on and plenty of people juggled jobs, partners, and families. But that's what it was – a juggling act. And that's why she'd told Jeremy they had to take it slowly. He understood. Even he had been forced to choose between his career and their relationship when he'd joined the Marines, and that was before kids. He'd chosen his career. And now she had the same choice to make.

Rebecca nodded. 'Fine, thanks, Dad. I ate some bad prawns yesterday. My stomach has been iffy ever since.'

'Did you cook the prawns?' asked Ryan. 'It was only last weekend you tried to poison us by making us eat duck that was more cremated than crispy.'

Rebecca winced at the memory. She couldn't explain how her oven had ended up on the maximum temperature, and despite the guilty glances her sons had given each other when smoke had spewed from the oven, neither of them had owned up to touching the dials. 'You can't get food poisoning from overcooked duck.'

Ryan looked at Alan, then flicked his eyes in Rebecca's direction. 'I can't believe you're going to leave your pension in this one's hands.'

Alan laughed. 'I trust my pension will be in safe hands with a very capable CEO and her new chief operating officer.'

'At least she'll be so busy it'll keep her away from the cooker.'

Rebecca gave Ryan a look. 'My first order of business might be to fire the new COO if he's not careful.'

Ryan held up his hands in mock surrender.

'Seriously, though,' said Rebecca. 'Shouldn't we talk about this?'

'About what?' asked Alan.

'The timing. It's a bit of a surprise. And the job shouldn't automatically be mine. Ryan works just as hard as I do.' In his time as production director, Ryan had opened a second factory in Edinburgh that had broadened their distribution and provided a significant boost to their already healthy seven-figure income.

A soft smile of affection formed on Alan's lips. 'Darling, if I was looking at who works the hardest, Elizabeth would be in contention, too. As master chocolatier, head of product development, *and* manager of the shop, the poor girl lives and breathes this business.'

Elizabeth had thrown herself into work when her fiancé, Steven, died on the eve of their Valentine's Day wedding from an undiagnosed heart condition. Despite her trauma, she'd channelled her passion and creativity into chocolate making and had more than doubled the range of products the business sold. She also hosted workshops and parties at the shop and loved it. Rebecca understood her sister's desire to bury herself in work, but she had kept up the same relentless pace for three years now. She made a mental note to invite Elizabeth over for a drink at the weekend just to check in with her.

'What exactly are the transitional arrangements you mentioned, Dad?' asked Ryan.

Alan sat up straighter in his chair. 'We will announce it in January, with Rebecca taking over as CEO at the start of the new financial year in April.'

Rebecca shifted her gaze to Ryan, who had slumped in his chair. He pushed back and balanced the chair on two legs, an action she had scolded one of her children for just the day before. Ryan was not just her business partner, he was also her kid brother, and he looked just as uneasy about this news.

'I thought you would be happier about this,' said Alan.

What could she say? *Actually, your timing is terrible, Dad. Can you hang on for another year while I see how things go with Jeremy?* Rebecca placed her hand over her chest, feeling the tightness within. 'We are happy for you, Dad. It was just a surprise.'

Alan shoved his chair back and stood up. 'Good. Have a think about it over the weekend. Let's keep it between us just now and we can discuss it further when Megan comes home next week. Oh, and Rebecca, a parcel arrived for you at the house.'

'Yes, sorry, I meant to mention that. I've ordered Christmas presents, but have arranged delivery to your place to keep them out of sight of the boys. There'll be a few more boxes coming. Hope that's OK?'

'Of course,' said Alan. 'I'll stash them in Megan's room alongside her boxes and the boys will never notice.'

Rebecca nodded. 'Thanks. Good idea.' Megan had packed up everything she owned and piled it into her childhood bedroom before she jetted off to Majorca earlier in the year. Much to Rebecca's frustration, she was showing no signs of coming home. And still had no desire to get involved in the family business. Megan was a drifter, and while that had been fine in her twenties, she was now thirty-two and Rebecca thought she should have worked out what she wanted to do with her life by now.

Alan closed the door behind himself as Rebecca kept her gaze fixed on Ryan. He rubbed his face in his hands. 'I know we've been talking about this for a while, but I can't believe he's really going.'

'You know Dad. He won't go far.' That was for her brother's benefit. The truth was, Rebecca had no idea what her father's plans were. The word 'retirement' had sounded so final.

'It's weird, though. What will he do?'

Ryan wasn't worried about what their father would do. He was more concerned about where he might go. They were as close as any family could be, and family mattered to Ryan in a way that none of the others could truly appreciate. Except Cat. He shared Rebecca's frustration that Megan was currently off travelling the world, although it was the distance rather than the lack of direction that bothered him most. When they'd looked at locations for their new factory, they'd considered locations in England for cheaper distribution rates, but Ryan had ruled out everywhere that wasn't Scotland, saying he wanted to drive home whenever he liked. He'd moved to a flat in Edinburgh, but Thistle Bay would always be home for Ryan.

'He'll take a few holidays and play lots of golf,' Rebecca said. Her words were like a stab in the chest, a painful reminder of her mother's absence. If her parents had made plans for their retirement, then life had intervened in the cruellest possible way. Her brother's face contorted into a deep frown. 'He's not going anywhere, Ryan. Not until we're all married off, at least.'

Ryan laughed and nodded, his mood lightening. 'You got off lightly on the Jeremy front.'

'For now.' Rebecca leaned forwards. 'Are you really OK with this? With me, I mean.' Ryan had joked plenty about her becoming CEO, but they hadn't ever had a proper conversation about it.

'Rebecca, you've been working for this since your first summer job here when you were fifteen years old. Taking over the business is your dream. It was never mine. I'm excited to see where you take it and proud to support you in any way I can.' Ryan came out from behind his desk and held his hand out for her to take. He pulled her to her feet and wrapped his arms around her, squeezing her tight.

Unlike her brother, Rebecca wasn't a natural hugger. Ryan was by far the most tactile of the Knight children. She had often wondered if that was because he was the youngest or because Gloria Murphy, who handed out hugs liberally, had effectively raised him after their mother, Catherine, had become ill. Or perhaps it was more rudimental than that. Ryan was the only Knight who didn't actually have Knight DNA.

After Ryan had learned that he was born to an unknown father and a drug-addicted teenage mother who had died a year after giving birth to him, he had shown no interest in trying to trace any other relatives. That may change at some point, but for now Rebecca was grateful he was content not to know. The Knight family had had their fair share of emotional situations and she would like their father's retirement to be the only big news in the next year. She allowed the weight of her head to rest against her brother's shoulder. If she took the job, her relationship with Jeremy was over before it had even started. But what choice was there?

2

Jeremy Lewis watched the small but thriving town he had called home since he was fifteen years old appearing on the horizon as Arthur's Audi trundled along the single-carriageway roads towards Thistle Bay. He had hoped Rebecca would meet him at the airport, as keen to see him as he was to see her. Instead, she'd sent her company's driver and said he was arriving home too late to see the boys. She had a point. Parenting twins was definitely easier to handle when everyone was well rested, but he wasn't sure he'd get through the next twelve hours without stopping off to see Rebecca.

He shifted his gaze to the foot of Blakely Hill and the six acres of land nestled between the rolling farmland and dense evergreen pine trees. Feelings of trepidation mired his usual relief at returning home safely. His military career, the only thing he had done all of his adult life, was over. Those six acres of land were now his to refurbish a home and set up his new business.

Being a Royal Marine had been more than a job for him. It had been his entire existence. That had only changed when Oliver and Liam had been born. When those two little bundles of energy had appeared five years ago, the fragility of life had come into sharp focus and planning for this day, the day he left the military behind him for good, had begun.

'Must be strange coming back this time knowing you're not leaving again,' Arthur said, as if reading Jeremy's thoughts. Arthur had worked for the Knight family forever and had given Jeremy many lifts to and from the airport over the years.

'It is. Good strange, though, I think.'

'Don't doubt it. You'll never regret spending more time with those boys of yours. They're not young for long.'

Oliver and Liam had already been two months old by the time he had first seen them. An overseas deployment meant he had missed the births and much of Rebecca's pregnancy. But he was here now and ready to do better. Rebecca Knight was the one for him; she always had been. Now all he had to do was convince her to think that way, too. But she was wary. He couldn't blame her. Their relationship had ended once before and it had been his fault.

When he'd stepped from the train onto the narrow station platform at Lympstone Commando, no amount of steady breathing had stemmed the swell of terror he'd felt. The Marines would push his body and mind beyond limits he hadn't yet known they had, but it was fear of failing that had almost been overwhelming. Almost everyone who had ever stood on that platform had failed their training. He'd glanced up and down the platform at the other passengers. The guy on his right looked at Jeremy, released a heavy sigh, turned, and slunk back onto the train. Jeremy had pushed his shoulders back and marched off the platform. He would not fail. Whatever it took, he would do it. And that decision had led to him ending his relationship with Rebecca.

Of course, the birth of their children had somewhat reignited their relationship, leading to a few weeks here and there of them looking and acting like a family. Things were different now. He was back in Thistle Bay full time and he wanted the boys, and the girl.

The car made its way down Main Street and Jeremy smiled at the explosion of twinkling lights and festive colours. Small towns knew how to do Christmas. Every pastel-painted shop front sparkled with fairy lights and a tree filled the windows. Wide strips of red and green ribbon were twisted around the Victorian-style lampposts. Even the hanging baskets had had a Christmas makeover and were brimming with evergreen foliage and clusters of red berries. The tree dominating the promenade at the end of the road must have been at least thirty feet tall. The warm glow from its lights reached the edge of the high tide as it lapped the shoreline. Switching on the lights was a ceremony that involved much pomp and pageantry on the first weekend of December, and Rebecca and the boys had been there to witness the show. Next year, he would be there, too.

Christmas had never been a big deal to Jeremy. His father had complained about the commerciality of it all and his mother had usually waited until the last minute to display their tabletop Christmas tree. It wasn't until he was a teenager and he and Ivy were on their own that he'd realised just how much his mother adored Christmas. The year after they'd left his father, Ivy had bought a tree so huge the star on top had skimmed the ceiling. She had seemed strangely jubilant about sweeping fallen needles off the floor every morning and he only realised later that her Christmas celebrations had been stifled for so many years.

The woman even had a festive name and yet hadn't been able to celebrate as she'd wanted to. At fifteen years old, Jeremy had acted too cool for Santa Claus, stockings at the end of the bed, and presents under the tree. He regretted that. It was only now he had his own children that he appreciated how much Christmas magic he and Ivy had missed out on over the years.

Arthur pulled up outside Gloria Murphy's quaint little bed and breakfast. The white walls and black trims of the two-storey building looked freshly painted. The seaside-facing windows radiated warm, inviting light.

Jeremy climbed out into the chilly night air and grabbed his luggage from the boot. He travelled light with only one bag. He'd left the rest of his belongings at Rebecca's house gradually over the last year and he'd posted gifts for the boys to his mum's house to keep them away from inquisitive little eyes. Jeremy thanked Arthur for the ride and headed indoors.

A bell above the door announced his arrival and a blonde girl who was little more than a teenager greeted him from behind the desk in the hallway. 'Hello, are you Mr Lewis?'

'I'm Jeremy, yes. Is Gloria not here?'

'No. She sends her apologies. She's been roped in to helping at the town planning meeting for Christmas events. I'm Susie.'

'I didn't realise Gloria employed anyone else.'

'I'm new. I just do a few shifts a week to help.'

Rebecca had been trying to get Gloria to hire someone for the last year. The bed and breakfast was small, with only half a dozen rooms, but Gloria managed it single-handedly, only hiring local kids to help serve breakfasts during school holidays. Rebecca had used her powers of persuasion to convince Gloria to at least appoint a small commercial cleaning company to take over the housekeeping, but Rebecca had said Gloria was determined to run everything else herself.

Susie checked him in, talked him through the dining arrangements, and showed him to his room. She had a quiet confidence about her that Jeremy immediately warmed to.

He ditched his luggage in his room – Gloria's favourite room, he knew, despite his instruction that she should place him in the small room at the back of the building. Jeremy had never had to win Alan Knight's seal of approval. Gloria was the hurdle potential dates had to jump over to take one of the Knight girls out. She'd taken a liking to him early on, though, and fearing that Rebecca was growing up too soon, Gloria had helped him get that first date with Rebecca. She'd thought Rebecca needed to be reminded she was just a teenager and there was more to life than looking after her siblings and working weekends in her father's business.

Jeremy left the bed and breakfast and stepped out into the darkness again, his eyes drifting skywards. The clear night sky sparkled with thousands of stars. The forecast predicted snow, but the air felt too crisp for snow tonight. He walked the deserted streets. The below-freezing temperature and the fact that nothing much was open beyond eight kept everyone indoors. Even the local bus didn't run at this time. Anyone looking for an evening out chose between The Smugglers Inn, the only pub in town, or a taxi to whisk them away somewhere else.

He headed straight for his mother's cosy two-bedroomed bungalow. The square-footage of the house was modest, but Ivy was proud to own every inch. She'd bought the house six months after they'd moved to town and hadn't ever considered selling it. Her sanctuary, she called it. And she meant it in the literal sense of the word. To Jeremy and his mother, Thistle Bay wasn't a suffocating small town. It was a place that embraced newcomers and welcomed them when Ivy had finally found the courage to leave her husband.

Jeremy tried the handle on his mum's door. It was locked, thankfully. Despite him urging her to keep her doors locked when she was home alone, the door was usually open for anyone to stroll in whenever they pleased. He dug his hand in his pocket to pull out his key, but then stopped. It didn't feel right to use his key when he wasn't staying here. He knocked on the door and stood off the doorstep so his mum would get a good view of him through her security spyhole.

Seconds later, there was movement behind the door and the key twisted in the lock. Ivy opened the door, and Jeremy frowned as he clocked her pale skin and tense smile. It was a look he'd seen too many times as a child. Jeremy had suspected his father's violence, but the first time he'd witnessed it had also been the time that violence came thundering down on him. His father's fist had hurtled towards his mother, Jeremy had lunged forward, and the punch had struck the side of Jeremy's face instead. Everything changed that night. Ivy and Jeremy had packed up the car and had driven as far as one tank of fuel would take them. They had arrived in Thistle Bay with two suitcases, the family Volvo, and bruises neither of them had needed to explain.

Over the next year, Jeremy had grown to six foot two, an inch taller than his father. He became a regular at the local gym and lifted weights. The decision to join the military followed soon after. He would never again feel as helpless as he had that night. He had been prepared for the day his father prowled back into their lives. That day had never come. Not following them had been the one good thing the man had done for his family.

'What's wrong?' Jeremy barged past his mother and into the house. He scanned the hallway, unsure what he was actually looking for. The house reeked of paint fumes, but otherwise, nothing was out of place.

'Nothing's wrong, darling. I didn't expect to see you tonight, and it's late, that's all.' Now in her early sixties, Ivy had kept her slim figure and naturally dark hair that grazed her collar, which she attributed to good genes from her father. Those genes had been watered down a touch by the time they'd reached Jeremy. He had a good thick head of hair, but a few wiry silver strands had appeared on his temples.

Ivy stretched up to give him a quick hug and led him to the snug lounge at the back of the house where she spent most of her evenings. Jeremy sank down onto the navy velvet sofa.

Ivy hovered by the door. 'Can I get you something to drink? Tea, coffee? Maybe a beer?'

'No, thanks. I'm good. Come and have a seat, Mum.' His gaze swept the room. 'Have you been decorating?'

Ivy came into the room, picked up a folded newspaper from the seat of the armchair, and tossed it onto the coffee table. Perching on the edge of the chair, she smiled at him. 'Just freshening up the hallway. It's good to have you back, son. How does it feel?'

'Pretty good.' He wasn't sure that was true. Edgy was more like it and he couldn't pinpoint why. Maybe Arthur was right and it was because, for the first time in over twenty years, he had no date to leave. Whatever happened from here on in was his choice and that was . . . new. 'You should have left the painting until I was back. I could have done it for you.'

'It was just a few walls.'

A door creaked in the hallway and Jeremy turned towards the door, expecting to see a ginger ball of fluff skulking into the room any second. 'Where is he?' he asked.

Ivy sat straighter on the chair. 'It's not like the cat to be so shy.'

His mum's cat had the very dog-like tendency of greeting visitors as soon as they arrived. The only time he'd made himself scarce was when the boys had been toddlers and didn't yet understand that pulling the cat's tail and squeezing his furry cheeks wasn't fun for the poor creature.

Ivy ran a hand across the back of her neck. 'It's getting late. He'll be looking for somewhere to settle down for the night.'

Jeremy noted the second mention of it being late and pushed himself off the sofa. 'It is getting late. Let's catch up properly tomorrow.'

Ivy sprang up from her chair. 'Oh, I didn't mean it was too late for you.'

'I know. But I'm still groggy from the flight. Do you have the parcel I sent here? It's gifts for the boys, so I'll take it away with me if it's easy for you to get.'

Ivy's cheeks flushed. 'It's in the bedroom. I'll get it.'

Jeremy followed her from the lounge. Ivy pushed open her bedroom door and lingered in the hallway for a few seconds before going in.

Jeremy peered into the room from the door. It seemed like her paint job was more than just a few walls. His mother's bedroom was wildly different from the last time he had been in it. He tried to recall when that was. Ever since the twins had been born, he had stayed with Rebecca when he was home on leave. Ivy had given her room the occasional fresh coat of paint over the years, but had changed little else. Now her wrought-iron double bedframe had been replaced with an oak king-sized bed with crisp white sheets, a comforter decorated with printed sunflowers, and a coordinating cushion propped up against the pillows. Her rickety wooden wardrobes had been removed to make space for the bed and a long, low chest of drawers had been added with a gap left for a cream chair that had been positioned by the window.

'I would have helped you to decorate, Mum.' Jeremy took the parcel from his mother's outstretched hand.

Ivy gave him a wide smile and reached her arms out to hug him again. 'It's done. It's so good to have you home, darling.'

Jeremy hugged his mother back and left with a promise to see her the following day. He waited until he heard her lock the door from inside before he stepped off her doorstep. He wasn't groggy at all and he felt a twinge of guilt at skipping out on his mother after only five minutes, but if his quick departure bothered Ivy, she hadn't shown it. He glanced at his watch. It was after nine. There was probably some murder mystery drama he had delayed her from watching. Ivy was a sucker for a brooding detective with a damaged heart and a dysfunctional relationship with alcohol.

Besides, there was another woman in town Jeremy was desperate to see.

3

Rebecca's cottage was tucked away in a quiet street, with a view of the play park and perfectly maintained communal green space. She'd had new windows installed before the boys had been born, opting for dark-grey sash windows made from modern UPVC but sympathetic to the original design of the house. Her car obscured her dining room window, to the left of her colour-matched grey door. The window on the opposite side was for a barely used living room and overlooked a square of grass. Jeremy glanced at the upstairs windows. The boys shared bedroom was to the front of the house and it was in darkness. Oliver and Liam were probably fast asleep and he wouldn't wake them. He'd tried that once and learned that young children and interrupted sleep weren't an ideal combination.

He tapped on the door. The lock clicked, and the door opened.

There she was. The woman who, at forty years old, still made his heart leap into his throat the way she had when they were teenagers. Her dark-brown hair skimmed her shoulders with a fringe framing her even darker brown eyes.

With no make-up on and wearing leggings and a chunky grey jumper, she was his Rebecca. She wasn't the businesswoman who favoured high heels and red lipstick. She was the woman that only he saw, and he knew what a privilege it was that she allowed him into this side of her life. His body was on autopilot. He stepped forward, threaded his hand through her hair, and met her mouth in a fiery kiss that she returned. Her lips were warm and he could taste a hint of red wine in her kiss. Every cell in his body fired up, and he knew he was home. Whatever nagging doubts he'd had about coming home for good were gone. This was where he was supposed to be, and Rebecca was who he was supposed to be with.

Rebecca broke off their kiss and held the door open wider. He squeezed past her. An air diffuser on the glass console table gave off the scent of cinnamon and cloves; the only sign of Christmas in the cottage. December was all business for Rebecca. There's nothing like Christmas to ramp up production for a chocolate company, but December was also the month in which her mother had died, and Rebecca had been burying herself in work and delaying the festivities ever since. He hoped to change that. This was the first Christmas he would spend with the boys since they'd become old enough to understand what the fuss was about, and he was going to make it a memorable one for all of them.

Rebecca touched a hand to her lips. 'I didn't expect to see you tonight.'

'That's what my mum said. I stopped in to see her, and if I didn't know any better, I'd think she couldn't wait to get rid of me.'

Rebecca laughed. 'I'm sure that's not true. She's been counting the days until you were back.'

Jeremy slipped off his shoes and padded up the hallway to the open-plan kitchen lounge. The back of the house was a slice of modern in the old cottage and was where his family spent most of their time. The curtains were drawn across the French doors, obscuring the long garden and the AstroTurf Jeremy had laid himself when Rebecca had flipped out after one too many incidents of their little football fans trailing mud into the house. A laptop sat open on the low coffee table in front of Rebecca's sofa, surrounded by papers and folders in neat little piles. The Marines had taught him to be organised, but Rebecca had been born that way.

'The cream sofa is holding up well.'

Rebecca smiled. 'Light colours and children are fine when everyone follows the rules.'

'That's right. No shoes, no food, no drinks without a lid.' He spotted a half-full glass of red wine on the table. 'For the kids, anyway. Got any more where that came from?'

'Sure.'

'Are the boys asleep?'

Rebecca poured him a glass of Merlot from an open bottle on the kitchen counter and rolled her eyes. 'Finally. Don't go up. It took them over an hour to fall asleep tonight. They're so highly strung at the thought of seeing you tomorrow.'

She handed him the wine, and he slowly caressed her fingers with his before taking the glass. 'I missed you, Bex.'

The familiar heat in her chocolate-drop eyes as she looked back at him made him breathe a little deeper. He wrapped his arm around her waist and pulled her closer. She wanted him just as much as he wanted her, but she was holding herself back. 'I can see you overthinking this, Bex.'

She fought his grasp and scurried towards the sofa, picking up her own glass. She raised it to him. 'Cheers.'

Moving into her space again, she took a step back, and he tapped his glass against hers. 'Cheers.'

They settled onto the sofa, with Rebecca avoiding eye contact and making small talk about the boys while Jeremy sipped his wine and stared at her mouth. She fidgeted with a cushion she held between them. This wasn't the order of events he was used to during previous stays in this house.

But he wasn't staying in the house this time.

He understood why Rebecca didn't want to just let him slot right into her life. His homecoming was permanent, and they had never reached that point in their relationship. They'd never discussed a future. Not even when the boys came along. He had selfishly presumed there would be a place for him in Rebecca's life, but he had given no thought to what that would look like.

Rebecca curled her legs under her body, and Jeremy clasped a hand around her bare foot. 'Will you come up to the farm with me on Saturday and look around?'

Rebecca nodded. 'The boys are itching to see the place.'

Jeremy leaned forward, drained his glass, and put it on the table. 'I'm going to take a peek upstairs.'

Rebecca sat forward and put her glass down beside his. 'If you wake them up, you'll be sorry tomorrow.'

Jeremy stood up and gave Rebecca a playful salute. 'I'm a Royal Marine. They won't even know I've been there.'

He climbed the stairs and pushed open the bedroom door, satisfied. He'd oiled that creaky door the last time he'd been home, and it still glided silently. Oliver's bed was closest to the door, and he was snoozing soundly with his hand clamped round his favourite stuffed robot. Liam had an arm and a leg hanging over the edge of his bed. Jeremy resisted the urge to tuck him back in. Both boys were light sleepers and Rebecca was right: if he woke them now, they'd be awake for hours. Besides, there was no need to wake them up. There were no limits on their time together. He would see them every day for the rest of their childhoods.

Jeremy crept back downstairs and returned to the lounge. He registered the change in Rebecca immediately. Gone was the tension, the stiffness he'd seen just minutes earlier. Instead, she was relaxed, her smile warm and her long legs once more curled underneath her body as she sat sipping her Merlot, nodding towards his refilled glass on the table. There she was. His girl.

He sat down, leaving his glass on the table, and entwined his fingers with hers. Something had shifted for her while he'd been upstairs, and he wasn't going to risk switching it back by asking her about it. He twisted round to look at her and her movements mirrored his own. Leaning forward until her breath caressed his skin, he paused, giving her the choice to back away from him or close the gap. Her eyes dropped to his lips, and he inhaled the fruity aroma from the glass she held in front of her. The fiery energy between them ached in his chest as he waited for her to make her choice. She closed the gap and pressed her lips to his. She chose him.

4
―――

Rebecca woke up as Jeremy twitched in his sleep beside her. Despite the darkness, her hand found the scar on Jeremy's shoulder. She traced its jagged edges with her finger. He'd been deployed to some of the most dangerous conflicts in living memory, and she could never truly understand how that impacted him. She only knew how it impacted her. She had taken the call when he'd been injured. He'd listed her as his next of kin and had asked her if anything ever happened to him to find out how serious it was before telling Ivy. His mother had had enough worry in her life and he didn't want to give her anymore if he could avoid it.

He'd told Rebecca he'd been lucky because he'd been shot by a handgun rather than a rifle and the biggest danger he'd faced was blood loss. A bullet had ripped through the flesh in his shoulder and he considered himself lucky. It was an explanation she hadn't been able to comprehend until she'd found out that not everyone injured on that day had made it. That knowledge and the unfair questions he still asked himself about what more he could have done were the scars that she knew still troubled him.

Jeremy stirred. Having him home for good meant she would never again have to fear receiving that call. Perhaps that was why she'd allowed her guard to slip last night and why Jeremy was now waking up in her bed. Her resolve to take things slowly had weakened the second she'd opened the door to him. Those brown eyes had been hungry for her. As their lips locked, she hadn't known she'd wanted that moment so badly. Her subsequent half-hearted attempt to keep him at a distance hadn't lasted longer than a few mouthfuls of wine before she'd allowed herself one more night with him. But that was last night. Now she had to deal with the consequences of her father's announcement. She just didn't see a way to make a relationship work when things were about to change so significantly elsewhere. She couldn't do it all.

Her phone alarm beeped on her nightstand and she reached across to silence it. The bedroom was pitch dark with not even a crack of light coming in through the edges of her curtains. Jeremy gripped her around the waist and pulled her closer to him, his lips nuzzling against her neck.

'We have to get up.' Rebecca rubbed at her heavy eyes, regretting the last glass of wine she'd had the night before. Jeremy groaned and squeezed her tighter. Oliver and Liam were early risers, and they'd have half an hour, if they were lucky, before at least one of their sons appeared. Using her feet, she shoved the duvet to the bottom of the bed, exposing both of their bodies to the chill in the air.

'That's harsh,' said Jeremy.

'That's reality.' Her eyes adjusted to the dark, and Jeremy propped himself up on his elbow. Her heart thumped louder in her chest. She flicked on her bedside lamp, grabbed her phone, and propped herself up on her pillows to check her emails. 'Do you want a shower here or will you shower at Gloria's?'

'Here. I'll go first, then I'll make some breakfast while you get ready.'

Rebecca glanced up from her phone. 'You can't make breakfast. You have to go.'

'Go where?'

She shrugged her shoulders. 'Anywhere but here.'

'I'm not following you,' he said.

Even with sleepy eyes and messy hair, the man could make her pulse throb in her ears. 'I don't want the boys to see you here in case they get the wrong idea.'

Jeremy sat upright and moved towards her. He waved his hand around the room. 'They've seen me in this bed a hundred times. What's different?'

'You're not leaving.'

He dragged his hand through his hair. 'Is that a question?'

'No. That's what's different. You stayed here to make the most of your time with the boys, then you would leave. It was straightforward. They know you're not leaving this time, and I don't want them wondering why you're here sometimes and not at other times.'

Jeremy leaned forwards, planted his hands either side of her body, and kissed her on the cheek, his lips lingering for a gratifying few seconds. 'There's an easy way to fix that,' he said. 'I'll just stay here all the time.'

Rebecca shook her head. 'And what happens when the farmhouse is ready? You'll move out and the boys won't understand.'

'There's an easy way to fix that, too. You can all come to the farmhouse and live with me.'

Rebecca rolled her eyes. 'You're insufferable at this time of the morning.'

'I'm serious.'

'Jeremy, we're not together.' He opened his mouth to speak, and she clamped her hand across his mouth. 'And I don't want to hear about your easy way to fix that.'

'Fine,' he said, the word muffled by her hand. He took her hand in his and lowered it away from his face.

'I'll get dressed and go. Gloria is probably dying to see me, anyway.'

'You didn't see her last night?'

'No. Someone called Susie checked me in.'

'I knew she'd recently hired Susie part time. It's not like Gloria not to be there for a guest checking in, though.'

Jeremy shrugged. 'It was only me.'

'All the more reason I would have expected her to be there. I'll swing by later and check on her.'

'Leave it. I'm there to check on her. Besides, there was a reason. She was away somewhere. I just can't remember where. Listen, Bex, I know me being here permanently is going to be an adjustment for us.'

Rebecca took a steadying breath. 'Look, Jeremy, the timing is just...'

'Timing is only an excuse if we allow it to be. I know you want to take things slowly. That's OK. I just need you to be sure that you want *us*.'

His expression was raw and exposed, his eyes glistening with a sadness that made her ache, and she wished she hadn't been the one to cause it. If he'd asked her yesterday, then she could have given him the reassurance he was looking for. She wanted them to be together, and if there was any doubt, their time together last night had confirmed it. But that wasn't enough. And she couldn't ask him to wait, to put his new life on hold, until she decided the time was right.

The bedroom door creaked open, bringing a stream of cool air in from the hallway. 'Mummy, I'm up,' said a sleepy figure in zebra-print pyjamas.

'Morning, Oliver,' said Jeremy.

'Daddy!' Oliver perked up and bounced towards the bed. He threw himself into Jeremy's arms.

Rebecca sighed. Jeremy had only been home a matter of hours and already their plan to keep things simple for the boys had failed. What did simple even look like now?

Rebecca dropped her phone onto her nightstand, kissed Oliver on the head, and padded towards her en-suite shower room. Heavy eyes and pale skin stared back at her from the mirror. Oliver's chatter in the bedroom was non-stop, and for once it wasn't directed towards her.

After a quick shower, Rebecca returned to an empty bedroom and got dressed. Her eyes lingered for a few seconds on the clothes hanging in Jeremy's half of the wardrobe before being drawn to her neatly made bed with perfect military-style tucked corners. Jeremy had even put the throw cushions in the right places. She skimmed her calendar on her phone, plucked her diary from the bag on top of her dresser, and flipped to today's date. She had forty minutes to get the boys dressed, drop them off at breakfast club, and hit the road towards Edinburgh if she was going to be on time for her first meeting of the day. She threw her diary back into her bag and marched towards Oliver and Liam's bedroom. The giggling she heard downstairs confirmed that both boys were now up and the comforting scent of hot toast reached her.

Downstairs, she crept into the kitchen to see Liam dressed in his school uniform and sitting on a stool at the breakfast bar, watching his dad in the kitchen buttering toast, cracking eggs, and pouring pineapple juice into glasses. Oliver was crouched beneath the counter wearing a fluffy, hooded onesie with spikes down its back over what she hoped was his clothes and not still his pyjamas. He looked like he was going to a Jurassic Park fancy-dress party instead of to school.

'I like the crusts cut off mine,' said Liam.

'That's right,' said Jeremy, who'd pulled on the clothes he'd been wearing the night before. 'It's only big boys who eat their crusts. I keep forgetting you're not old enough to do that yet.'

'I eat my crusts,' said Oliver from his hiding spot.

'I'll eat my crusts, too, Daddy,' Liam added. 'I'm old enough to do that. Mummy just always cuts them off.'

'What's Mummy getting the blame for?' Rebecca asked, making her presence known.

'Cutting off my crusts,' said Liam.

'That's because you like your crusts cut off,' said Rebecca, giving him a kiss on his cheek as she passed him while pretending she hadn't spotted Oliver. With his hair sticking up in all directions, Liam resembled his father more than usual.

'I'm old enough to eat my crusts now,' her son said.

'That's good,' said Rebecca. 'But maybe just eat one slice of toast because you're going to breakfast club this morning. You'll probably want to eat something there, too. Now, where's your brother?'

'ROAR!' came a voice from behind her.

Jeremy yelped and bounced back from the counter. 'You scared me. I thought I was being attacked by a scary dinosaur, but I see now it's Oliver.'

'I'm not scary,' said Oliver. 'I'm a stegosaurus.'

'Well, a stegosaurus would be pretty scary if it were in the kitchen. It might think I'm breakfast and eat me.'

'Silly Daddy,' said Oliver. 'I'm a vegetarian.'

Jeremy peeled his son's fluffy hood off his head. 'I'm a little relieved to hear that. Come and sit down and have some breakfast. Who wants sausages? I spotted some leftovers in the fridge.'

Oliver giggled and looked up at his dad. 'Daddy, sausages come from a pig and I don't eat pigs anymore.'

Jeremy turned to Rebecca. 'We're still talking about the dinosaur, right?'

She waved a hand at him in a gesture to indicate they would discuss it later. From the look on his face, her response wasn't as reassuring as he had hoped it might be.

Rebecca helped Oliver out of his onesie and onto the stool beside Liam. She slid a slice of toast onto his plate. 'We've got twenty minutes before we need to go to breakfast club, so munch up.' She joined Jeremy at the cooker and plugged in the coffee machine on her counter.

'Breakfast club?' he asked.

'I'm heading to Edinburgh, so I'll drop the boys off at school early. They'll eat and play in the gym hall until school starts.'

'I can take them to school,' said Jeremy. He put a generous scoop of butter in a frying pan and leaned towards her. 'Don't tell me,' he said, lowering his voice, 'that I have a vegetarian five-year-old.'

She pressed the button on the coffee machine, hoping to drown out their conversation further. 'I'll explain later, but he's pretty adamant. I made him a lentil curry with cauliflower rice the other night. He hates cauliflower, but he grimaced his way through it and finished the lot.'

Jeremy sighed and poured the eggs onto the heat. 'I'll do

drop-off.'

'It's fine, really. They only go to the club once in a while and they like it.'

'Still, I'd like to take them. You can have breakfast and head off whenever you're ready. Eggs?' Jeremy asked.

Rebecca smoothed down her slim-fit trousers and nodded. There were definite advantages to having Jeremy here in the mornings, but having a tidy bed, a shower with no one bawling through the door, and breakfast cooked for her didn't make up for the confusion her boys would surely feel when the farmhouse was renovated and Jeremy moved out. She and Jeremy had just had their last sleepover.

After a quick breakfast, there was just enough time for Jeremy to give the boys their presents before Rebecca had to leave for work. They moved onto the sofa and Jeremy handed them each a parcel wrapped in uninspiring brown paper.

'Are these from England?' asked Liam.

'No. Before I was in England, I was in a place called Guam. It's a tiny island with beautiful beaches and lots of green space.'

'Just like where we live,' said Oliver.

'That's true. Only it's much hotter than here.'

Liam, almost vibrating with excitement, tore open his parcel while Oliver picked the tape off one end of his.

'This is so cool,' said Liam, whirling around his die-cast model ship. 'Look, Mummy.' Rebecca leaned forward and made appropriate noises to show how impressed she was. 'It's a boat. Is that the one you were on, Daddy?'

'No. This is a replica, a copy, of a ship that has been resting on the bottom of the sea near Guam for more than one hundred years.'

'Wow! That is so cool. Can I take it to school with me?'

'You can take it for Fun Friday,' said Rebecca. 'Just be careful not to lose it.'

Liam's head bobbed furiously as he clutched the gift to his chest. 'I won't.'

Jeremy turned to his other son, who had delicately opened one end of his parcel. 'How are you getting on, Oliver?'

Oliver tipped his package up. Three oval pebbles tumbled into his hand. The boy grinned as he turned the stones over in his hand, inspecting the smooth silver surfaces. He held up the flattest of the three. 'I'm going to paint the flag for Guam on this one.'

'That's so strange,' said Jeremy. 'That's exactly what I thought when I found that one. I was walking on the beach and I saw something glinting on the sand. I picked it up, that one you're holding, and thought, I bet Oliver could paint a cool flag on this stone.'

Oliver beamed at his father. 'I already know what the flag looks like. Mummy showed me when you were away. It has a boat on it.'

'Is that so?' asked Jeremy. 'I can't wait to see it on your stone once you've finished it.'

'I'm going to start it now so you can see it before you have to go away again.'

Jeremy smoothed Oliver's hair down. 'Daddy doesn't have to go away anymore. I live here now.'

'With us?' asked Liam.

The hope in his son's voice slammed into him like the punch he'd once taken to the shoulder when he'd allowed his guard to slip momentarily during a training exercise. Rebecca stiffened beside him and he placed a hand on her knee. 'Well, up at the farm eventually,' he said. 'But you'll see me every day.'

Oliver shuffled along the sofa closer to him. 'Did you and Mummy get a divorce?'

Now there was a word Jeremy hadn't even realised was in his son's vocabulary. 'No.'

'Do you know what that means?' asked Rebecca.

Oliver nodded and looked down at the stones he was cradling 'Aiden's mum and dad got a divorce and now he only sees his mum on a Sunday.'

Rebecca moved to sit on the coffee table in front of the boys. Jeremy could see the anguish in her eyes and knew these questions were why she'd wanted him gone this morning. 'Some parents don't live together and there are lots of reasons for that,' she said. 'But we all live in the same town now, so you'll see lots of us.'

Jeremy scanned his children's faces, hoping to see the natural cheeriness that came with being five years old. Instead, their expressions were of concern and confusion. Oliver's bottom lip quivered and Rebecca's fear leached into the room. Leaving the base for the last time ever had been more gut-wrenching than deployment. At least in a conflict zone, he knew what to expect. He was trained for it. There were rules and procedures and contingency plans. His life had been structured in the same way since he was eighteen years old. Everyone on his team knew the rules. Rebuilding his family, his new team, was unfamiliar territory, and he hadn't yet figured out the best way to approach it. And he knew Rebecca was going to make it harder than it needed to be.

5

Jeremy dropped the boys off at breakfast club with a promise to see them again as soon as they finished school for the day. He fired off a text to Rebecca to let her know he would pick them up later. The strain in the atmosphere that morning had been about more than the risk of confusing the boys. It had been her own feelings she was wrestling with. She had wanted him to stick around last night. She had wanted him there in the morning. Until she'd flicked the light on and her fear got in the way. Luckily, he didn't scare easily.

He checked the time. His mother was an early riser. He could stop off for a coffee before heading back to the bed and breakfast. Something weird had been going on with her last night and his mind was taking him back to a time he had chosen to never revisit. Returning home from school, seeing the dread on his mother's face, her sallow skin and eyes full of shadows, feeling the tension in her embrace as she sheltered him from whatever trauma had happened while he'd been gone. Those days had ended when they'd arrived in Thistle Bay. But last night there was tension in her hug. She was keeping something from him and she only ever did that when she thought she was protecting him. He needed to remind her he was all grown up and she no longer needed to do that.

Despite the early hour and still-dark sky, Ivy's front door was unlocked and Jeremy let himself in. He immediately clocked the golf bag resting against the wall in the hall and poked his head into the front sitting room, which his mother only used at Christmas or when she had company. It was empty, and the patterned wallpaper surrounding the fireplace had been stripped and the wall painted a muted neutral shade. Muffled radio voices came from the other end of the cottage and Jeremy headed towards the kitchen.

'Mum? You here?'

There was no answer. The bathroom door creaked behind him and Jeremy turned around, expecting to see a ginger ball of fluff stalking him up the hallway. Instead, what greeted him was a flash of naked flesh.

'Oh my God.' He averted his eyes from the man in front of him before registering his mother's voice behind him.

'Jeremy!' Ivy said from the kitchen doorway. Her complexion was pale and her eyes wide, but thankfully, she was fully dressed.

Jeremy shuddered. 'I just came by to say hello, but we can catch up later.' He spun around, his elbow clattered against the tall shoe cabinet in the hallway, and he cursed out loud. He all but sprinted back to the front door, ignoring his mother as she hurried after him calling his name.

'It's OK, Mum,' Jeremy called without looking back. 'We'll talk later.' He slammed his mother's front door and stalked away from her cottage. Caffeine, lots and lots of caffeine, was needed to process what the hell he'd just walked in on.

The sight of Mystic Coffee with its navy-blue signage, block white letters, and the guarantee of something hot and strong to counteract his racing heartbeat was a small comfort. He shoved open the door and felt a wall of warmth from the fire flickering away inside. He took a deep breath and inhaled the deep earthy aroma of the coffee shop.

'Hey, welcome home!' Ryan Knight, Rebecca's younger brother, got up from a table near the counter and grabbed Jeremy in a bear hug before he could say a word. Ryan released him and squeezed his shoulder. 'It's good to have you back.'

'Thanks. Shouldn't you be in Edinburgh? Rebecca is on her way there.'

Ryan glanced up as if trying to picture his calendar for the day. 'Nah. She's off to a board meeting at that Puddle Jumpers charity thing.'

Jeremy looked past Ryan and locked eyes with the woman at Ryan's table. She was sitting beside Nick Bell, local photographer and art gallery owner, and had swivelled round in her chair to follow the commotion Ryan had caused. Her hair was a lot lighter than Rebecca's and her eyes were more green than brown, but Jeremy had spent enough time around the Knight sisters to recognise the family resemblance straight away.

'It's Cat, isn't it?' he said.

'Yeah.' Her eyes darted towards Ryan.

'I'm Jeremy.'

Cat stood and reached out to shake his hand. 'Oh, right. You're Rebecca's . . .' Yeah, he didn't know how to finish that sentence either. 'Oliver and Liam's dad,' she added.

'I am.'

'They're such sweet kids. You must be very proud of them.'

Jeremy smiled. 'They're why I'm here.'

Ryan leaned closer and muttered under his breath, 'Are they the only reason?'

Jeremy ignored Ryan's quip. 'It's just amazing that you're here after all this time, Cat.'

Mystic Jones, the cafe's owner, appeared from behind the counter and herded the group back towards Ryan's table. 'You lot are blocking my thoroughfare.' Mystic, with a tangle of chestnut curls that she'd attempted to tame by tying them in a high ponytail, clasped her hands on Jeremy's forearms, her sparkling green eyes radiating warmth. 'It's good to see you home safe, honey.'

'Thank you,' said Jeremy. 'I'll join the queue. Can I get anyone else a refill while I'm up there?' The rest of the group shook their heads and Jeremy followed Mystic up to the counter, taking his place behind two elderly women.

'Is he your boy?' one of the women asked Mystic while tossing her head in his direction. Jeremy guessed Mystic was in her early fifties, which would have made her a teenage mother if he had been hers. Mystic didn't seem put out by the implication, though.

'No, he's Ivy's son,' the other woman said. 'Mystic doesn't have children.'

'Why not?' the woman asked, looking directly at Mystic for an answer.

'I'm happily childless,' said Mystic with no hint of irritation or offence in her voice.

The nosey customer screwed up her face in disbelief, as if that wasn't a choice someone was entitled to make. People were like that on relationships, too, he had found. They asked questions that were a little too personal, and then judged your answer. He'd lost count of the number of times he had been asked why he and Rebecca weren't together.

The timing wasn't right for them had been his stock answer and had satisfied most people until the twins had come along. People had then looked for a deeper reason, and when he had none to give, they screwed up their face in the same way Mystic's judgemental customer had just done.

The two women shuffled along to the end of the counter and Mystic turned to Jeremy. 'What can I get you, honey?'

'Just a black coffee, thanks.' It wasn't normal for guests to walk naked through their host's hallway. Whatever was going on at his mum's place, he wasn't ready to deal with it. 'With an extra shot,' he added.

Jeremy fetched his drink and lowered himself into the vacant chair beside Ryan. 'So, Cat,' Jeremy started. 'I hear you're sticking around in Thistle Bay. That's great news.'

Cat nodded and grinned. He smiled back, happy to see her so content with her decision. Rebecca had told him about the mess she'd made in dealing with the situation. That was how she'd put it, at least. To Jeremy, it sounded as though everyone had agreed with the decision to wait before telling Cat she was their sister. They should have told her the truth as soon as she'd arrived instead of having her work for them for a fortnight first, but he understood why they'd done it. Their dad's reaction had backed them into a corner and they thought they were doing what was best for him.

The guilt was just like Rebecca. She'd felt responsible for her family since she was a teenager. At fifteen years old, she hadn't even been able to commit to a burger on a Saturday afternoon until she'd checked where each of her siblings was going to be.

They'd met in high school. Rebecca was struggling with her mother's mental illness, and Jeremy and Ivy had moved to town only a few weeks before. Being raised by one parent was the only thing they'd had in common. She was determined to stay in Thistle Bay and help her father run his business. He planned to join the Marines and see the world. There was never any question that she wouldn't work in the family business. She loved the business. Her job was a huge part of her identity and he understood that because his job was a huge part of his identity. Or at least it had been.

'I really love it here,' said Cat. 'I felt so at home from the first day I arrived.'

Nick squeezed Cat's hand as it lay on the table, and their fingers intertwined. Jeremy pointed back and forth between them. 'Ah, I hadn't heard about you two.'

Cat's cheeks flushed a little pink. 'Rebecca didn't mention it?'

'We haven't had much time to talk. Our calls get hijacked by the boys.'

Mystic appeared beside them and put a plate with four shortbread biscuits in the middle of the table. 'Is anyone planning to eat?'

'Yes, please,' said Nick. 'Bacon rolls for me and Cat. Anyone else?'

Jeremy and Ryan declined. Mystic winked at Nick, pressed her hand to his cheek, then wandered off.

Jeremy put his head in his hands. 'Bacon rolls. I take it you know about Oliver?'

'That he refuses to eat anything with a face? Yep,' said Ryan.

'How's that going down with the meat-eating military man?' asked Nick.

Jeremy looked up, frowned, and slumped back into his chair. 'Not great.'

Ryan was the first one to dive into the biscuits. 'It's just a phase. Kids do that, don't they? Are you heading up to lord over your empire this morning?'

Jeremy snapped a biscuit in two, shoved one half in his mouth and shook his head. 'I was keen to get started, but Archie Henderson has asked me to wait until Sunday. He wants a final look around. Given that my plans involve ripping out his kitchen and bathroom, I thought I'd best leave everything alone until Archie has been up there one last time. I'm picking up my new car today, though.'

'What are you getting?' asked Nick.

'I got a good deal on a Land Rover. Ex-company-car stock. Two years old with less than thirty thousand miles on the clock. There are a few scrapes on the paintwork, but with a farm and two boys, I don't mind that.'

'Sounds like a steal,' said Ryan. 'Do you need a lift?'

Jeremy shook his head. 'I'm not getting it until this afternoon. My mum is going to drop me off.'

'You sure? I can take you after one o'clock.'

A lift from Ryan would help him avoid seeing his mum for at least another day. Obviously, they had to talk about what had happened, but that was a conversation he was quite happy to put off for as long as he could. 'Actually, a lift would be great. Thanks.'

Ryan nodded. 'No problem. Have you guys heard about his plans?' he said to Cat and Nick. 'Jeremy is setting up an adventure experience on the outskirts of town.'

'What's an adventure experience?' asked Cat.

'I bought six acres of land at the foot of Blakely Hill,' said Jeremy. 'I had imagined one day building a big fancy house on the land. Turns out I'm not allowed to demolish the old farmhouse on the land, but I got planning permission to gut it inside and create an adventurers' retreat. I haven't worked out all the details. Maybe it's some kind of endurance course for people who want to play commandos. Or maybe it's just clay pigeon shooting and archery, maybe quad biking, something like that. The only bit I'm certain of is camping cabins. They're being delivered on site in a couple of weeks.'

The camping cabins had been months in the planning and had required planning permission and specialist ground crews to install utilities. Contractors had carried out the bulk of the work over the summer. There was just a week of onsite installation, and then Jeremy could be ready to launch his business. He just had to figure out what activities he wanted to offer.

'Ooh, are they like those little wooden tents?' asked Cat.

Jeremy laughed. 'I guess so, only my wooden tents have a separate bathroom and an open-plan bedroom, living room, and kitchen.'

'Sounds very fancy.'

'I hope so. I'll be living in one of them until I renovate the house.'

'You're not staying with Rebecca?' asked Cat.

Jeremy cleared his throat and looked out of the window at a gloomy Main Street. The fluorescent green cross above the chemist flickered to life, its edges blurred by a heavy morning fog that seemed in no hurry to clear. Faceless figures surged by in dark winter coats, heads down against the biting December chill, like the cast of a Lowry painting. 'We thought it might be too confusing for the boys.'

Ryan laughed. '*We?* That sounds like a line straight from my sister's mouth.'

'She's right, though.' Jeremy smirked at the look Ryan gave him. 'OK, she thinks she's right.'

'So are you back at your mum's?' asked Nick. 'That must be quite the transition.'

Jeremy shook his head, his stomach suddenly queasy at the thought of his mum's house. He rammed a piece of shortbread into his mouth and chewed. 'No. Mum only has two bedrooms and my old room is currently housing a set of bunk beds for the boys that I didn't fancy squeezing myself into. I've slept in worse conditions, but I also haven't stayed with my mum for more than a night or two since I was a messy teenager. I'm staying at Gloria's bed and breakfast until my camping cabins arrive.'

'Aww,' said Cat. 'I loved my time at Gloria's. I stayed in the room at the front with the bay window and it had the comfiest bed.'

'I'm in that bed. Most beds are comfier than the beds I've slept in, but it is a good bed.' Jeremy pointed to Nick and Cat. 'Actually, it's good timing running into you both. I'm having the opening weekend on the twentieth of December.'

'Wow, you don't hang around,' said Ryan.

'It's just a dry run with friends and family, having some food and a couple of drinks. I'll launch properly in the New Year. But I've told everyone to expect to be on camera.' Jeremy turned to Nick. 'I was hoping you could come and take some photos that I could use on my website.'

'Sure,' said Nick. He stepped away from the table for a few seconds, then returned with bacon rolls.

Ryan rubbed his hands together with a cheeky grin on his face. 'When do the quad bikes arrive?'

Jeremy shook his head. 'I haven't ordered anything yet.'

'Cutting it fine, aren't you?' said Ryan.

'I just haven't figured it all out yet. Maybe I'll just open for camping while I work out what to do with the rest of the space. I need a website, though. I asked Rebecca to help me write something and her exact words were, "*No chance. Hire*

Cat." You free for a job?' Jeremy said to Cat. 'I thought I would talk you through my plans, then you could come for the opening weekend and see what it's all about and help me write something up for the New Year.'

Cat nodded. 'Sounds fun.'

She took a bite of her bacon roll and rolled her eyes to the ceiling in appreciation. At that moment, she looked like Rebecca at her most relaxed. The free spirit who played on the floor with the boys, read bedtime stories, and took her turn being goalkeeper when the boys nagged her enough. The girl who had laughed until she cried the last time he had been home and they'd played Twister with the boys and Jeremy had tried to cheat by tickling the back of her knee. That was the girl he'd come back for.

'What's Puddle Jumpers?' Cat asked in between bites of her breakfast.

Jeremy deferred the question to Ryan. 'It's a charity that takes kids on outdoor adventures. They work with young carers, foster kids, and any other young person who needs a break from whatever they've got going on in their lives. They take kids to the beach, woodland walks, farm visits, even camping trips a few times a year.'

'Hmm. Maybe I should include that on your website,' Cat said to Ryan.

Ryan shook his head. 'It's not connected to the company. Rebecca sits on their board and uses her contacts to help with funding and venues, but otherwise she stays pretty quiet about it.'

The charity had inadvertently played a pivotal role in Jeremy's life, too, although he kept that to himself. Liam and Oliver's very existence was the result of an evening off for him that coincided with Rebecca being in London for the night representing Puddle Jumpers at a charity awards ceremony.

The charity hadn't won, but they had also asked Rebecca to present an award. He'd taken the train to London without telling her he was coming and blagged his way into the conference room in time to see Rebecca on stage. She'd seen him. He'd slipped out of the door before she left the stage, leaving it up to her to decide whether she'd come to find him.

When he had crept out of her hotel room early the next morning, neither of them had suspected the change that had already been set in motion. His seven-hour round trip had been worth every second he got to spend with her that night and now they had their two amazing little boys.

Cat looked down at her now empty plate and Jeremy thought about how difficult this must be for her. There was so much she didn't know about these strangers who considered her family, although that seemed to be the theme of the day. He hadn't known his son was a vegetarian or that his mother had a . . . oh hell, that was another sentence he didn't know how to finish.

Jeremy had spent longer than he intended to hiding in Mystic's, but after two coffees and a cherry scone, he made his way back to the bed and breakfast that he'd dumped his gear in the night before and hadn't been back to since. He pushed open the door and a familiar voice chirped from the dining room on his left. 'Jeremy, I thought that looked like you coming around the corner.'

Jeremy turned to see Gloria Murphy with her trademark, as far as he was concerned, jubilant smile. Gloria was now the proprietor of Thistle Bay Bed and Breakfast, but when he'd first met her, she'd already had a prominent role in the Knight family. As Catherine Knight's oldest and best friend, Gloria stepped in to help Alan Knight look after the couple's four children after Catherine became ill. She'd become Alan's housekeeper, nanny, and best friend all rolled into one and supported him for almost twenty years. She'd opened the bed and breakfast once Ryan, the youngest of Rebecca's siblings, had gone off to university.

'It's so good to see you back home.'

'Hi, Gloria.' Jeremy wrapped the woman in a warm embrace.

Gloria squeezed him back with affection. 'Is your room OK for you, son?'

'It's perfect,' he said, releasing her from his hug. 'Thank you. You shouldn't have gone to any trouble. It's only me.'

'I pride myself on every guest leaving with the best possible impression of our small town. You're no different. You'll get the full guest experience while you're under my roof.'

'Rethink that strategy or I might never leave.'

Gloria chuckled. 'It'll all come together for you soon enough.'

He hoped so. He had a to-do list a mile long and felt too far away from being able to cross items off it. Top of that to-do list, Rebecca, was proving to be just as challenging as he had anticipated. He looked around the dining room and took in the wine glasses begging to be filled and half a dozen bottles of red wine waiting to be uncorked on the sideboard. 'How's the bed and breakfast business? Are you doing lunch now, too?'

'Oh, it's for this afternoon, but never mind about that. I

want to hear all about you. Rebecca mentioned your plans for Archie Henderson's land. How exciting!'

He suspected Gloria had had to prise details of his plans out of Rebecca. He couldn't imagine her voluntarily getting into a conversation that included Jeremy and his future plans, given her reluctance to even discuss the topic with him. 'It is exciting. A big change, but I think it'll be good.'

'Definitely, son. You've travelled the world long enough. It's time to settle down with that beautiful family of yours.'

'I'm trying my best there.'

'She'll come around,' Gloria said with a comforting confidence in her voice.

'She wants to take things slowly.'

'She thinks that way carries the least risk.'

Jeremy fidgeted with the zip on his coat. Everything came with risks, just varying degrees of it. He and Rebecca had settled in to a routine built around Jeremy's blocks of leave and centred on Oliver and Liam. Their romantic relationship had been at a standstill and it hadn't worried him because he'd kept his focus on the future knowing Rebecca would be a part of it. But he could tell from her hesitation that morning when he'd asked if she wanted them to be together that they had gone backwards and he hadn't seen it coming.

'Yoo-hoo, Gloria,' a voice shrilled from somewhere in the hallway.

Gloria grasped Jeremy's arm. 'That's the Wintersons. Make sure you tell them you're happily married. Nick Bell was in here yesterday, dropping off some new prints for the bedrooms, and they detained him for over an hour as they tried to fix him up with their granddaughter.'

The Wintersons turned out to be identical twins who he guessed were in their eighties. Their dark-grey hair was pulled back and twisted into matching buns on the back of their heads. The black metal frames of their glasses had pointed edges, which did nothing to soften their old-school headmistress appearance.

'Good morning, Mrs Winterson. And Mrs Winterson. Is everything OK in your room?' Gloria asked with polite professionalism.

'Oh yes, dear,' they said at the same time and Jeremy suddenly got an image of Oliver and Liam still talking in unison as adults. Despite his and Rebecca's attempts to nurture their children as individuals first and twins second, there were instinctive similarities that he presumed only twins had. Although as an only child, Jeremy supposed some similarities were a trait in many sibling relationships and not unique to twins.

'Have you met Jeremy Lewis?' Gloria said, introducing her guests to each other.

'We haven't, no,' said one lady. 'Are you single?'

Jeremy smiled at the woman's directness. He supposed there was no time for beating about the bush in later life. 'I'm not,' he said. 'I'm happily married.'

The other woman took Jeremy's left hand. 'I don't see a ring.'

'It's er . . . in the jeweller's being cleaned,' he said. The woman rummaged in her handbag and produced a small black photo album, and Jeremy feared he was going to have to sit through the same granddaughter sales pitch Nick had gone through. 'We've got two boys. Twins, actually. They're five years old.'

'Oh, how wonderful,' said the other Mrs Winterson. She shook her hand towards her sister, who obliged by slipping the photo album back into her bag. 'You should bring the boys in to see us one day. We'd love to meet them. And your lovely wife, of course. What did you say her name is?'

'Rebecca.'

'Childhood sweethearts,' Gloria added.

'So rare these days,' the women said at the same time. Despite their earlier directness, if they wondered why he was staying at Gloria's and not with his wife, they didn't ask.

'I'll bring the boys in one day, but for now I'm afraid I've got some work to do upstairs. It was a pleasure meeting you both.' Jeremy ducked upstairs to his room before any more lies came spilling out of his mouth. He hoped the Winterson sisters weren't staying long enough to spread the news of his fake marriage around the town. Rebecca was a delicate operation and the last thing he needed was her getting freaked out by a fake marriage when she wanted to take it slowly.

6

Rebecca crawled her sleek black MG into the space on her narrow driveway. She squinted as the light from her headlights bounced back at her from their reflection in her dining room window. Glancing at the twinkling lights on her neighbours' houses on either side of her cottage, she sighed. It was only four in the afternoon. It was far too early in the day for outdoor lights and it was far too early in the month for Christmas decorations.

To her left were the Campbells, a retired couple in their sixties who spent their weekends asking their three children to hurry along the delivery of grandchildren. To her right was a single man named Brian who spent a lot of time yelling into his mobile phone. In the fifteen years that Rebecca had lived in her cottage, the house next door had changed hands every couple of years. Brian had been the longest owner of the property, having lived there for four years now. She hadn't noticed the decorations that morning and wondered how Brian had found the time to string icicle lights around his guttering when she presumed he should have been doing whatever busy work it was that provoked his temper every time he left or returned to his house. A flashing Santa Claus caught her eye in one of Brian's upstairs windows. It seemed he had even found the time to decorate inside.

'Hi there!' came the voice of Mr Campbell as soon as Rebecca stepped out of the car.

'Hi,' said Rebecca. She connected her car to the charger and strolled towards her neighbour, ready to make polite small talk. 'Lovely decorations,' she said through gritted teeth, trying to avoid looking directly at the inflatable snowman billowing at the end of her neighbour's driveway.

'Thanks. It's taken me all day to get to this point.' Mr Campbell put his hands on his hips and examined his handiwork. 'Of course, I stopped for a bit to give Brian a hand with his lights. I was going to offer to help you with yours, but I see Jeremy is home.'

'He is, yes. And I don't bother with lights outside.'

'Yes, I remember.' Rebecca felt the judgement from Mr Campbell despite his smile. 'I thought with the children being older this year, they might have persuaded you. They were admiring old Frosty there.' Mr Campbell pointed to the blow-up snowman. 'He'll do until we get some snow on the ground. I've got a reindeer in the garage that I didn't get round to putting up today. I was thinking I'll tackle it tomorrow in the daylight, but I'm happy to put it up in your garden if you think Oliver and Liam would like it.'

Rebecca shook her head. 'That's so kind of you, but don't worry. Jeremy has plans to decorate with them and I wouldn't want to get in the way of that.'

Mr Campbell smiled again. 'That's wonderful.' He looked up and down their street. 'I think we might be the most festive street this year. It's just such a shame they cancelled the festive prizes.'

'Isn't it?' said Rebecca. The town's self-appointed Christmas committee had previously judged their fellow residents' Christmas decorating skills and awarded first, second, and third place rosettes to the top three homes. The competition had been cancelled two years ago after it had been revealed that two of the top three had hired professional decorating firms to design and install their decorations. Mr Campbell had been one of the most vocal voices demanding the return of the rosettes. Following the controversy, the Christmas committee had voted by a majority to cancel the competitive element of the festivities. 'Right, I need to get the boys off to football now.'

'Ah yes, all that fresh air and exercise will help them sleep tonight. Tell Jeremy to give me a shout if he needs any help with your decorations.'

'Will do,' said Rebecca.

Her cottage was cosy in all senses of the word when she entered. The heating was on, the bright ceiling lights were off in favour of the warm glow from her lamps, and the scent of freshly baked bread lingered in the air.

Rebecca reached the back of the house and crept into her open-plan kitchen and living space.

'It's so quiet,' she said, putting her handbag and laptop case on the sofa before joining Jeremy in the kitchen.

He leaned towards her and kissed her cheek. 'I've just sent them upstairs to change into their football kit. I figured it was too early for dinner, but they needed a snack before football, so we had nibbles.'

Rebecca looked at the leftovers on the counter. There were chunks of baguette, a few soggy pieces of cucumber, and the telltale slick of red oil from some pan-fried chorizo. Jeremy creased his forehead as he glowered into the space behind her. She picked up a piece of bread and tore a corner off. 'OK, out with it.'

'Out with what?'

'I can see you've got something to say.' Now wasn't the time for a heart-to-heart with Jeremy, but they had such little time to talk without the boys overhearing that she thought it best to let Jeremy say whatever was on his mind.

'Did you know my mum's ...'

She watched him wrestle with himself as if trying to find the right word or phrase. 'Seeing someone?' Rebecca added, grateful that this wasn't a conversation about the two of them.

'You could say that.'

'Did Ivy tell you about him?'

Jeremy shook his head. 'No. I dropped into her place this morning, and whoever he is, I saw more of him than I would have liked. I was so shocked I just ran out of there.'

Rebecca laughed. 'Oh my word. Were they ...'

'*Don't* finish that sentence.' Jeremy opened the fridge and grabbed a cold bottle of beer from the top shelf. He spun around, yanked open the cutlery drawer, and dug around for the bottle opener. 'He was either going in or just coming out of the shower. At least I hope that's what was going on.'

Rebecca gripped the beer bottle as Jeremy popped the metal cap off. 'It's a bit early, isn't it?' she said.

'Really? I was thinking it's a bit late in life for that kind of business.'

'I meant the beer.'

'Oh.' He took a long gulp and handed Rebecca the bottle. 'I need something to take away the image.' Rebecca took a swig. 'I mean, who has tan lines on their backside in December?'

Rebecca's mouthful of beer came spurting out of her lips and they both jumped back to avoid the liquid as it splashed onto the kitchen floor tiles.

'Anyway, I'd rather not think about it anymore today.' Jeremy spun around and picked up a plate from the counter. 'We kept you some food.'

Rebecca smiled at the plate brimming with green salad, chunks of Brie, slivers of fig, and a scoop of chorizo clinging to the edge. 'Amazing. Thank you. I'm actually starving. I missed lunch.'

Jeremy handed her a fork. She plonked herself down on a barstool and dug in. 'So what's the deal with our veggie son?' he asked, wiping up the beer spillage and dropping onto the chair beside her. 'Oliver wouldn't eat the chorizo.'

Rebecca shoved a forkful of salad into her mouth and unlocked her phone. She scrolled through her photos until she found the image of Oliver and Liam sitting behind the posters they had designed for school. Their smiles were wide with pride at having finished their first piece of homework. She handed her device to him. 'They did a class project on dinosaurs, and when Oliver found out that the stegosaurus was a herbivore, it led to some pretty awkward conversations.'

Jeremy shook his head. 'What do we do?'

Rebecca shrugged and speared a chunk of cheese. 'Just go with it and see if it fizzles out.'

'Why are they doing class projects, anyway? They're in primary one. Shouldn't they just be playing with modelling clay and digging in sandpits?'

Rebecca laughed, then spotted the look on Jeremy's face. 'I'm trying not to overthink it. Last week Liam's favourite fruit was bananas. This week he hates them. Kids go through phases all the time. Oh, by the way, I told Mr

Campbell next door that you're going to be putting up Christmas decorations with the boys, so he might mention it.'

'Noted. I was going to go at the weekend and pick some up.'

'You don't have to. I only told him that to stop him putting an inflatable reindeer in our front garden.' Why had she just said *our*? It was *her* front garden. Jeremy didn't live here.

Jeremy laughed, the lines across his forehead softening. 'Yeah, I spotted the snowman on the way in. Very tasteful.'

'Mummy!' the boys yelled in unison as they bounced their way into the kitchen and launched themselves at her. 'Daddy's taking us to football,' said Oliver.

'I know. Very exciting.' Rebecca knew it was just as exciting for Jeremy as it was for the children. He'd once told Rebecca that although he didn't miss the man himself, he'd missed having a father every week at football. Ivy would stand on the edge of the pitch with the other mothers during weekday practice sessions, but on weekend match days, she'd been surrounded by dads cheering on their kids and yelling the occasional expletive at the coach or the volunteer referee. The perimeter of the football field was much more diverse now, but Rebecca still remembered the boys' club it used to be when Ryan played as a youngster. Jeremy had talked about coming home for good ever since he'd found out he was going to be a father, but it had been Oliver scoring his first, and so far his only, goal that had been the final push for Jeremy to set his theoretical plans in motion.

∼

They dropped Oliver and Liam off, and with Jeremy offering to hang around on the sidelines for the entire match, Rebecca thought she could skip away and finish a few work tasks to get a head start before the weekend. Besides, standing in the dark on the sidelines of a soggy football field wasn't her favourite Thursday night activity. She drove into town and found a parking space on Main Street, just off the promenade. The shops were closed and the streets were empty, a stillness settling over the town. Only the soft, rhythmic sound of the tide lapping the shore filled the air around her.

She headed straight to Mystic Coffee. The deep smokiness of freshly brewed coffee was immediately comforting and the crackling of the fire on the back wall tempted her to linger. As long as she was back before the final whistle, the boys would be none the wiser.

Mystic greeted her with a cheery smile. 'I rarely see you in here at this time of day.'

'I've just dropped the boys off at football.'

'Ah. It's a cold one tonight. You'll be needing something to warm you up then.'

'Yes, please. Just a coffee,' said Rebecca, loosening the scarf around her neck and unfastening her coat.

'Sitting in?'

Rebecca nodded, and Mystic grabbed a mug. 'The boys probably won't even feel the cold. Running around and burning off all that youthful energy.'

'I know. They're just in football strips. They ditched their fleecy tops as soon as they stepped onto the grass.'

Mystic flicked a switch and the coffee machine roared into action. 'Fancy trying our Christmas blend?'

Rebecca grimaced. 'No, thanks. It'll be another few weeks before I'm up for that.'

Mystic laughed. 'You realise it's only three weeks until Christmas?'

'Uh-huh.'

Mystic placed the mug on the metal tray of the coffee machine and jabbed a couple of buttons. 'What's the essential Christmas toy this year?'

'I think I'm still a year or two away from that trauma. Everything on their lists was easy to order.'

'I hear Jeremy has bought Archie Henderson's land.'

'Yes.' Rebecca pursed her lips at Mystic's not-so-subtle segue from Christmas to Jeremy.

'Well, now he's home for good, maybe the time is right for you to rekindle that love. You're good for each other.'

Mystic slid the mug of steaming-hot coffee across the counter and Rebecca tapped her phone against the card reader. The payment-processed chime came at the same time as the quaint metal bell above the coffee shop door tinged, and Rebecca sighed at the sight of Gloria striding in. Rebecca had yet to see Gloria since Jeremy had come home, but Gloria had been dropping Jeremy's name into every conversation they'd had over the last fortnight. She plastered a smile on her face and picked up her coffee.

Gloria shucked off her coat to reveal a camel-coloured jumper and chunky jewellery that complemented her silver hair and matched her bright-pink lipstick. Today's choice was fuchsia dot earrings and matching necklace. Fuchsia was Gloria's colour. She'd been wearing the same shade on her lips the entire time Rebecca had known her.

'Rebecca! What an unexpected and lovely surprise,' said Gloria. Her tone suggested there was nothing unexpected about it. She'd probably spotted Rebecca parking from the bed and breakfast windows and dashed across the street. 'How is that handsome Marine of yours?'

Rebecca cleared her throat. Gloria was straight to the point as ever. 'He's not my Marine. And Mystic has already given me the rekindled love chat, so you can save your speech.'

'I have,' said Mystic, leaning on the counter as though she was settling in to watch some kind of show.

Gloria cupped Rebecca's face with her hand. 'Oh, hen, there's nothing to rekindle with you two. That spark never left either of you.' Gloria rubbed her fingers across the top of Rebecca's hair to mess her fringe up a little. It was a move she'd been doing since Rebecca was a teenager. It used to be accompanied by the phrase *soften your edges a touch*, but Gloria had long since stopped saying that. Messing up Rebecca's neatly combed fringe was enough for Rebecca to know exactly what Gloria thought she should do.

Rebecca caught the look that passed between Gloria and her coffee shop owner friend and knew they were scheming. The pair were enthusiastic matchmakers. They usually confined their love matching to the boys in their lives. Ryan was a key target, but he had so far evaded every potential match. Their other frequent victim had been Nick Bell, local photographer and Thistle Bay Art Gallery owner. Now Nick and Cat seemed happily loved up, Rebecca hoped they weren't switching their well-intentioned meddling to her romantic relationship.

'While I'm seeing you, Gloria,' said Rebecca, forcing a change of subject, 'your boiler is due its annual service. I've booked the engineer to come on Tuesday next week between one and four in the afternoon. Just let me know if you won't be there and I can swing by and sort it.'

'I'll be there,' said Gloria. 'But didn't you tell me last year that you'd give me the paperwork so I can sort out things like that myself?'

Rebecca nodded. 'I'll get it to you.'

Gloria gave her a doubtful look. Rebecca rattled off an excuse about catching up on some work and took her coffee to a table in the corner. This was going to be the worst part about Jeremy being home. The entire town would watch them, willing them to get together. They had history, and they had the boys, but rekindled love rarely worked out and definitely not when it was under the glare of an entire town. She opened her laptop and retreated to the place she felt most comfortable.

After clearing a bunch of emails, Rebecca checked the time on her phone and took a gulp of her coffee. She had ten minutes to finish her drink before she had to head back to the football pitch.

The bell above the door tinged again and a rush of cool air brought a shivering Cat Radcliffe clutching her laptop to her chest into the coffee shop. With her light-brown hair pulled back into a messy bun, there was a passing resemblance to Elizabeth . . . and to their mother. Rebecca blinked hard and pushed thoughts of her mum away. Cat seemed stuck in the doorway, as if deciding whether to come in or beat a hasty retreat. Rebecca smiled and waved, and was a little relieved when Cat finally stepped inside and closed the door.

As Cat placed and waited for her order, Rebecca contemplated what to say to her. They were still at the stage of tiptoeing around each other. Cat's entirely justified anger at the secret Rebecca had kept from her had faded, but they hadn't found the sibling camaraderie that Cat seemed to have already developed with Ryan and Elizabeth.

Cat collected her drink and hovered again until Rebecca called her over. 'Cat, will you join me?'

She slipped into the chair opposite Rebecca with a

tentative smile and placed her laptop on the table. 'On your own tonight?'

'The boys are at football. I need to collect them shortly.'

Cat kept her coat on and rubbed her hands together before warming them on her mug. 'They must be freezing.'

'You'd think, but they don't seem to feel it. I'm glad I bumped into you. We've got another meeting on Wednesday with the conference venue supplier. It's one of the last steps to taking forward your idea. We'd love for you to come if you're free.'

Cat shook her head. 'Sorry, I've got a meeting on Wednesday with a potential new client.'

Rebecca didn't expect Cat to drop everything to work for the family business, but she had so far resisted every attempt by Rebecca to get her involved even a little. 'How are things going with Nick?' Rebecca asked, changing the subject.

Cat smiled, the tops of her cheeks turning pink. 'It's early days, but pretty great so far.'

That's what Rebecca would have liked to be saying about her relationship with Cat. It was indeed early days, but there was nothing great about it. There was an awkwardness there that Rebecca didn't know how to fix. After decades of trying to find Cat, they'd finally found her, and Rebecca had driven a wedge between them and she only had herself to blame. She was the one who had insisted they delay telling Cat why they had tracked her down. Cat's arrival had transformed her calm and in control dad into an anxious and uptight version of himself that Rebecca hadn't seen in a long time. Helping him through that had felt like the priority, but she hadn't considered Cat's needs and was now paying the price for that.

'I'm glad it's going well.' Rebecca took a last gulp of her

coffee. 'Sadly, I need to brave the cold again and watch the last ten minutes of a football match and pretend to be interested. Don't work too hard.'

Cat laughed and Rebecca caught a flash of how things could be between them. 'I won't.'

Rebecca placed her mug on Mystic's counter and said goodnight on her way out. She wrapped her scarf tighter around her neck and dug her hands into her pockets as she walked back to her car. At least things between Nick and Cat were good. Nick and Ryan had been friends since they were kids, and Rebecca knew he was a good guy. She just hoped he didn't screw up his fledgling relationship. Cat had so far decided she wanted to stay in Thistle Bay, but there was nothing like nursing a broken heart to make someone leave town, and Rebecca really didn't want to lose her sister all over again.

7

Early on Saturday morning, Jeremy flicked his car's hazard warning lights on, stepped out onto the grass verge, and peered over the fence that bordered the arable farmland he had bought from old Mr Henderson a year ago. He'd never owned a home and now he was jumping into six acres of land that was all his.

Archie Henderson had one son and he used to say he was a banker in the City. When the banking crisis happened and the economy was on the verge of collapse, Archie switched to simply saying his boy worked in the City. Whatever Gregor Henderson did, he had no interest in small-town farming, and Archie put the farm up for sale when he finally retired at age seventy-five.

Jeremy had been apprehensive about telling Archie that he wanted to buy the land and convert it to an adventure experience. He had thought nostalgia would make Archie struggle to sell it to anyone who wasn't a farmer. But if there was one thing he had learned about living in a small town it was that you were better off being honest with people. As far as Jeremy knew, Archie had no plans to move away. Jeremy would see him regularly, and if he weren't straight with Archie about what he planned to do, someone else would end up telling him. Jeremy's offer for the land had included a note of his intention to transition away from farming.

Archie had been ready to accept the deal and Jeremy had scheduled a few days' leave to get the deal signed when a sheep farmer from the Borders made a last-minute offer that was higher than Jeremy's. Jeremy thought he was out of the running. Instead, Archie had summoned him to the farm early one morning and subjected him to what had felt like an interview.

'What's the first thing you'll do if you take over the farm?' Archie had asked him as they had strolled among the barns and into one of the barley fields.

Jeremy recalled glancing down at his feet, grateful he had rethought his footwear and replaced his trainers with working boots. 'Nothing immediately. It'll be towards the end of the year before I'm able to do anything major. Once I'm back in town permanently, I plan to strip out these fields and replace them with grass, mostly. Some bark depending on where each activity ends up.'

Archie had scratched at the back of his neck. 'What exactly do you plan to do here?'

'It'll be an adventure playground for grown-ups. Archery, clay pigeon shooting, corporate team-building events, and maybe a military-style assault course for those who don't mind a bit of a workout and getting muddy. I'll have onsite accommodation, too.'

'Tents?'

Jeremy had shaken his head and noted a glint of relief in

Archie's eyes. 'Camping cabins. They're wooden houses, but small. I'm going to start off with four cabins, accommodating up to sixteen people, and I hope to scale this to eight cabins once the business is generating income. I'm also planning a barbecue cabin in the middle where guests can chat around the log fire or grill meat from Hugh's butcher shop. It'll be a social place for everyone to get together, whether they're camping in a group or travelling on their own.'

'Why do you want the land?' Archie had asked.

'To start my adventure business.'

'I know that, son. But *why*?'

Jeremy had stared out over the landscape. The early-morning mist had cleared to reveal the rolling hills, the quaint town, and the sea, which could alternate between serene and savage over the course of half an hour. The glistening beachfront was a favourite with his children. They played on the sand, paddled in the water, and ate ice creams or pastries, depending on what took their fancy that day. It was idyllic. 'I'm not looking to farm,' Jeremy had said. 'Nor am I looking to build an empire. My business proposal gives tourists another reason to come to our town and I think that's good for everyone. But even that's not what's driving me. I just want to be here with my family, and I need a way to pay for that.'

Archie Henderson had extended his hand. 'That's good enough for me, son.' A handshake first thing in the morning and the contracts had been signed by noon. Archie had even offered to stay on as farm manager until Jeremy was ready to take over.

In the months that followed, and with Archie's help, Jeremy accelerated his plans. Archie had ploughed the fields, ready for planting. Field grass and turf had replaced his wheat and barley fields. He had overseen the repair of a few collapsed dry-stone walls and the replacement of the weather-beaten fences that marked the perimeter of the six acres. Archie had even insisted on being there when his barns had been demolished and when the foundations for the cabins had been dug in to ready the land for Jeremy's new business venture.

Now, here Jeremy was, unlatching the wide metal gates that led to his very own plot of land in his hometown. He pushed the gates open, hopped back in his car, and headed straight for the ancient stone farmhouse that sat proudly at the end of the wide gravel driveway. The two-storey house was over three hundred years old, and the one and only time Jeremy had seen inside, it was cluttered with Archie's belongings. Archie had moved out in the autumn and had told Jeremy, 'I've left a few bits and pieces of furniture that I don't need. They might come in handy for you since you're starting from nothing.'

He was starting from nothing. Jeremy hadn't lived in the town for more than a few weeks at a time since he was eighteen years old, but the last twenty-two years faded into the background as his future dangled in front of him just waiting for him to grab it. He parked in front of the house, made his way across the drive to the edge of the fields, and stared at the sunken concrete plinths awaiting his camping cabins.

The central platform would house his barbecue hut. He could almost see his guests coming together, warming up around the fire, cooking some food, and enjoying each other's company. He furrowed his brow, and kicked at the edge of the grass. That was where his vision ended. He'd seen others struggle with life away from the Marines. The ones who succeeded had found another purpose. Something else they went all in with. He surveyed his land again. This was the right place. He just had to decide which activities to offer.

At the boundary of his land stood a compact barn with light panelled wood and a sloping grey roof. It was the newest structure, surrounded by grass and a solid fence, and the only structure that Archie Henderson had suggested Jeremy keep. Jeremy had agreed, seeing it as an ideal storage place for the equipment he would need for his adventure business. Now he just had to figure out what equipment he needed and get it ordered. There wouldn't be any complicated setup or construction, so he could indulge himself with another week of procrastinating before he had to decide.

Tyres crunched on the driveway behind him and he turned to see Rebecca's car slowing to a stop.

'Daddy!' He heard his boys' voices through the closed car windows and Jeremy smiled. Children shrieking in enclosed spaces burned through Rebecca's already short fuse faster than almost anything else.

Jeremy opened the rear door to the black MG and put his finger to his lips. 'Shh. I saw rabbits on the grass and we don't want to scare them away.'

Jeremy leaned in and released their seatbelts. The boys wiggled out of their car seats and charged towards the grass without silence or stealth.

'I'm on my second round of headache pills already today.' Rebecca strolled around the front of her car.

Jeremy placed his hands on the side of her head and massaged her temples. 'They're full-on when they're excited, huh?'

'You have no idea.'

'That's something I'm here to change.' He clocked the regret in Rebecca's eyes at her choice of words. He slipped one hand around her lower back and her body tensed as he kissed her on the cheek.

A child crashed into his legs. 'Daddy, Liam scared away the rabbits.'

'Nuh-uh,' protested Liam. 'I was as quiet as a mouse.'

'That's the problem,' said Oliver haughtily. 'Mouses are not quiet. They scurry around scratching the floor and chomping on things they're not allowed to eat and they keep you awake all night because of their noise.'

Liam nodded his agreement, having got over the accusation levelled in his direction by his brother.

'We had mice in the cottage,' said Rebecca.

'Ah,' said Jeremy. 'Do you need me to get some traps?'

Liam shook his head and clamped his little hands on his hips. 'Me and Mummy already caught them. We used a stinky cheese at first, but the mice didn't seem to like it, so we used peanut butter instead and caught three.'

'Three? Wow! Well done. It's difficult to catch mice. You must have the magic touch.' Jeremy ruffled his son's hair and Liam's grin lit up his entire face as he revelled in the compliment.

'We took the boxes to the field behind our house and let them go.'

Oliver tucked his hand into Jeremy's. 'I stayed home with Auntie Elizabeth,' he mumbled. 'Do you think there will be any mouses in your new house, Daddy?'

Jeremy squeezed Oliver's hand. 'I don't think so. But if there are, it sounds like your brother and Mummy are expert rodent catchers, so they won't be there for long. Come on, shall we have a look inside?'

The heavy wooden front door had seen better days and would feature high on the upgrade list. Daylight poured through cracks in the wood that maybe weren't big enough to let a mouse sneak in but were definitely big enough for heat to escape and wind to blow through. Jeremy crept across the threshold and into the first ever home he'd owned. He half expected Archie to appear in the doorway, but he found the house deserted and eerily quiet. Even his boisterous boys had quietened down as they tiptoed into the house behind him.

Rebecca's hand touched him between the shoulder blades and she nudged him further inside. 'Let's get in and have a proper look around,' she said. She sailed past him and into the kitchen, flicking on lights and pulling back dusty old net curtains as she went.

He smiled, seeing Rebecca's shoulders tense up. This place wasn't her idea of a home. There was too much dirt, dust, grime, and old things for her liking. The kitchen alone was tired and dated. It was large, but drab, thanks to dark wooden cabinets and cluttered counters. The stone floor revealed traces of rust-coloured linoleum tiles that had once been glued on top of it. Rebecca's style involved clean lines and light furnishings. How she maintained an immaculate house with two five-year-olds, he had no clue.

The farmhouse desperately needed refurbishment, but it still gave off a homely vibe. A water-marked wooden table and four chairs was the first piece of Archie's abandoned furniture to catch Jeremy's eye. The deep scratches on the flat surface and several gouges on the chunky wooden legs showed it had been well used. A coffee mug on the surface pinned a scrap of paper in place. Jeremy noted the name scrawled on the paper – Mitch Adams, who owned the neighbouring farm – and a phone number scribbled underneath. He snapped a photo of the note with his phone, crumpled up the paper, and tossed it into the corner of the room, which seemed to have become the dumping ground for junk mail and jagged scraps of wood.

Rebecca gathered a pile of mail addressed to Jeremy that was strewn on the other end of the table. 'This was the heart of the home,' she said.

Jeremy suspected she was picturing Archie Henderson at the table with his working overalls and muddy wellies. He wasn't, though. He was picturing a sleek new kitchen and a roaring fire in the brick fireplace with an Aga in the corner and a pot of chilli bubbling away on top. Chilli was a family favourite because the boys got to dip nachos in the saucy meat and they loved fiddling with their individual bowls of guacamole, sour cream, salsa, and of course cheese. It was a meal he always made them when he was home on leave and the first meal he would make them when the farmhouse was habitable.

He reached for Rebecca, and this time she didn't tense up. She wrapped her arm around his waist and he rested his chin on the top of her head, taking in the faint scent of her coconut shampoo. Rebecca was meant to be at that table with them. He had never been surer of that.

They strolled through each of the rooms with Jeremy keeping an eye out for pieces of furniture he thought he could reuse. He left the boys marvelling over a handcrafted toy truck they'd found in the living room and climbed the dusty wooden staircase to the bedrooms. The master bedroom boasted spectacular views across the entire town and the sea on the horizon. The rest of the room, however, was so far out of date it couldn't even be called retro. Every wall was covered in grimy cream wallpaper with brown swirls he feared would make him nauseous if he stared at them for too long. A black metal bedframe rested in the centre of the room with a mattress he'd mistaken for being disgustingly stained. On closer inspection, he realised it wasn't staining. It was a forest design in a rather unfortunate shade of beige.

Three paintings hung on the back wall – Victorian-style portraits of two women and a man. Jeremy made a mental note to check with Archie if they were relatives of his and if he wanted them back. The eyes on each painting seemed off. They were unnaturally bright in comparison with the rest of the painting and almost looked like someone had painted them on at a later date. He unhooked the portraits from the wall and stacked them against a creaking dresser with half-opened drawers and a cracked mirror above it.

Jeremy had slept in some questionable locations, but none had made him feel as uneasy as this room currently did.

The other three bedrooms were, thankfully, less like something from a horror film. Each room was empty and clad with padded wallpaper with a similar pattern to the one on the roll of kitchen towel in Rebecca's house. Jeremy suspected the rooms had been papered in the eighties to disguise cracked and uneven walls. There were no dents on the copper-coloured carpet that indicated furniture had ever been there. It appeared Archie only ever lived in the master bedroom and the rooms downstairs.

Jeremy left the bedrooms and found Rebecca checking out the family-sized bathroom. 'I think they call it avocado green,' she said, gesturing towards the freestanding bathtub and colour-matched sink and toilet.

'Yes, if we had sliced the avocado through the middle and left it out on the counter all night.'

'What are the bedrooms like?' asked Rebecca.

'Decent sizes. The view from the master is as good as it gets.'

Rebecca wandered along the hallway to check it out. 'Whatever you do, don't look at the paintings on the floor by the dresser,' Jeremy called out after her.

He found the boys searching through a pile of rubbish in the kitchen, looking for more toys. 'Watch your hands. There are sharp bits of wood in there. I don't think there are any more toys.'

'Aw,' said Liam with a huffed breath.

'Do you want to come and see the fields?'

'I do,' said Oliver.

'Off you go,' said Jeremy, opening the door in the kitchen. 'I'll wait for Mummy.'

Rebecca's footsteps on the stairs echoed around the house, and Jeremy waited for her by the door.

'I will not sleep tonight,' she said, returning to the kitchen.

'You looked at the paintings, didn't you?'

She nodded.

Jeremy put a hand on her shoulder and steered her out of the house. 'I warned you.'

'Yeah, well, telling someone not to do something just gives them an overwhelming urge to do it. No matter how old you get.'

Jeremy laughed as they followed the boys out into the fields. 'OK. Whatever you do, *do not* kiss me before we leave here.'

'You're hilarious,' said Rebecca in a monotone, striding ahead of him.

He loved her, and he knew she loved him, too, although neither one of them had ever said it. Their lives were always going in different directions and acknowledging that they were completely and hopelessly in love with each other was a level of complication they avoided. He never expected her to wait for him. Throughout the years, he had tried to prepare himself for the day she met someone else and the magic was dead. It had never happened.

Now, the only adult life he had ever known had ended, and he had to start all over again. He was just glad he got to do that with the three people traipsing ahead of him. His family. The people he loved most in the world.

The boys stopped, and Jeremy and Rebecca caught up with them. Jeremy looked at Oliver's sullen face. 'What's wrong, buddy?' he asked.

'Where are the animals?'

'What animals?'

'From the farm.'

'There weren't any animals.'

'You said you were buying a farm.'

'Mr Henderson grew crops for making bread.'

Oliver's bottom lip trembled and the disappointment in his dark eyes was like a punch in the gut to Jeremy as the little boy trudged away after his brother.

'Am I going to have to get a couple of sheep and a goat?' Jeremy asked under his breath.

Rebecca shook her head. 'He'll get over it.'

'Maybe I'll get a few chickens. The guests might like to pick their own eggs.'

'They might not appreciate the five o'clock wake-up calls, though.'

'Isn't that just roosters?'

'Aren't they the same thing?'

Jeremy shrugged.

'Exactly my point. Get a farm cat if you really need an

animal. They look after themselves and they'll keep the mice out of your house.'

Jeremy's shoulders slumped at the thought of the four faces that would keep him awake tonight – a disheartened Oliver and those three creepy Victorian portraits.

8

After an hour up at the farm, Rebecca had whisked the boys away for their Saturday activities: swimming lessons, followed by craft club for Oliver and touch rugby for Liam, then an afternoon birthday party at a soft play centre, which had left Rebecca with another throbbing headache. It was dark by the time she edged her car into her driveway, but her cottage windows glowed with warmth and life. Instructing the boys to keep their seatbelts fastened until she had connected the charger, she hooked the car up and waited until the lights flashed to confirm the power was flowing before she opened the rear door for her twins to climb out.

'Straight into the house, boys.'

'Please can we just go to the park for five minutes?' begged Liam. It was the question he asked every evening and the one downside to living directly opposite the children's play park. The swings and slide seemed to call to him. Rebecca didn't want to wish away their childhood, but still there were some days she wished they were old enough to go to the park on their own for a little while.

'I think Daddy's inside,' she said, hoping the lure of Jeremy was stronger than the desire to burn off the sugar the boys had consumed at the birthday party. It was. The boys sprinted towards the house, flung open the front door, and abandoned their shoes in the hallway as they ran inside.

For the second time in two days, Rebecca's house had the comforting scent of a meal that she hadn't cooked.

'Perfect timing,' said Jeremy. 'Take a seat.'

Jeremy had set the coffee table with napkins, cutlery, and glasses of water. Cushions from the sofa had been placed on the floor as makeshift chairs. Oliver and Liam grinned at her from their seats around the table.

'What's this?' asked Rebecca.

'Casual family dining at its best.' Jeremy carried plates to the table. Venison burgers, plus a veggie one for Oliver, topped with red onions, tomatoes, and cheese, and accompanied by sweet potato fries. 'I hope you're hungry. Dig in, boys.'

The boys didn't need to be told twice and rammed their burgers into their mouths within seconds. Jeremy kissed Rebecca's cheek and took his place on the floor. Sitting on the floor to eat was something they only did when Jeremy was home. He always said the dining table was too stuffy and the boys chatted more when they were relaxed. Rebecca suspected Jeremy was more comfortable on the floor given that the boys talked non-stop regardless of where they sat.

A game of swing-ball tennis in the back garden followed dinner, then a magic show where Rebecca and Jeremy had to pretend to be amazed by the mystical powers of their children. Rebecca had opened a bottle of red wine, which helped to both ease her headache and make the show more entertaining.

By the time eight o'clock came, the boys were on the sofa

snuggled up on either side of their dad and Rebecca was more than ready for the day to end. 'Right, brush your teeth and get into bed,' she said.

'Can Daddy read our story?' asked Oliver.

'Sure,' said Jeremy.

'Can we read *Where's My Teddy*?' Oliver asked. 'It's my favourite.'

'And *The Snail and the Whale*?' asked Liam. 'That's my favourite.'

Jeremy squeezed his children closer. 'Definitely.'

The boys wriggled off the sofa and scampered upstairs to brush their teeth. 'Goodnight, boys,' she called out after them. Rebecca laughed and turned to Jeremy. 'I don't even get a look-in now that you're home.'

Jeremy sat forward and pressed his hand to the back of the seat, his forearm skimming Rebecca's hair. He leaned forward and kissed her, his lips lingering on hers for a few seconds. 'It's good to be home.'

Jeremy sauntered from the room and Rebecca refilled their wine glasses. Jeremy returned only minutes later and looped his arm around her shoulders, pulling her closer. She felt like a teenager in the back row of the cinema, debating whether to rest her head on his shoulder. A familiar warmth stirred inside her and she sank towards him.

'They were asleep before I had finished the first story.'

'Worn out by the excitement of the last few days, I imagine.' Rebecca allowed herself to imagine having him here every night. One of them would cook dinner while the other kicked the ball around in the back garden, their children's favourite pastime regardless of the weather. They would take turns reading bedtime stories and could snuggle on the sofa for a precious few hours of kid-free time before it all started again at the crack of dawn the following day.

But that wasn't real life. Tonight had been perfect because the boys were excited to see their dad. Rebecca hadn't been working, and Jeremy's business was nothing but an idea and a pile of paperwork. Real life involved skinned knees, temper tantrums, late-night emails, and exhausted parents sniping at each other. And with her new job, how could they possibly make it work? She had been old enough to witness her parents' marriage disintegrating, and she didn't want that for her children. Her father had tried to shelter his children from the stress of their mother's illness and the toll that took on their relationship, but she had seen it.

Jeremy shifted in his seat, and his words cut through her thoughts. 'Did you know about Mum and this, whoever he is?'

'Why are you so bothered by this?'

'I don't know. She's just never been with anyone before.'

'That you know of.'

Jeremy glared at her. 'Do you know differently?'

Rebecca shrugged. 'I've seen her out and about with the occasional man before, but it never seemed like anything serious.'

'Well, this man was naked in her house. I would say that's pretty serious.'

'That would be good for her, right?'

Jeremy moved to the edge of the sofa and put his wine glass on the table. Rebecca reached out a hand and rubbed the spot between his shoulder blades. He sighed and tilted his head back until the ends of his hair tickled her fingers.

Her heart thudded in her chest. They'd spent the years since the boys had been born slotting their lives together whenever they got the chance. But everything was about to change. Her father was retiring. She was going to run the business. It was a role that came with a whole new level of expectations. When Jeremy had ended their relationship shortly after he'd joined the Marines, he'd said that divided loyalties just meant doing a bad job in two areas. She would always prioritise her children, but if she could only succeed in one other area, her focus had to be on the business that sustained her entire family.

She pressed her palms into the sofa to get up. Jeremy reached his arm across her body and blocked her from moving. He grinned at her with the same boyish charm that had first caused Rebecca's stomach to flip. Her head told her she was making the right decision.

'Tell me why we're doing this again?' he asked.

'Doing what?'

'Doing nothing. Me constantly leaving kept us apart all these years.' He took her hands in his. 'For once, I'm going nowhere. Maybe this is a good time to keep exploring what we have here.'

Rebecca took a deep breath. If she could just explain about her dad, then it would all make sense to him. Jeremy, of all people, would understand. But it was only right that her siblings heard the news first. 'What have we really had? In the years since we were kids this has been purely physical.' She caught the flash of hurt in his eyes. 'You know how I feel about you, Jeremy, but we haven't spent more than a few weeks at a time together since we were kids. We're at the beginning of a new phase in our relationship. I would dive in headfirst if the boys weren't here. But they are here and I'm not prepared to take the chance that this won't work out. I'm not willing to risk our children being raised by parents who hate each other.'

'I could never hate you.'

'You say that now, but I'm not an easy person to live with. I know that.' She pulled back just the slightest bit and fought for another breath. 'It can't happen, Jeremy. I don't know how to run a business and be a mother and be what you need me to be.'

'I don't need you to be anything other than what you already are. It's you I fell in love with and I love everything about you.' Jeremy put a hand on her knee. 'I should have told you that a long time ago, Bex, but I'm here now, and not just for Oliver and Liam; I'm here for you.'

She could feel the truth in his words, and a surge of desire rose in her body, threatening to engulf her. Blinking hard, she glanced up at the ceiling, determined not to let tears fall. She desperately wanted to tell him she loved him, too, but that could only make it harder for both of them. 'The timing is just . . .' She paused, her throat aching with emotion as she tried to swallow it down.

'It won't work and the boys will be the ones who suffer,' she said, her voice a whisper.

He kissed her once more, his hand tangled in her hair, and she didn't resist. When he pulled back, his eyes were heavy and his face held a shadow of exhaustion. She felt a stab of guilt about her part in that. After everything he had been through and everything he must have seen in his life, she hated that she was the one causing him to look in such pain.

'Bex, what makes you so sure it would end badly?'

She blinked away the moisture in her eyes. 'Nothing lasts forever.'

There was nothing else to be said. Rebecca followed Jeremy up the hallway and closed her front door quietly behind him. Receiving his green beret had symbolised more than the passing of his commando tests, it had confirmed to Jeremy who he was. Or rather, who he wasn't. He wasn't a coward like his father who would attempt to prove otherwise by overpowering his wife and child. He was someone who could be relied upon to protect people. In the worst of circumstances, he would stand up and do the right thing, no matter how challenging the world seemed. And if the right thing meant giving her up, then she knew he would do it. They were finally on the same page. Rebecca clasped the door handle and dropped her forehead onto the cool wood, wondering why the wave of relief she had expected to feel was absent.

9

Jeremy had given Rebecca her space. He'd woken up at the bed and breakfast after a fitful night's sleep, courtesy of a dream he'd had too many times to count. He was lying face down in a field with the taste of sour earth on his lips. The deafening crackle of gunfire raged around him. Above the ringing in his ears, his mind screamed at him to return fire, but his hand wouldn't grip his weapon. His fingers twitched in the treacly mud that seemed to hold the rest of his body prisoner.

The dream always ended when he heard the rotor blades of the helicopter. The whirring inside his head jolted him awake, and he lay in the darkness, his memories giving him another few seconds of the nightmare: powerful hands peeling him off the ground, his legs somehow carrying him forward, then nothing.

Memories of the following two days existed only in the depths of his subconscious. He had come around on day three in a stark room with blinding strip lighting and a nauseating aroma that combined antiseptic and the blood that had seeped through the bandages across his shoulder. Rebecca sat alongside his bed, her skin pale and her eyes heavy from a lack of sleep.

He'd been lucky. He'd escaped with nothing more than a bullet to the shoulder and a concussion. Death and human destruction was an inevitable sight for a Marine. Over the years, he'd seen those around him, people he was fortunate enough to call friends, bleeding with injuries he could instantly see were life changing, with fear in their eyes at the thought that they might not make it home. Those were the scars that he still carried.

Jeremy threw on his running gear and headed out for a few laps of the town. No one else seemed to be awake as he sprinted up the wide pavements of Main Street. The festive hanging baskets glimmered under a light spray from the gentle ocean breeze. He circled the town's border, glancing up towards Blakely Hill and his land at the foot of it as he passed. The familiarity of his hometown brought a sense of comfort he had found nowhere else.

His feet pounded the pavement as he ran back towards the beach, taking in the salty scent of the ocean. He crossed the street, and somehow missed the edge of the kerb, landing awkwardly on the side of his foot. 'Damn it!' It had been less than twelve hours since he'd told Rebecca he loved her and it was already driving him to distraction. Her response hadn't been what he'd hoped for. He'd expected her to change her mind once he was home and forget this 'taking things slowly' nonsense. But it didn't matter. He wasn't going anywhere. Rebecca could have all the time she needed to realise her feelings for him. He was glad he'd told her how he felt. He didn't want her ever questioning that.

Jeremy arrived back at the bed and breakfast dripping with sweat. His stomach grumbled as the enticing smell of a home-cooked breakfast drifted towards him when he passed the dining room.

'Jeremy?' a voice called from inside the room.

He peered around the doorframe and grinned as the other woman who had been a big presence in his life since his teenage years greeted him with a warm smile and a glint in her blue eyes. 'Morning, Gloria. I'll save my hug for when I'm showered.'

Gloria moseyed towards him with a pot of coffee in one hand and a plate of scrambled eggs with smoked salmon in the other. 'Come down when you're better dressed and I'll make you some breakfast. What would you like?'

'Is a Gloria special still on the menu?'

Gloria gave him a wide grin and nodded. 'It is for you. See you shortly.'

After showering with the sea kelp body wash Gloria provided for guests, a refreshed Jeremy sat in the window of the dining room tucking into the breakfast he'd eaten most Sunday mornings at the Knight house. Just like how he remembered it, his plate now was overflowing with bacon, sausages, haggis, baked tomatoes, mushrooms, beans, and two poached eggs. Jeremy picked up a triangle of toast from the middle of his table and used the corner of it to puncture his eggs and release the bright-orange yolk onto his plate.

'There's nothing quite like local eggs,' Jeremy said to Gloria as she placed a pot of coffee on the edge of his table.

'There's no comparison. What are your plans for today? Are you off to fetch those gorgeous boys of yours?' Gloria asked.

Jeremy nodded as he finished his mouthful of breakfast. 'I'm going to take them up to the farm with me this afternoon.'

'Oh lovely. I do hope they get along well with your new neighbours.'

'That's one of the good things about the place: our nearest neighbours are a good few acres away. The boys can make as much noise as they want and Mitch Adams won't hear a thing.'

Gloria cast a glance towards Susie, who was clearing the table in front of Jeremy's. 'That's just lovely, isn't it, Susie? It's so good when we have neighbours we can get along with.'

Susie clattered dirty cutlery onto a stack of plates and smiled. 'Um, yeah,' she said and scooted past them towards the kitchen.

'She's a good girl,' said Gloria. 'Shy, but a hard worker. And she doesn't mind early mornings.'

'Or late nights,' Jeremy added, recalling Susie checking him in. 'I'm glad you've got someone helping. You always take on too much.'

Gloria placed a hand on his shoulder. 'Only if I love to do it. Have fun with those boys.' She skimmed her other hand through the air in a rainbow outline in front of her. 'Try to see the bigger picture when you're up at the farm.'

Jeremy cocked his head, unsure what she meant. Gloria just smiled and busied herself clearing more tables. Jeremy watched her work, savouring the taste of a home-cooked breakfast on his tongue. Gloria and Rebecca were as different as two people could be in all other respects, but the one trait they shared was taking on too much and never asking for help. By the time Jeremy had come on the scene, Gloria had been working for the Knight family for five years already. She'd lived in the house and seemed to have no set working hours and no set days off. Many times he'd heard Alan telling her to take herself out for the day and leave the children to him on the weekends, but she wouldn't hear of it. She was as present in their lives as another parent. Perhaps because of that, she hadn't had children of her own. A choice he wondered now if she regretted.

By the time Jeremy had lingered over his breakfast, the dining room was empty of other guests and every other table had been cleaned. Jeremy picked up his dirty dishes and wandered into the kitchen with them. Gloria was at the kitchen island with her hands in a bowl of flour and chunks of butter. 'It's a winter berry crumble for this afternoon,' she said. 'Something nice and comforting to warm everyone up.'

'Sounds amazing.' Jeremy dumped his dishes in the sink and turned the hot tap on.

'Leave that, son. I'll stick everything in the dishwasher later.'

Jeremy spotted the stainless steel dishwasher in the corner and pulled the door open. 'I can do that. You've got your hands full. What's happening this afternoon?'

'Nothing in particular, but I like to serve some food in the dining room at around four. Nothing fancy. Just a few finger sandwiches and biscuits or a dessert.'

'Around four. Got it!' said Jeremy as he loaded his plates into the dishwasher. He was always up for food he didn't have to make himself.

'You should bring the boys along today if you'll still be with them.'

The *if you'll still be with them* stung. Part of being home was being here with his boys. But he wasn't. He couldn't even see them first thing this morning because they had another batch of activities planned. Rebecca called the shots and he couldn't complain about that because she'd looked after them on her own for almost six years. He was going to have to muscle his way into being more involved in their lives, and he knew Rebecca would struggle with that. She liked to be in charge, and he couldn't push it too hard too soon or she would dig her heels in and be even less receptive to his plans for their joint future.

Jeremy shut the dishwasher door, rinsed the sink, and left Gloria to her baking. 'We'll see you at four for crumble.'

'Good luck,' Gloria called behind him and he wasn't sure if she meant with the farm, the boys or with Rebecca. It could apply to all three.

Jeremy spent the morning driving around building-supply stores and timber yards, collecting the tools and materials that fitted in his Land Rover and arranging delivery of the rest. When he arrived back in town, he called his mother and rabbited on about the boys, about his plans for the farm, and even the generous dimensions of the back of his car. Never before had they had such a one-sided conversation. He knew he was being childish, but he also knew what Ivy wanted to talk about if he let her get a word in.

With a promise to see her soon, he hung up and ducked inside Mystic Coffee, smiling at the lady herself as she waited to take his order. He ordered and moved to the end of the counter to collect it.

'Susie, what are you doing here?' he asked, seeing Susie fixing the lid of his drink in place. 'First you get me breakfast, now you're getting me coffee. Are there any other places I should expect you to pop up today?'

Susie laughed. 'I'm just part-time here and with Gloria, so I can fit in both. I also work at the library on Thursday nights, just in case you're ever there.'

'Noted. Thanks.'

He took his coffee and spotted Cat huddled over her laptop in the far corner. Jeremy still remembered the day he'd found out about Cat's existence. He'd known for years that there was a family secret, but Rebecca had always told him the time wasn't right to talk about it. Then when Rebecca's brother, Ryan, turned eighteen, Alan Knight told him he wasn't biologically related to his siblings or either of his parents, and Rebecca had blurted out everything when Jeremy was home on leave just a few weeks later. Her sobs were as shocking as the night one of his fellow Marines crept up to his bunk and tore him from his sleep by drenching him with a bucket of icy water. He'd never seen her so out of control, and all he could do was hold her in his arms until her trembling limbs stilled. The flood of emotions was driven by a combination of fear about what the secret was going to do to her family and relief that she was finally unburdened and no longer had to carry this ticking time bomb of a secret.

Jeremy made his way towards Cat. 'How's life as an entrepreneur?' he asked when she looked up from her screen. According to Rebecca, Cat was determined to make a go of her new copywriting business, and while she had agreed to help maintain Thistle Bay Chocolate Company's website, she didn't want to get any more involved in the family business.

Cat glanced back at her laptop screen and shrugged. 'This week I'm making my fortune rewriting a website that sells premium cat food.'

'Should be easy for you, *Cat*.' Jeremy smirked at his own poor excuse for a joke. 'Sorry, total dad-joke. It's spending all this extra time with the kids.'

Cat smiled and held out her hand, indicating for him to

take a seat. 'I'm more of a dog person. I'm finding it a challenge to get inside the mind of a cat lover.'

'That's where you're going wrong.' Jeremy slid into the seat opposite Cat. 'Dogs want to please their owners. They wag their tails, give a paw, and run to see you when you've left them alone for two minutes while you're in the bathroom. Cats don't care about their owners. It's the owners who are desperately trying to get love and affection from their cats. You need to get inside the head of the cat – they're in charge here. So, what is it that the cat would want its owner to know about your cat food?'

Cat opened up her Internet browser and talked as she typed. 'How do I get my cat... *to like me* is the second result after *to come home*. You might be onto something. You a cat person, Jeremy?'

'Nope. But my mother is, and she gets more excited when the cat shows up than when I do.'

'Aw, that's cute.'

'The worst part about playing second fiddle to a feline is when my mum asks me to go out and call the cat in for his dinner.'

'I thought cats just roamed around and appeared whenever they felt like it.'

'So did I. But this cat doesn't stray too far and apparently always comes home when called. He's never yet appeared on demand for me. Although I refuse to stand in public calling his name.'

'Let me guess. He's called something like Buttons?'

'Worse.'

'Mittens?'

'Third time lucky.'

'Puss in Boots?'

'Nope. Snuffles. Or Mr Snuffles Purrington, if my mum is annoyed with him for bringing home a dead bird.'

Cat placed a fist in front of her mouth to stifle her laughter.

'I know. I keep telling her that even the cat is embarrassed by his name and that's why he stays so close to home.'

'Mr Snuffles Purrington. How did she even come up with that name?'

'She got it from a teenagers' magazine she read in the hairdresser's. It was one of those articles where you find your cat name by looking up the first letter of your name and your month of birth, or something like that. She'd texted it to me as a bit of fun. This was before she had a cat. Once she got him, she remembered the article and said it was a shame she couldn't remember her cat name.'

'Oh my goodness. Mr Snuffles Purrington was *your* cat name, wasn't it?'

Jeremy nodded. 'Unfortunately, I have an excellent memory for random bits of information.'

Cat laughed again and took a gulp of her coffee. 'I met your mum for the first time only a couple of weeks ago. She was walking along the promenade with Oliver and Liam. You must be so pleased to be home.'

He was pleased to be back, but he didn't yet feel at home. There was too much uncertainty over what was going to happen with Rebecca and what he planned to do with the farm. And he still couldn't bring himself to talk to his mum about whatever was going on in her life.

'Sorry, I didn't mean to pry,' Cat added, bringing Jeremy back into their conversation.

Jeremy dragged his hand through his hair. 'It's not your fault. It's a Knight family trait.' He caught the flicker of uncertainty in her eyes and realised that was a stupid attempt at a joke. She was a Radcliffe, although from what he had seen, in name only. The Knight women were strong, independent, and sure of themselves, and those same traits existed in Cat. 'It's my turn to be sorry,' he said.

She shrugged it away graciously. 'It's still all a bit weird,' she said. He was relieved not to feel any awkwardness coming from her.

'You might find it stays weird. Families are like that. You've only known the Knights for a short time, but I'm not sure it's any easier with family you've spent all of your life with. Last time I was at my mum's, I found a naked man in her house. I didn't even know she was seeing anyone.'

She sucked in a breath and covered her eyes with her hands. 'Oh no.'

'Exactly. I turned, thinking it was Mr Purrington and got an eyeful of something very different.' Jeremy shook his head, trying to dislodge the vision. 'But enough about things neither of us wants to think about. When are you free for us to get together and talk about a website for the farm?'

'I've got to head off for a call soon, but I've got time late afternoon if that suits you?'

'I've got the boys later. I can catch you during the week. I'll give you my number and you can text me whenever suits you.' Cat passed over her phone and Jeremy saved his number.

'I just need to know a bit more about your business and the target market you have in mind.' *Target market?* Jeremy drew his eyebrows together. Cat, as if sensing his cluelessness, added, 'I'll ask you some questions to help prompt your thoughts. Nothing too taxing. For example, is your business for adults or families?'

Jeremy thought for a moment. That should have been a straightforward question to answer. 'Both, I guess.'

'That's fine. I presume you have some way of managing the bookings?'

The way she drew out the question suggested that she doubted he would answer positively. Jeremy shrugged and took a gulp of his coffee. 'No wonder Rebecca didn't want to help me with this. I sound like I have no idea what I'm doing. Are you already regretting saying you'd work for me?'

Cat shook her head and closed her laptop. 'Trust me, I've had worse clients. Everything is do-able; you just need to be clear on what you want the result to be. I can do the words for you, but you'll need some kind of booking-systems solution to separate guests by type. I'm thinking families want to avoid booking on the same weekend as a stag do and vice versa.'

Jeremy turned his head towards the window. 'That's not going to work, is it?'

'From a copywriting perspective, it can. We keep the home page simple, then have two gateways – one button says "click here to book your family holiday", and the other says "click here to book your adults-only weekend". Although I'll think of something other than "adults only", since that sounds a bit . . . well, you know.'

Cat's cheeks pinked a little and Jeremy laughed. 'Like they're booking a weekend in Amsterdam?' he said.

'Exactly. I can put some feelers out and get a booking system recommendation. Your website can have two personalities as long as we steer customers to the right pages. You just need to be happy that your business has two personalities.'

'If the boys have anything to do with it, it'll have three personalities. Oliver is gutted there aren't any animals. Rebecca says he'll get over it in a couple of days, but you know what he's like.'

Cat twirled a strand of her hair around her finger. 'I haven't spent much time with the boys, actually.'

'That's something we have in common.'

Cat gave him a sympathetic smile and left to take her call, leaving Jeremy to ponder his split-personality business – for all of a minute, before Rebecca bundled into the coffee shop with her mobile phone glued to her ear. Jeremy caught her attention and slid around into the seat Cat had not long vacated. Rebecca ordered and collected her drink, finished her call, then strode towards Jeremy's table.

'You just missed your sister,' said Jeremy, keeping the chat neutral. Now wasn't the time to rehash last night's conversation.

Rebecca pointed towards the top end of Main Street. 'I just saw her up at the shop. She's working on a new recipe while the shop is closed.'

'Not Elizabeth. Cat.'

Rebecca slumped down in the chair opposite Jeremy and put her hands to her head. 'It's maybe just as well.'

'How so?'

'I'm still trying to get her more involved in the business. She's not keen and I'm not sure how many other ways I can ask. It would be good for her. I want her to feel part of things instead of on the outside of it all.'

'Maybe you should stop trying to make her part of your business and focus on making her part of your family.'

Rebecca dropped her hands into her lap and he knew his words had landed. Her eyebrows drew together as her mind tried to figure out a new strategy for dealing with Cat. That was a continuous source of frustration for him. She never allowed herself to be guided by her emotions. Everything had to be planned out. Pros and cons were weighed against each other. Obviously, the cons of being with him had trumped whatever good she thought they might find together. Jeremy picked up his paper cup, concentrating on not squeezing it too tight and sending scalding coffee everywhere. He left Rebecca alone and headed straight for the farm.

10

Jeremy stood at the edge of his fields, gazing out across the landscape. The Royal Marines had trained him to build something from nothing and then dismantle it again, leaving no trace he'd ever been there. It was a fundamental survival skill. Now, here he was, about to craft something on the landscape that would leave its mark. When the concrete had been poured, he had taken the first steps towards changing the purpose of this land.

It was the depths of winter, but the landscape was still a patchwork of green. He looked forward to seeing it changing with the seasons. Spring would bring even brighter greens, fields of bold yellows, and a kaleidoscope of colours from the wildflowers that he knew would grow.

Tyres on the gravel behind him alerted Jeremy to Archie Henderson's arrival. Jeremy sauntered over to meet him. 'Afternoon, Archie.'

Archie, still looking every inch the farmer despite his recent retirement, hovered outside his muddy car.

'Shall we start in the house? You've left a few things that

I thought you might want,' said Jeremy, thinking about Archie's creepy pictures. 'Do you want to look?'

'No. There's nothing else I need, so just get rid of it. If you think there's anything of value, you can always ask Fred Cromarty about it.'

Fred Cromarty had owned the antique shop that now housed Nick Bell's art gallery. 'I thought Fred had given up the antique business.'

'Just the shop. He still trades antiques from his garage.' Archie raised his eyebrows and his jaw slackened.

'Everything OK?'

Before Archie could answer, Jeremy heard a grunting behind him and turned to see two sheep wandering up the field and clomping towards them. Jeremy stood up taller. 'Erm, I think we need to call the neighbouring farmer. It seems a couple of his flock have strayed.'

Archie cleared his throat and strode toward the approaching sheep. 'Yeah, I've been meaning to mention the girls to you. They're why I'm here.'

Jeremy followed, but drifted a few feet to the left of Archie. Like a muddy dog that senses when someone isn't a dog person, the sheep altered course to match Jeremy's new position, and he could have sworn they skipped just a little faster. 'The girls?' he asked.

Archie made some kind of clucking noise, and the sheep slowed to a stop in front of Jeremy. One nibbled on the hem of Jeremy's trousers while the other kept her eye on Archie.

'This one here is Chop,' said Archie, patting the sheep on her head. 'And I called your one Rump because she's kind of an ass.'

'My one?' Archie simply nodded, as though no further explanation was needed. 'What are they doing here, Archie?'

'They live here.'

Jeremy's gut twisted as he felt the beginning of bad news heading his way. 'When are they moving out?'

'That's the thing I've been meaning to talk to you about, son. You see, last winter one of Mitch's fences got blown over in a storm. No one realised until the following day when their morning commutes were interrupted by forty or so sheep running around the town. Everyone came together, as you would expect, and we rounded up Mitch's sheep in under an hour. All except these two. Chop here was the most skittish sheep around, and no one could get close enough to touch her. Anyone who got too close to her was head-butted by Rump and the only thing we could do was herd them toward the fields. We made it as far as my land. Now your land, son. And since virtually the entire town was involved in their rescue and witnessed both their primal desire to live and Rump here putting herself in harm's way to save her buddy, the town feels invested in their future.'

Jeremy could picture the scene: bleating sheep scurrying everywhere to escape a mob of people who had convinced themselves they were helping the poor beasts. 'It's a touching story, Archie. What's that got to do with me?'

'Everyone in town feels they've earned the right to stay on this land. It's somewhat of a package deal.'

'There was nothing in the deal I signed that mentioned sheep.'

Archie Henderson sighed and petted one of the sheep on her head again. 'Look, I realise this is unexpected. But Chop and Rump live here, and if you want them gone, you'll have to evict them. I couldn't bring myself to do it.'

Jeremy laughed. 'Are you being serious?' The look on Archie's face told him this wasn't some practical joke being played on the newcomer. 'But you're a farmer.'

'An arable farmer. There's a reason I couldn't farm animals.'

'Can't Mitch just take them back?'

'Only if you want them . . .' Archie made a slicing movement across his neck with his hand and Jeremy got his drift. It almost appeared as though Rump understood, too. She chose that moment to lunge forward and head-butt Jeremy in the centre of his thigh. 'I told you to behave, girl.'

Jeremy cursed under his breath and dragged his hand down his now aching thigh. 'Well, they can't stay here. I can't have them wandering around the grounds while I have guests, especially not if they're aggressive.'

'Oh, don't worry about that. Rump will calm down, and they've got their own field.' Archie pointed to the grassy field at the foot of Jeremy's land with its own perimeter fence and small barn. 'That's their space there.'

Jeremy took a deep breath as it all slotted into place. 'I don't know how to look after sheep.'

'It's easy. They'll keep your grass trimmed most of the year and I'll tell you how to top up their feeds the rest of the time. Mitch will send someone round to shear their coats in the spring, so you won't get any parasites from them.'

'*Parasites?*'

'They won't bring you any trouble. Come on, I'll help you put them back into the field.' Archie shoved at the sheep in front of him to turn her around and the duo shuffled down the grass together.

Jeremy glared at the sheep at his feet, who he swore was glaring back. He had the feeling these were the neighbours Gloria was talking about and he was being well and truly stitched up.

The sheep were back in their enclosure and Archie Henderson had scarpered before Jeremy got another chance to object to their presence on what was now *his* land. Pushing all thoughts of farmyard animals to the back of his mind, he set to work. There wasn't much he could do outside until the camping cabins were in position, so he focused on the pile of rubbish that had accumulated in the kitchen.

Having yanked on a pair of leather rigger gloves, he spent an hour transferring random cuts of wood, scrap wire, and a ridiculous number of broken plastic plant pots into the skip he'd hired. Once the kitchen was cleared, he refilled it with tools he unloaded from his car. He wiped his forearm across his sweaty brow and pulled his phone from his pocket. Two missed calls he hadn't heard coming through. He dialled the number back.

'Hi, this is Serena from Cosy Cabins,' came the cheery voicemail. 'Please leave a message after the tone and I'll call you back.'

Jeremy left a message, opened his phone settings, and turned the ringer volume up. He was about to shove his phone back in his pocket when the same number called back.

'Serena, hi.'

'Mr Lewis, I'm glad I caught you. It was just a courtesy call to make sure the foundations were on track for the installation team's arrival.'

Jeremy stared out across the smooth grass and sunken concrete plinths of what was to be his camping field. 'They sure are. I'm looking at the area now.'

'Great. I was hoping to come onsite next week for a quick look before the install begins so I can take some before and after photos. Do you mind?'

Jeremy suspected Serena's visit was less about capturing the transformation and more checking he was ready. As his project manager, she hadn't been overly enthusiastic about his choice to lay the foundations himself. He knew the price she'd quoted had a ridiculous mark-up and he planned to be as cost-efficient as possible in launching the business. The land had been expensive enough. A former military mate had started his own building company, and Jeremy had hired his guys to do the groundwork. What he'd saved on the foundations he'd added to the budget for the cabins. They would be his primary source of income for the first few months, and he wanted them to be perfect.

'Sure you can come onsite,' Jeremy said. 'I'm up here every day, so just tell me when suits you.'

'Great. I'll drop you a text with my travel plans. I'm looking forward to it,' said Serena, and she ended the call.

With the light fading and Gloria's winter berry crumble calling, Jeremy headed back into town to pick up the boys. A quick call from Rebecca and Jeremy diverted to Mystic Coffee to find the boys petting Nick's black working cocker spaniel, Skye, while Rebecca waited for a coffee.

'How's the farm?' asked Rebecca.

Jeremy looked down at his grubby clothing. 'I made a start. But it turns out I have a couple of squatters.'

Rebecca's eyes widened, and she took a sharp breath in. 'Oh no. Are they in the house? I don't remember seeing any signs of squatters when we had a look around. Archie Henderson said he was up checking the place every day. That's why I didn't bother going up.'

'He was up there every day, but he wasn't checking on the property. He was feeding the squatters.'

'He's *allowed* them to stay there and hasn't mentioned it? Who are they?'

'They go by the names of Chop and Rump.'

Rebecca looked appropriately confused, which reassured Jeremy that she wasn't involved in what he now feared was a conspiracy to get him to adopt the beasts. 'Wait, are you talking about those sheep that were running around Main Street earlier in the year?'

Jeremy nodded. 'That's the ones.' Rebecca's laugh irritated him. 'This isn't funny. I don't want sheep.'

'Sorry, but it's a bit funny. Just give them back to Mitch Adams. They were his sheep first. Let him deal with them.'

'That was my first thought, but Archie says Mitch will slaughter them and the town will never forgive me.'

Rebecca pursed her lips as she stifled another laugh. 'The town will get over it. Just don't mention this to the boys or you'll end up with an entire flock.' She picked up her coffee and something in a paper bag that he would put money on being a red velvet cupcake. She didn't usually have a sweet tooth, but red velvet cupcakes were her one weakness. Rebecca moved away, then paused and turned back to Jeremy. 'How come we didn't see any sheep when we were up there yesterday?'

'I had the same question. Apparently, Chop and Rump were away getting their hair done to make them look extra adorable for the new owner. I think Archie just wanted me to love the place before he introduced the squatters.'

Rebecca didn't even try to hold her stifled laughter in any longer, and Jeremy wished he had something to throw at her as she strolled over to the boys.

Susie passed Jeremy a takeaway coffee and leaned over the counter towards him. 'On the house. You look like you could use it,' she said. 'You should know, Chop and Rump's barn was paid for by the locals. Local businesses donated money and put out collection tins for customer donations. If you're not keeping them, you'll need to find those sheep a happy home the townsfolk approve of.'

Jeremy rubbed his hand across his jaw. 'Thanks, Susie. For the coffee and the insight.'

'Good luck,' she said with a sympathetic smile. 'If you ever need a hand with the sheep, just let me know. My grandparents had a smallholding in the Borders and I worked there every summer.'

'How big is your garden?'

Susie smiled again. 'Sorry, I'm in an upstairs flat.'

Jeremy's shoulders sagged as he realised there was no easy way out of this mad situation.

11

Jeremy arrived at the bed and breakfast, minus the boys, who had decided it was more fun to accompany Skye on her afternoon walk. He found Gloria sitting in the guests' lounge with a laptop across her knees and Rebecca's youngest sister, Megan, filling the screen. A lamp beside her cast a soft, amber light that created a warm and inviting atmosphere.

'Oh, that's good timing,' said Gloria. 'Come and say hello to your sister-in-law.'

Jeremy thought about correcting her, but quickly realised there wasn't any point. And no one else was around, so what did it matter? He sat on the low sofa, his bulk making Gloria rise on the end of the seat. 'Hi, Megan. How's life in the sunshine?'

'So great. How's life in the snow?'

'The snow hasn't started yet, but life is good.' He feigned positivity, choosing not to mention the fact he was living in a bed and breakfast, avoiding his mother, the woman he loved had rejected his advances, and now it seemed he had become the custodian of two sheep who had somehow been given protective status as though they were the town's official mascots.

Gloria patted his knee in a gesture he took to mean he wasn't fooling her. He took no comfort from it, though, especially given his suspicions that dear old Gloria had known exactly what awaited him at the farm that morning.

'I'll see you in a day or so. I'm flying in for Dad's party. You'll be there, right?'

'I will be. The boys will love seeing you. Especially Oliver. He loves having someone to talk about painting with.' Jeremy considered himself pretty handy, but that meant he could build things from wood and plaster a wall. He couldn't paint a picture, and neither could Rebecca. His son's artistic nature, which seemed much more advanced than his years, came from whatever gene he shared with his artistic auntie rather than from either of his parents.

Megan grinned. 'I've got him a set of ceramic tiles that come with various shades of aquamarine paint colours. There are templates, too, so he can create intricate patterns easily. They're beautiful.'

'He'll love that. Thanks so much.'

'Don't you think Gloria deserves a break? I was just trying to convince her to take a few days off and come and visit me.'

Gloria sighed theatrically. 'And I was just telling Megan that I can't drop everything and jet off to Majorca. I've got bookings right through the Christmas period.'

'So go in the New Year,' said Jeremy. 'I'm sure Susie can manage on her own for a bit. She seems very capable.'

'Susie who?' asked Megan.

'Susie . . .' Jeremy turned to Gloria for her to fill in Susie's surname.

'Susie Jacobs. She's working with me for a few hours a day.'

'My goodness.' Megan's face filled more of the laptop screen as she leaned towards her camera. 'Jeremy, put your hand on Gloria's forehead and see if she's feeling OK. I've only been begging Gloria for the last year to get some help.'

Gloria clamped her hand against Jeremy's and rested it on his knee, as if making sure he didn't put his hand anywhere near her forehead. 'The girl needed a job and I'm busy enough, so I thought, why not?'

Megan leaned back again, her face shrinking away on the screen. 'Seriously, I'm glad you've got some help.'

'Megan . . .' Gloria started before Megan cut her off.

'Fine, I'm glad you're helping out Susie. That was a very nice thing for you to do for her.'

'It's what neighbours do in this town.' Gloria glanced at Jeremy. 'They look after each other when they need it most.' And with that, Jeremy's suspicions were confirmed. 'Anyway, I'd better let you go, love, and try and sort out your flights.'

'OK. Love you both.' Megan gave a last wave into the camera before she hung up.

Gloria shook her head. 'Poor thing had her flight home cancelled by the airline. Just like that.'

'They'll rebook her on the next available flight.'

'That's what she was hoping for, but the next two are full. She'll figure something out. She's resourceful, that girl. Now, where are those gorgeous boys of yours?'

'Lured away by a fluffy black dog. They're walking Skye along the promenade. Nick's going to drop them off on his way back.'

Gloria stood up. 'Excellent. I'll get the crumble out of the oven.'

'Then we need to talk about those new neighbours you knew I was going to meet today.'

Gloria chuckled and disappeared through to the kitchen as Jeremy stomped into the dining room like a petulant child. The sideboard held tea, coffee, and fruit juice. Three of the bottles of red wine that Jeremy had spotted earlier were uncorked to breathe, which seemed excessive, given he was the only one here. Bowls, plates, and cutlery were stacked neatly at one end beside a platter of gingerbread.

'Jeremy, is that you?' came a voice behind him. He turned to see the Winterson twins entering the dining room with cheerful grins on their faces. They wore identical pine-needle-green skirts sitting just below their knees, cream blouses with loose bows tied in front, and chunky cardigans, one of which was a pale yellow and the other a burnt orange. They scanned the room and their smiles faltered ever so slightly, as if seeing him here alone was a disappointment.

'Good afternoon, ladies. My sons have gone to walk a dog, but they'll be here in just a few minutes. Can I get you both something to drink?'

'Oh, you have a dog?' asked one of the ladies.

'No. They're just helping to walk a friend's dog.'

'Nicholas Bell's dog?'

'That's right,' said Jeremy. Both ladies seemed to perk up at Jeremy's confirmation and strutted their way to the sideboard. One of the ladies scooped up a bottle of wine and poured it to the brim of a wide goblet on the sideboard. She filled a second glass and Jeremy now realised why Gloria had opened three bottles.

Gloria returned with a large dish in her oven-mitted hands and placed it on a mat on the sideboard. 'Good afternoon, Mrs Winterson. And Mrs Winterson. I'll leave this here, but be careful because the dish is still super hot.'

'Can I give you a hand with anything, Gloria?' asked Jeremy.

'There's a jug of custard in the kitchen. Can you fetch it for me, please?'

Jeremy cupped his hands around the warm ceramic jug, carried it back to the dining room, and placed it on the sideboard. He heard a commotion behind him and knew without turning around that it was his children. Kids have this way of announcing their presence without having to say a word.

'Nana Gloria,' the boys yelled at the same time. They dashed towards her, their strides in sync, and flung themselves into her open arms. Gloria had played such a massive role in the Knight kids' lives that it was only right that she was a grandmother to their children. Who knew if things might have been different for Gloria if she hadn't stepped in to help raise her best friend's children. Gloria loved Rebecca and her siblings as any mother would love their children, and now she loved Jeremy's children in the same way his own mother loved them.

Nick hovered in the doorway, his eyes a little wider than usual as the Wintersons made a beeline towards him.

When the boys had finished squeezing the life out of their nana, Jeremy shepherded them towards the two women, who appeared to be grilling Nick about something. His love life, no doubt. 'Oliver, Liam, I would like to introduce you to Mrs Winterson and Mrs Winterson. They're twins, just like you.'

'Wow, really?' asked Liam, his head tilted back to stare up at them. He swayed slightly, examining the ladies from every angle as if to check their similarities. 'You still look the same.'

'We do,' said the Wintersons.

'My mummy said that me and Oliver will look different as we grow up.'

'Well, yes,' said one of the ladies. 'Sometimes that happens as you develop your unique styles. We looked very different growing up.'

Jeremy couldn't imagine that and wondered at what point that had changed, given their hairstyles, glasses, and most of their clothing was identical.

'You staying for crumble?' Jeremy asked Nick.

Nick made a show of glancing at his watch. 'I would love to, but I've got to meet my girlfriend for dinner.'

Jeremy smirked at Nick's unusually loud voice. The Wintersons seemed pretty taken with the children, so Nick had probably escaped another hour of the ladies trying to set him up with their granddaughter. 'Boys, what do you say to Nick for letting you help with Skye?'

'Thank you, Nick.'

'Anytime. Skye loved her walk.' Nick hurried out of the bed and breakfast just as Jeremy's phone gave an ear-splitting ring in his pocket. Oliver and Liam jumped and clamped their hands across their ears. Jeremy's ringtone had gone from too quiet to obscenely loud. He sent the call to voicemail, not daring to answer it given the look of displeasure on the Winterson sisters' faces.

Gloria was busy serving up bowls of crumble and custard to more guests who had slipped into the dining room as they'd all been chatting. He recognised the couple as the guests in the room next door to his. Jeremy gave them a nod, and they nodded back. They were a friendly couple, probably retired, and limited their conversations to the weather and Gloria's excellent breakfasts. He noted they avoided eye contact with the Wintersons, who had now plonked themselves down at the same table as his children. He snagged a couple of bowls of crumble and delivered them to the boys.

'Now tell us, boys, what's your mother like?'

Jeremy caught Gloria's eye. A hint of dread churned in his stomach as he wondered how long it would take the boys to reveal that he was not in fact married to their mother.

12

The start of the new week passed by in a blur for Rebecca. She hadn't even eaten the sandwich she'd picked up for lunch before it had been time to collect the boys from school.

She knew what question was coming as soon as she pulled into her driveway. 'Please can we go to the park for five minutes?' begged Liam.

Rebecca wrangled the boys out of the car and herded them towards their house. 'Sorry, not today. I've got a call in fifteen minutes and I need to see if Grandpa has left the paperwork inside for me.'

The boys' shoulders drooped and they trudged towards the house. The flexibility to pick her children up from school was an invaluable perk of her job, but when her workday wasn't yet over, it could also be a major guilt trip.

'Hi.'

Rebecca turned to see Cat standing on the pavement at the edge of the driveway. Leggings and a heavy burgundy jumper beneath a bottle-green waterproof coat had replaced her usual work attire of patterned dresses and thick tights. A small bag with a narrow strap lay across her body and one arm gripped a stack of manila envelopes.

'Auntie Cat,' said Oliver. He ran towards Cat and hugged her waist. Liam followed his brother's lead and thrust his arms around her, too.

Rebecca felt a sharp twinge in her chest and wondered if Cat was aware of just how much she looked like their mother. Their father had told her, of course, but Cat could only look at photographs. She'd never had the opportunity to see Catherine the way Rebecca had seen her. She gave Cat a smile and shifted her gaze to the envelopes. Now wasn't the time for nostalgia.

'These are for you.' Cat held the envelopes out above the boys' heads. 'Alan was bringing them around, but I offered to do it since I'm all but passing, anyway.'

'Thanks.' Rebecca took the envelopes. She peered inside and was relieved to see the contracts inside with her father's familiar handwriting scrawled on the first page. He only had a couple of comments by the looks of it. The boys released their hold on Cat and headed back to the house. 'I'll never understand why he can't just email me his comments like everyone else.'

Cat shrugged. 'Old-school, I guess.'

Rebecca nodded. 'That makes two of them. Still, Dad's not as bad as Harry Mitchell on the other side. That man has had a dozen changes on every draft.' She pointed towards Oliver and Liam, who were waiting on the doorstep. 'Do you want to come in?'

Cat shook her head. 'Another time. I heard you say you have a call shortly.'

'I do. That's why I needed these,' Rebecca said, raising the envelopes. 'It's a meeting with the lawyers to give our feedback on the conference centre contract. You're welcome to join me if you want to see how it's going.'

'I'm not sure I'd be any help with that. I can sit with the boys, though, while you're on the call if it helps'

'Oh, don't worry. I'll only be half an hour and they're used to sitting quietly with snacks while I'm working.' Rebecca glanced back towards her children. 'They're used to sitting with snacks, anyway. The quiet thing is a bit hit-or-miss.'

Cat laughed and leaned closer to Rebecca. 'I've got half an hour. Why don't I take them over to the park?'

'I couldn't ask you to do that.'

'You didn't. I offered.'

Cat glided past Rebecca and asked the boys if they wanted to go to the park with her. Squealing was the only sign of their agreement. Rebecca unlocked her front door and Oliver and Liam threw their schoolbags inside.

'We'll see you in half an hour,' Cat said. 'But just text me if we need to make ourselves scarce for longer.'

Rebecca smiled. 'Thanks, Cat. Half an hour will be great, and then I'll have a glass of wine inside with your name on it.' Cat hesitated for a second and Rebecca felt like a puppy begging for a treat. It wasn't a feeling she was used to.

'Thanks, but I'd better not,' said Cat. 'Nick wants us to hike part of the way up Blakely Hill tonight so he can take photos of the Main Street Christmas lights. I think the dark will be challenging enough without adding alcohol to the mix.'

Rebecca nodded and watched the trio skip off towards the park. Cat paused at the foot of the driveway, stepped onto the grass, and scooped up a rugby ball that had been abandoned in the garden at some point. 'Anyone up for a game of touch rugby?' she asked before they crossed the road and ran onto the grass on the other side.

Rebecca cursed herself for asking Cat to join the meeting. She had made it quite clear she didn't want to get involved. Jeremy was right: Rebecca did need to focus on their personal relationship. That was easier said than done, though. When running a family business, the lines between business and personal were blurred; at least they were for Rebecca. Still, it warmed her heart to see Cat bonding with Oliver and Liam. Her mother would have liked that, too.

Inside, Rebecca shook off the wave of memories that had washed over her and fired up her laptop. She called Megan while she waited for her emails to load. The international dialling tone cut off when her sister answered after only one ring. 'Hey, Rebecca.'

'Megan, why didn't you tell me your flight was cancelled?'

'Hello, Megan. How are you today? I'm well, thanks, Rebecca. How are you?'

Rebecca sighed. She didn't have time for her sister's games or social niceties. 'Be serious. Gloria told Jeremy, who told me, that your flight was cancelled. What's happening?'

'It's all sorted. I didn't tell you because there's nothing to tell. My flight was cancelled, but I handled it. I've got another flight. A day later than planned and arriving in Glasgow instead of Edinburgh, but still plenty of time before the party.'

Rebecca opened up the dial-in details for her call. 'You should have told me.'

'Why? Don't you think you've got enough on your plate?'

'I could have helped you.'

'I didn't need help. I'm a grown-up and a seasoned traveller who can book a flight.'

'I know that. Send me your new flight details and I'll ask Arthur to pick you up.'

'Already done. I emailed him an hour ago.'

Rebecca sighed again. 'Next time, just tell me.'

'Next time, just trust me,' Megan retorted.

'I trust you.'

'Then trust that I'll call you if I need help. Now, where are those gorgeous nephews of mine? Let me say hi.'

'They're at the park with Cat. Ryan and I are about to dial in to a call.'

'Well, don't let me keep you. I'll see you soon.' Megan hung up and Rebecca clicked the link to enter her conference call. Alan was waiting until Megan was home to tell her about his retirement plans. Until then, Rebecca couldn't tell Jeremy, and telling him would help her explain why she was keeping him at a distance. Now that conversation was delayed by another day. She had almost told him the other night. Not that she didn't trust him to keep the news to himself, it was just that her siblings had a right to know before anyone else. All she had to do was make it until Megan was home, then Jeremy would understand everything and he would stop looking at her like she'd stomped all over his dream.

13

The first flurries of snow and a biting icy wind coincided with the school Christmas fair. Rebecca rushed towards the main building, keeping close to the metal railings in case she slipped on the slushy snow beneath her feet and had to grab something. Once inside, she looked at the sea of people who seemed to know exactly what they were doing and where they were going. She fiddled with her phone for a few seconds, trying to make herself look less lost, then followed the general stream towards the gym hall at the rear of the building.

Rebecca caught sight of Joanne Ferrier at the back of the hall and took a deep breath. Joanne had styled her bleached blonde hair with a Santa hat headband and she was gripping a clipboard that Rebecca doubted was actually necessary for the smooth running of their tiny school's Christmas fair. Joanne had been an organiser in high school. She was on the school newspaper, the pupil council, the dance committee, and, in their final year, the yearbook committee. She liked to be in the middle of things and it seemed not much had changed.

'Rebecca,' Joanne said as soon as she spotted her. 'I'm so glad you could make it. I wasn't sure you would manage it, given how busy you are these days.'

'Happy to help,' said Rebecca with as much of a smile as she could muster. She *was* busy, but she suspected that was a dig from Joanne. The woman spent her days trying to guilt-trip parents into getting involved with the school. There seemed to be a fundraising need, a school event requiring parental supervision, or a playground clean-up every week. As irritated as Rebecca was by Joanne, she was also grateful that there were parents like her who were prepared to do these things. Being busy was actually just an excuse. Rebecca could have made the time if she really wanted to, but she didn't. Carving out time to spend with twenty-five children who weren't hers just wasn't something she was prepared to do.

Joanne flipped a page over on her clipboard and tapped the edge of the board with her pen. 'We have you running the tombola. Does that work for you?'

'Great,' said Rebecca. 'Just tell me where.'

Joanne gave her unnecessarily detailed directions to the tombola table in the back corner of the hall. Rebecca headed straight there and found Chad Hernandez, the local estate agent and part-time barman at The Smugglers Inn, turning all the bottles on the stall to face outwards.

'Hi, Chad. How did you get roped into this?' Chad didn't have children and was, in fact, not long out of school himself. He was the product of a short-lived holiday romance and had a thick Fife accent and fiery ginger hair that didn't match his name at all.

'Hi, Mrs Knight. Ms Knight, sorry.' The boy's freckly face flushed. His pale skin must be a nightmare when he visited his Spanish family, Rebecca thought.

'I've told you before, Chad. Call me Rebecca.'

'Right, sorry, Rebecca.' He nodded in Joanne's direction. 'Joanne came into the pub to see if we could donate some booze. I only handed over the bottles and then she started gushing about how fantastic it was for me to volunteer and I didn't know how to get out of it.'

Manipulating the poor lad. It was a skill Joanne had perfected in high school when she hadn't been offered a place on the hockey team. Three days after the team was confirmed, Abigail Fox, who also happened to be Joanne's next-door neighbour, had quit the team and Joanne had taken her place.

Rebecca studied the tombola table, her job for the next two hours. Her shoulders slumped as she took in the array of prizes, which included a dozen bottles of booze, too many bottles of glitter bubble bath to count, no fewer than five squeezy bottles of ketchup, and a jar of mayonnaise. If by some unfortunate turn of events she found herself on the tombola stall for the school's spring fair, she would tell whoever was in charge of communications to be a bit more specific about what kinds of bottles they were looking for. She fired off a text to Jeremy asking him to stop by the shop to pick up some chocolates from Elizabeth. It would be bags, rather than bottles, but at least it would make her feel better about someone winning ketchup if she could give them a bag of sweet treats, too.

Only ten minutes after arriving, the stall was ready, and the kids streamed in with their soggy, snow-covered parents, most of whom looked like they'd rather be anywhere but their children's school gym hall on a dreary winter's day.

Their first four customers took home a bottle of gin and three of the bottles of wine, to the obvious delight of their worn-out-looking parents. Child number five wasn't as lucky. Jodie Hopkins, who was in primary six and lived just a few doors down from Rebecca, pulled out her winning ticket. The poor girl's face fell when Chad handed over the solitary jar of mayonnaise. She soon brightened when Rebecca slipped her a ten-pound note alongside her creamy condiment.

By the time Rebecca had given away a bottle of ketchup and the last note in her purse, Jeremy had arrived with Oliver, Liam, and Elizabeth in tow and weighed down by a cardboard box that she hoped was brimming with bags of chocolate. Rebecca slid a chair towards Jeremy and he lowered the box onto the seat. She rummaged in the box and thanked her sister for the stash of chocolate buttons and fruit-centred truffles.

Elizabeth bought two raffle tickets from Chad and handed them to Oliver and Liam to open.

'My number is forty-three,' announced Liam.

'Sorry, pal,' said Chad, who had turned out to be a natural with the kids. 'The number has to end in a zero or a five to be a winner.'

Oliver took his time unfolding his little white ticket. 'My number is one hundred and five.'

Liam hooted and jumped up and down. 'You've won something, Auntie Elizabeth.'

'So I have,' Elizabeth said, leaning over to give a beaming Oliver a kiss on the top of the head. 'My lucky charm,' she said, ruffling his hair.

Chad moved round to the front of the stall. 'Can you boys help me find number one hundred and five?' The boys scanned the stall's goodies and Rebecca watched as Chad, who knew exactly where the winning bottle was, steered their gazes towards the alcohol end of the table.

'I found it,' Oliver called out. 'It's wine.'

Chad scooped up the bottle and handed it to Elizabeth. 'It's gin, actually. Congratulations, Mrs Knight, I mean Ms Knight.'

'Thank you, Chad. And please just call me Elizabeth.'

Elizabeth waved her raspberry gin prize in Rebecca's direction. 'Got time for a drink on Friday night?'

'If you don't mind coming to me. I'll have the boys.'

'I can take the boys,' said Jeremy. 'They'd love a sleepover at Nana's bed and breakfast.'

'That's really not a good idea. With two five-year-olds in your bed, you won't get a wink of sleep. You could always ask your mum to babysit.'

Jeremy scoffed. 'Nope. Still avoiding seeing her in person.'

Rebecca gripped Jeremy's shoulders and gave them a playful shake. 'You're going to have to have the conversation with her at some point. The longer you leave it, the more awkward it's going to be. Just get it over and done with.' She pushed away thoughts of their own awkward conversation. Jeremy had told her he loved her and she'd shut him down without being truly open about her reasons. That kind of declaration needed a discussion, but Jeremy hadn't pushed her, and she was doing her best not to bring it up again until Megan was home.

'Yes, boss,' said Jeremy, turning to the boys. 'Is Mummy right?'

Liam grinned. 'Always.'

'Not always,' said Rebecca. 'But I am right in this case.'

'I'll make you a deal,' said Jeremy. 'I'll ask Mum to babysit on Friday if you come to dinner with me.'

Rebecca tilted her head and pouted. 'Sorry, can't. I have plans with my sister.'

Elizabeth stepped forward. 'Actually, I just remembered I told Ryan I'd see a movie with him on Friday. So it looks like you're free after all.'

Rebecca glowered at her sister, and Jeremy grinned. 'Come on,' he said. 'We haven't exactly spent much time together, just the two of us, since the boys were born.'

Rebecca weighed up the various scenarios. If Jeremy wanted to talk, she couldn't. And if it wasn't that, then a romantic dinner for two was not a good idea. Her head was screaming at her to say no, but against her better judgement, she asked, 'Where are you planning to take me?'

Jeremy grinned. 'The Smugglers Inn. Alex is making some kind of cheese-stuffed pie. It sounds amazing.'

'That's very... public.'

'It'll be fun.'

Rebecca rolled her eyes and chewed her bottom lip to stop herself from smiling. 'Fine. If you see Ivy, I'll come to dinner.'

'Excellent. It's a date.' Jeremy steered Oliver and Liam together. 'Shall we check out the bake sale? I'll buy you something nice and sugary before I leave you with Mummy tonight.'

'Yes!' the boys cheered in unison.

'Can I get my face painted before we buy cakes?' asked Oliver. 'I want to be a tiger.'

'I wanted to be an elephant,' said Liam. 'But Auntie Cat said I would probably end up looking like a mouse, so I'm going to be a cat instead. A grey one with a pink nose.'

'Lovely,' said Rebecca, trying not to worry too much about how long it was going to take to scrub their face paint off in the bath that night. She leaned forward to Elizabeth. 'Cat's here?'

'Yep,' her sister confirmed. 'We saw her on the way in. Mystic roped her into helping with the face painting.'

'I'll stop by and see her when I can get away from here. And by the way, thanks a lot, traitor. I think what you did here just violated some sister code.'

Elizabeth laughed and cupped Rebecca's cheek with her hand. 'It's for your own good.'

Rebecca shook Elizabeth's hand away and turned to Jeremy. 'Not too much sugar, please.'

He gave her an exaggerated military salute and kissed her on the cheek.

Rebecca pulled back sharply. 'That's one of the reasons everyone thinks we're rekindling our romance.'

'Aren't we?' The amusement in his eyes quickly faded as he looked over her shoulder. 'Oh hell. You're my wife. Just go along with it,' he whispered.

Rebecca turned to see two women barging towards them. The women must have been at least eighty but were still sprightly on their feet. She guessed these were the Winterson twins. The boys had mentioned meeting them at Gloria's, having been fascinated by how alike the ladies looked despite being, in their words, way old. 'You must be Rebecca,' one of the ladies said. 'You're a lucky girl to be married to such a boy. As the young people say, he's a catch.'

'I don't think young people say that anymore,' said the other woman.

'Of course they do. It's a timeless expression.'

'And I suppose we are at the seaside, so the fisherman connotations are probably stronger here.'

Rebecca stifled a laugh as best she could. Cat and Nick arrived at the tombola stall. The anguished look on Nick's face told Rebecca this wasn't the first time he was meeting the Wintersons. He threw his arm around Cat's shoulders and one of the ladies made a scoffing sound.

'Oh, Nicholas, did I show you this?' The woman rooted around in her burgundy handbag and produced a photo album. She opened it and thrust a photo towards Nick of a young blonde woman smiling at the camera. 'This is our granddaughter.' The only family resemblance was the less than perfect vision, which she had corrected with trendy full frames. 'You two would make a very attractive couple.' The woman brazenly looked Cat up and down. 'No offence intended, dear.'

'None taken,' said Cat, shooting a look Rebecca's way. Rebecca gave a quick shrug.

'And you're both natural blondes. You would make delightful babies.'

Nick kissed Cat on the top of her head. 'I'm afraid I have baby plans with someone else,' he said.

Rebecca noticed the fleeting panic in Cat's eyes before she wiped her hands down the front of her dress and gave the women a phoney smile. 'I'm afraid I must be going. I've got some face painting to do. You ready, boys?'

Oliver and Liam grasped Cat's hands and skipped away with her, Nick scurrying behind them. Jeremy made a show of giving Rebecca another kiss, only this time it wasn't on the cheek. He pressed a kiss to her lips, sending that all too familiar tingle up her spine. He then took off after the children before she could say anything else, followed by the Winterson sisters. Elizabeth raised her eyebrows in Rebecca's direction, then wandered off behind her nephews. Rebecca really had to speak to Jeremy about the public displays of affection, matchmaking twins or no matchmaking twins.

She turned her attention back to the stall and repositioned a few bottles to fill the gap left by Elizabeth's gin. 'Most of the good stuff is gone,' she said to Chad.

Chad grinned and looked down. 'I stashed some extras underneath the table just in case there was an early winning streak on the alcohol.'

Rebecca peered at the hidden supplies – two boxes of wine carrying six bottles each. 'Excellent thinking, Chad.' She picked up a raffle ticket book and taped numbers to the extra bottles of wine.

Chad rifled through the box on the chair. 'Elizabeth has given us so much chocolate that I think there's enough to give a bag away with every bottle.'

'Great, let's do it,' said Rebecca. 'How many tickets would you like?' she asked her next customer.

An hour and a half later and the tombola stall was officially empty. The chocolates had gone down well and the sparkly bubble bath had been better received than Rebecca had expected – by the kids, anyway. The parents hadn't seemed so keen on glitter for their bathrooms.

'Incoming,' muttered Chad.

Rebecca glanced up. Joanne Ferrier was striding in their direction, making a show of ticking things off on her clipboard and just generally trying to look important. 'You take off, Chad, before you're assigned another job. I'll clean up here. I couldn't have done it without you. Thank you.'

Chad hesitated for a split second before grabbing his things from under the table and dashing off in the opposite direction to Joanne.

'Hi, Joanne,' Rebecca said. 'We're all done here. Just tell me who to give the cash to and I'll get things tidied up.'

'Oh, I'll take that,' said Joanne. Rebecca clipped the lid in place and handed Joanne the plastic box, the coins rattling around inside. 'Thank you so much for helping,

Rebecca. I know how busy you are. You have two young children, twins at that, plus you're running a business and,' she leaned forward and lowered her voice, 'I heard about that business with Cat Radcliffe. No one ever really knows what's going on in other people's lives, do they? And now a new relationship. Or should I say, a rekindled relationship. I don't know how you keep all of those plates spinning.'

The woman was fishing for information and Rebecca left her hanging. 'You've got plenty of plates spinning yourself, Joanne. But only another, what, six months, then Felicity will be done with primary school and you'll have more than done your bit for the school community. They'll find it hard to replace you on the committee.'

Joanne's nostrils flared and she gave a phony smile that didn't reach anywhere close to her eyes. 'You're sweet.' She brushed her hands down her sleeve and repositioned her Santa hat headband. 'I must see if Nancy needs a hand with the toy swap. It can get pretty frantic there in the last hour.'

Joanne pranced off to the other side of the gym hall and Rebecca cringed at the low blow she had just delivered to her former classmate. Joanne wouldn't be itching to relinquish her position as head of the parent teacher committee. The committee had become a big part of Joanne's identity. The look on Joanne's face had suggested the woman was all too aware of the impending void in her life and she wasn't exactly happy about it. Although no one else was champing at the bit to step into her shoes, so Joanne might try to hang on to her position after Felicity left for high school. Rebecca made a note to seek Joanne out at the end of the fair to thank her, genuinely, for organising the event. These events gave their small-town school some much-needed extra funds, and they only happened because people like Joanne, as frustrating and condescending as she could be, put in the time and effort to organise them.

The word *rekindled* was really starting to irk Rebecca, but it was Joanne's plates-spinning comment that had got to her most. It was a reminder that her life was at capacity, precariously balanced at best. She wasn't sure what Jeremy wanted out of dinner on Friday, but if he was hoping for more than a meal, she'd have to set him straight.

14

Jeremy had arranged to meet Cat at Mystic's on Thursday morning. He slouched on the sofa in front of the fire, sipping his coffee and running through his plan to tackle the old fireplace in what would become his new living room. The red bricks on either side of the hearth looked like they'd been added in the eighties and no amount of whitewash could save them. Jeremy could knock them out while the electrician tasked with rewiring the place got to work.

The man sitting on the sofa opposite him shuffled forward and heaved himself off the seat with a loud groan.

'Do you want the paper, son?' He held out his folded newspaper.

Jeremy reached out and politely took the paper. 'Thanks.' Mr Dennison had been the high school janitor and had chased Jeremy and his friends on more than a handful of occasions when they'd been hiding out behind the gym hall instead of going to class.

Jeremy placed the paper, still folded, on the sofa beside him. As a Royal Marine, he was frequently cut off from what was happening outside of the environment right in front of him. He had quickly learned that none of that stuff really mattered. If there were a political or world event that impacted the task in front of him, someone would tell him. Otherwise, it was just noise that was best filtered out.

The man inched past the table. Time hadn't been kind to him. Too many cigarettes had aged his skin beyond his sixty-something years and he moved as though every joint in his body creaked. Mr Dennison paused when he got to the edge of the table. 'It's very good of you to allow those poor sheep to see out their last days in the place they think of as home. They're so happy there. It would have been a shame to move them. You turned out all right, son, all things considered.'

Jeremy laughed. 'Thanks, Mr Dennison.'

Mr Dennison stepped to the side to allow Cat to pass him. She thanked him, dropped onto the sofa beside Jeremy, and slipped her coat off. 'Hey. I heard you've got a couple of unwelcome guests on your land.'

Jeremy nodded. 'That I do. Were you asked to sign a petition to get me to keep them?'

'There's a petition?'

'Wouldn't surprise me.' He nodded towards the departing Mr Dennison. 'Everywhere I go, people keep telling me how amazing I am to give those poor creatures who have been through so much a happy home to see out their last days.'

Cat laughed, and Jeremy flicked her on the arm. 'Far too many people are laughing instead of helping me to come up with an arrangement that's acceptable to everyone. Now, getting down to business.' Jeremy tossed Cat a one-inch-thick pile of paperwork. 'This is my plan.'

Cat flicked through the papers and plucked out one of

the many handwritten lists. 'It seems your plan is pretty advanced.'

'The plan is. The execution isn't. That one is a list of furniture I need. It's premature given I've still got lots of work to do before I move into the house, but I had time to kill while I was away, so I spent my evenings making lists of everything.' Everything, that was, except what exactly he planned to do with the land.

He watched Cat scanning his list. She flipped the page over and kept reading. 'This list is very comprehensive.'

'Well, I've spent the last twenty years living with very few possessions. I've never owned a piece of furniture.'

'I can relate,' said Cat. 'I'd lived in furnished apartments my entire adult life. Bed shopping turned out to be a lot of fun, though, and crawling into a king-size bed that no one else had ever slept in was magnificent.'

'I'm not sure I even know what to look for.' Jeremy held up his hand and counted out a shopping list on his fingers. 'A bed, a set of drawers, a table and chairs, a sofa, beds for the boys. I know the individual items I need. Pulling it all together into one cohesive look is another story. I fear my beautiful old farmhouse is going to end up looking like student digs.'

'Nah, it'll be fine. Ask Rebecca to help. She has style by the boatload.'

'Hmm, furniture shopping. That might be too relationship-y for her.'

'Relationship-y?'

'Rebecca is a work in progress. She hasn't yet accepted the fact that us ending up together is inevitable.'

Cat shifted in her seat and he sensed a reluctance to talk about her oldest sister's relationship.

'I don't know Rebecca all that well, but . . . ' Now it was

Jeremy's turn to shift in his seat. He got the feeling Cat was about to tell him something he didn't want to hear. 'I know that she's a perfectionist,' she said.

'What's more perfect than being with the father of her children?'

'Nothing. If it works out. If it doesn't work out, she has far more to lose with you than with any other man.'

'How do you mean?'

'I've been in plenty of relationships.' Cat paused and he could see her wrestling with something as her eyes darted up to the ceiling. 'Plenty isn't the right word,' she continued. 'It's more like a handful, or a few.' She shook her head. 'Terminology isn't important right now. My point is, I don't speak to any of those ex-boyfriends. I don't need to. A clean break all round makes it easy to move on. You can't do that when you have children. You're bonded for life, no matter how your relationship ends. She seems to set higher standards for herself than she does for anyone else and I'm not sure she can throw herself into a relationship if she doesn't feel certain she can make a success of it.'

'So I need to give her that certainty.'

'Well, that's impossible. Nothing is certain in life. But you can show her you understand why she's so hesitant.'

Jeremy nodded. He could do that. He bumped his arm into Cat's. 'Thanks. Cat Radcliffe, Copywriter and Counsellor Extraordinaire.'

They spent the next hour flicking through a demo site for a booking system that Cat had found. Cat clicked back to the home page. 'It's not the cheapest option, but it allows you to configure your own rules, which will help to keep your family bookings and your *others*, as I'm calling them for now, separate.'

'It seems to have everything I need. Honestly, I had in

mind I'd be using a diary, a spreadsheet if I really had to, to make my bookings.'

Cat shook her head. 'Definitely don't do that. You'd have to man the phones constantly. You want to automate as much as possible, and a system like this enables your customers to book online, which is what everyone expects these days. It's sleek and will save you so much time.'

'I'm sold. You should be on commission for this company.'

Cat closed her laptop with a satisfied grin on her face. 'What's the plan for the rest of the day? Have you started smashing up your new house yet?'

Jeremy sighed and scratched the back of his neck. 'Yes, but first I'm off to visit my mum. Not something I'm looking forward to. I had a rather weird encounter last time I was there.'

Cat nodded and pursed her lips in a sympathetic smile. 'With a naked Lennox.'

Jeremy needed to find a way to stop shuddering every time the man's name was mentioned. 'I told you, didn't I?'

'Yes. Lennox told me, too.'

'You know him? And who is Lennox? That's the first time I've ever heard that name.'

Cat took a mouthful of her coffee. 'He's a friend of Josef's. They play golf together,' she said, as though that explained everything. 'Although I suspect Lennox plays and Josef chats.'

'Who is Josef?'

Cat grinned, her eyes wide. 'That makes me feel less like the newbie around here. Josef runs the bakery kiosk on the promenade.'

Jeremy gathered up his papers and stacked them into a pile. 'I can't picture him, but I think I bought the boys a pretzel from him last time I was home. Where's Lennox from?'

Cat shook her head. 'I don't know. I thought he'd lived here for years.'

Jeremy shrugged. 'Maybe.'

'Does he have a familiar face?' Cat pulled a water bottle from her bag and took a gulp.

'Unfortunately, it wasn't his face my eyes were drawn to.' Cat snickered and clamped a hand across her mouth until she'd swallowed her mouthful of water. 'If he was laughing with you about our interaction, I didn't find it quite as humorous,' said Jeremy.

'He wasn't laughing, he was mortified. And he only told me because he was asking how to make you like him.'

'Really?'

'Yes. I suggested he start by keeping his clothes on in your vicinity.'

'Good advice.' Jeremy took a gulp of his coffee and winced. It was stone cold, and he was a forty-year-old man. It shouldn't bother him if his mum was in a relationship. He should be happy for her. But his only experience of his mother's choice of partner was his dad, and that hadn't been good for either of them. 'Do you think it's serious between them? Just from what you know.'

'I can't speak for your mum. I've only met her a couple of times, not even to talk to. We've just said hello in passing. Lennox, though, seems a decent man. The fact he was asking me about you, that he was looking for ways to connect with you, tells me he plans to be spending a lot more time with your mum. Your approval being important to him should tell you everything you need to know, in my opinion.'

Jeremy smiled and clinked his mug against Cat's water bottle. 'Thank you again for your sage wisdom, Cat.'

'I'm not done yet. I actually might have a plan for your sheep.'

'Seriously?'

She nodded with a grin on her face.

'Thank goodness, because I'm at a loss.'

'You get some chickens ...'

Jeremy raised his hand and cut her off. 'I'm trying to get rid of two animals, not adopt a pile more.'

'No. You're trying to launch a successful business, part of which involves giving families a memorable outdoor experience. Just picture little kids heading towards a chicken coop and picking up fresh eggs to fry in the barbecue cabin and eat alongside some veggies they've harvested from your land.'

'I don't have vegetables.'

'*Don't* have doesn't mean *can't* have. It's the perfect solution.'

Cat folded her arms across her body, an act of satisfaction rather than defensiveness. With that one action, the quiet confidence that all the Knight women shared shone through. 'Your name might be Radcliffe, but your personality is Knight all the way.' Jeremy gulped his cold coffee, pleased to see Cat smiling at his comment this time.

Jeremy arrived at his childhood home, having successfully avoided it for the last week. His mother hadn't pressured him to come round, which he guessed was on purpose. She'd learned over his teenage years to let him sit in his sulk, knowing he would come to her when he was ready to talk.

He paused at the gate. The windows of the fancy living room were open. His mum never left the windows open when she went out. He half hoped Lennox was home alone. That had to be less awkward than listening to his mum talking about her love life.

The door was unlocked, and the house smelled of bleach. Not a good sign. Always tidy but never particularly house proud, Ivy cleaned when she was anxious.

'Jeremy, is that you, honey?'

Jeremy took a deep breath and strode through to the kitchen with Rebecca's words ringing in his ears. *Just get it over and done with.*

His mother was at the sink wearing pink rubber gloves and scrubbing the metal shelves from inside the oven. The fumes from the white foam sprayed all over the inside of the oven hit the back of his throat despite the door to the garden being open and the two windows pushed as wide as they would go.

'You're cleaning the oven,' he said.

'I want to get it spotless for . . .' Ivy paused and wiped her brow with the back of her arm. 'Christmas,' she added.

It seemed to Jeremy that cleaning the oven should have been a New Year job, given the amount of food likely to be splattered all over it while cooking Christmas dinner, but what did he know? He checked the kettle had water in it and flicked it on.

Ivy peeled off her rubber gloves and plucked a carton of milk from the fridge while Jeremy grabbed tea bags and dropped them into a couple of mugs.

'I'm glad you stopped by, honey. I wanted to talk to you about Lennox.'

Jeremy felt oddly relieved that his mother was getting straight to the point. 'I know, Mum. You're seeing him. We really don't need to talk about this.' Jeremy made two cups of tea, scooped the teabags into his mother's kitchen compost caddy, and poured the milk.

Ivy moved the teas to the kitchen table while Jeremy returned the milk to the fridge. 'We do need to talk about it. I know this must be uncomfortable for you.'

Jeremy shook his head. 'It's not uncomfortable. I'm a grown-up. I can be happy for you.'

His mother picked up on his choice of words straight away. 'You can be. But are you?'

He took his time answering. He didn't know the man. Cat seemed to think highly of him, but he didn't know her very well yet either. Still, her professional advice had been spot on so far and the fact that the Knights were embracing her had made him quick to trust her. 'It was just a surprise. You haven't been involved with another man since, you know.' He couldn't even bring himself to say the word *Dad*.

His mum reached forward and clasped his hands in hers. 'After everything we went through, I thought we needed time. And some stability, I suppose. A couple of years turned into a couple of decades before I knew it. But sixty is the new forty, so they say?'

'You're sixty-six.'

Ivy shrugged. 'Close enough.'

Jeremy scanned the kitchen worktops. 'Is it too early for a drink?'

'Honey, I'll always be a mum and a grandma. But at some point I recognised I was also a person, and I needed something in my life that wasn't all about you and the boys.'

He smiled at her. 'I'm happy for you. I just wasn't expecting it.'

Ivy laughed. 'And I wasn't expecting your first time meeting Lennox to go quite like it did. How about I invite Lennox over for dinner tomorrow tonight and I can make the introductions properly?'

Jeremy shook his head, and his mother's eyes dulled. 'It's just that I have plans with Rebecca tomorrow night. I was actually hoping you could keep the boys for us.'

Ivy's eyes brightened again and a tension line across her forehead that he hadn't noticed earlier smoothed out. 'Of course I'll keep the boys.'

'But we will get a dinner organised. Maybe next week after Alan's birthday party.' A thought suddenly occurred to Jeremy. 'Is Lennox going to the party?'

Ivy shook her head. 'I'm not either, actually. Lennox's daughter Samantha has just moved house, and she invited us for dinner.'

His relief was immediately followed by a pang of guilt. He wasn't ready to see his mother flaunting her new relationship around town, but he hated to think she might not be going to Alan's party because of him. 'After Alan's party then. Let's get takeaway, though,' said Jeremy. 'I don't want you cooking and messing up that oven.'

15

Rebecca slipped her feet into her newest pair of high-heeled shoes. Glancing down at her pencil skirt and green and gold sequined top, she sighed. She had probably overdressed for a cosy dinner in the local pub, but she had bought this top last January and hadn't yet had occasion to wear it. It was too sparkly for work and too expensive for weekends traipsing around football fields with the boys. She refreshed her emails one last time. Nothing new appeared, and she closed her laptop. Her phone buzzed on the table and she glanced at the screen. 'Hey, Ryan, what's up?'

'Just checking you got those financials I sent through. I've run the numbers three times and I keep coming up with the same answer.'

'I got them, thanks. I haven't had a look yet, though.'

'Do you want me to take you through them now?'

Rebecca re-opened her laptop and hesitated. Ryan's numbers had never been wrong before, and there really wasn't a reason for her to check them tonight. 'Actually, I can't. I'm on my way out to meet Jeremy.'

'It's a bit late for the boys, isn't it?' said Ryan.

'They're with Ivy. It's just me and Jeremy.'

'Ooh, date night. Have fun.'

'It's not a date,' she said, knowing Jeremy had called it a date and she hadn't corrected him.

'Where are you going?' asked Ryan.

'Just to the pub.'

'Drinks, dinner, or both?'

'Both. Why?'

'Sounds like a date to me.'

'Ugh. You're infuriating.' Rebecca banged her laptop closed a touch harder than she'd intended to.

'That's what little brothers are for.'

Rebecca's doorbell rang, and she slipped the laptop into her bag. 'Someone's at the door. I have to go.' Ryan made kissing noises down the phone, just as he used to do when he was a kid and Jeremy came over to the house. A smile tugged at the edges of her mouth and she thumped the screen on her phone to cut him off.

She opened her door, and her smile widened at the sight of Jeremy standing on her doorstep. He gave her a boyish grin and goose bumps popped up on her arms despite the heat inside her cottage. A dark-blue jacket and smart trousers peeked out from beneath his long navy coat. It seemed he, too, had overdressed for dinner at the pub. 'I thought I was meeting you there,' said Rebecca.

'I was passing. I've just dropped Archie's creepy pictures off at Fred Cromarty's.'

Rebecca shuddered. 'Thank goodness they're gone. I just need to grab my bag.'

Jeremy waited in the hallway while she grabbed her bag from the kitchen counter. She followed him out of her front door, locking it behind her, and onto the street. Jeremy took her hand, and she fought the urge to snatch it back. They strolled to The Smugglers Inn hand in hand. Jeremy's grip on her was a reminder of the effect his touch had on her hormones.

Her mind drifted back to the night in London that had resulted in her pregnancy. They had dashed back to her room hand in hand through the narrow corridors of the hotel and they had both known exactly what was going to happen that night. Tonight, the boys were on a sleepover, and there couldn't be any awkward questions in the morning. With her fingers entwined with Jeremy's, she knew exactly how this night could end if she wasn't careful.

The Smugglers Inn was tucked away in an alley close to the beach. A soft glow from the pub's windows lit up their path. Jeremy opened the door, allowing a rush of heat to escape. She wriggled her hand free from his and followed him as he weaved his way through rustic barrels converted into tables. Candlelight flickered off their surfaces.

As they settled at a table tucked in the corner beside the edge of the bar, Rebecca dodged eye contact from the other patrons. The folks in Thistle Bay did not conceal their gawping and interest in other people's lives.

The pub had changed hands and been redecorated more times than she could remember, but it had always kept both its name and its place at the heart of the community, meaning it was always packed with locals. Rebecca had come to this very pub to celebrate her eighteenth birthday with some friends and her dad had received calls from three different people reporting her presence. Apparently, the *I Am Eighteen* badge her friends had made her wear hadn't been enough to convince some patrons that she could legally drink alcohol.

Rebecca tucked her bag under the table, removed her coat, and draped it over the back of her chair just as Christos, one half of the Greek couple who had taken over the pub a couple of years before, appeared and handed them menus. 'Tonight's special is deep-fried crispy monkfish, and it's dee-licious.'

'Sounds great,' said Jeremy, 'but it's got to be Alex's cheese-stuffed pie I've heard so much about.'

'Spanakopita. It's feta, spinach, and filo pastry. It's one of his specialities and a fine choice.' Christos turned to Rebecca. 'Do you need a few minutes to browse the menu?'

'Nope. The monkfish special for me, thanks.'

'Excellent,' said Christos. 'Are you having wine?'

Rebecca looked to Jeremy, who nodded. 'Whatever wine you recommend is good for us.'

'I have a lovely red from Santorini. It goes well with the meatiness of the monkfish.' Christos headed off to place their order and get their wine.

Charlie, a regular at The Smugglers Inn for longer than Rebecca had been alive, swivelled around on his bar stool and raised his glass of whisky to them. 'I hear you're taking over responsibility for those sheep,' he said to Jeremy.

Jeremy turned to Rebecca, rolled his eyes, and turned back to Charlie. 'I haven't figured out what I'm going to do yet, but I can't keep the sheep.'

'Why not?'

'I have no idea what I'm doing with sheep.'

Charlie's deep laugh reverberated around the pub. 'You're a military man. You'll figure it out.'

'Plus, I'm a dog-friendly business. Other people's dogs and sheep don't work.'

'Archie made sure you had a good fence.'

'He did. But it's not a high fence. It's too easy for a dog to jump it.'

Charlie looked up, his eyes scanning the ceiling before

he confidently announced, 'Electric fencing. That's what you need.'

'Not ideal for a dog-friendly *and* family-friendly business.'

'Hmm, maybe not,' said Charlie, brow furrowed in thought as he downed his drink.

Rebecca had to laugh at the fact that to Charlie electric fencing around kids was only a *maybe* not. The man was quite the character. With his sharp tongue and politically incorrect views, she wouldn't have expected him to be rallying for two sheep. She would have guessed he was the type who preferred his sheep on his plate with gravy and roast potatoes.

'Well, like it or not, laddie,' Charlie added, 'you've inherited a couple of sheep. I know you'll do the right thing.'

Charlie spun back to the bar and tapped his now empty glass. Jeremy put his head in his hands, and Christos gave Rebecca a sympathetic smile as he poured a generous measure of whisky into Charlie's glass.

'I need to find somewhere else for those sheep to go,' said Jeremy.

Christos delivered their wine, then their meals, and Rebecca and Jeremy chatted easily as they ate and drank. Rebecca stuck to conversation about the boys and avoided anything too sensitive, such as Ivy's new relationship and what on earth they were planning to do about their own relationship.

'Was it weird for the boys when you introduced them to Cat?' Jeremy asked, veering towards edgier territory for Rebecca.

Rebecca shook her head. 'Actually, no. They took it at face value. I've asked them a couple of times if they have questions about it, but they both looked at me like I was slightly bonkers.'

'The questions will come as they get older, I think. It's a pretty incredible story. I honestly never thought you'd find her.'

'I'd doubted it myself over the last couple of years.'

'I like her. She's given me a lot to think about.'

'Like what?'

Jeremy gazed straight through her. 'Just the direction I want to take the business. The questions she asked have got me thinking about whether I've made the right decisions for the right reasons.'

Nerves nibbled away inside Rebecca's stomach and she took a deep breath. She didn't want to ask the obvious question, but she had to. She'd only torture herself later if she didn't. 'Are you questioning your decision to come back?'

Jeremy reached across the table and took her hand. 'That's the one part of my plan I'm certain about.'

Rebecca should have been relieved, but she wasn't. Coming back wasn't the same as being with her. And she knew that question shouldn't even be in her mind. He had said he wanted to be with her and she had already said no, a position she planned to restate tonight. He told her he loved her, and she had said nothing. She had given up any right to ask if he had changed his mind. If he was rethinking his desire to be with her, she should be happy with that. They could raise their children without the complication of a romantic relationship that would likely sour, anyway.

Christos came to clear their plates and Rebecca snatched her hand away from Jeremy's. 'All good with your food?' he asked.

'Superb,' said Jeremy, eyeing Rebecca curiously.

'Did you not like the monkfish?'

Rebecca glanced down at her plate. She'd spent more time fiddling with her food than she had eating it and still had half of her meal spread across her plate. 'It was delicious, really. Just a bit much for me tonight.'

Christos stacked their plates on top of each other.

'Hey, Christos. Alex uses a lot of lamb in his cooking, doesn't he?' said Jeremy.

A thud made Christos jump a little, and the cutlery clanged on their piled-up plates. Charlie bashed the handle of his walking stick on the top of the bar, and Christos and Rebecca exchanged glances. 'Not with the meat you have in mind. That would put us out of business.' Christos glanced towards Charlie, who couldn't hide the fact he was leaning back slightly to overhear their conversation. Christos leaned closer to Jeremy. 'Whatever you do with those sheep, it can't involve eating them. They're local treasures. Space for dessert?'

Rebecca held her hand to her stomach and shook her head. 'Not tonight.'

'I've suddenly lost my appetite,' said Jeremy. 'I'll take a coffee, though. Bex?'

'Coffee would be good, thanks.'

Christos disappeared with their plates, and Jeremy emptied the last of the wine into Rebecca's glass. 'Local treasures. Is that a thing?'

Rebecca shrugged. 'Seems to be.'

'Maybe I should rename them Judy and Maggie.'

Rebecca smirked. 'That's Dame Judy and Dame Maggie, thank you.'

'I can see me having to keep that troublesome pair. Do you remember Ailsa Barnes who lived next door to my mum?' Rebecca nodded. 'I saw her in Mystic's yesterday and she told me my mum would be so disappointed if anything happened to those sheep. And Mr Dennison told me it was good of me to allow them to see out their last days in the place they've come to think of as home. Everyone seems to know.' Jeremy put his hands on the table and pushed himself up. 'I'll be back in a minute, then there's something I want to talk to you about.'

Rebecca watched Jeremy heading toward the bathrooms. Christos returned with their coffees and set them down on the table. Jeremy's mobile phone screeched somewhere inside the coat hanging on the back of his chair.

'Wow, that's quite the ringtone,' said Christos.

Charlie spun around on his stool and glared in her direction.

Rebecca jumped up. 'Sorry. I don't know why he has his phone so loud. I'll turn it off.'

'No problem,' said Christos.

'Maybe not for you,' grumbled Charlie from the bar. 'Some of us are too old to be startled by loud noises. Makes the old ticker beat just a little too fast.'

Christos moved away, leaving Rebecca to rifle around in Jeremy's pockets to find the offending phone. The call had gone to voicemail before she found it. She pulled the phone out of Jeremy's inside pocket and froze. Her hand had brushed against something else in the pocket and, like Charlie, her heart beat a little faster. She dug her hand back into the pocket and clasped her fingers around a small velvet box. No, not velvet; that was just the soft lining of Jeremy's coat. The box itself was smooth and cool to the touch.

'What's up?'

Rebecca flinched at Jeremy's voice behind her. 'Your phone,' she said.

'Sorry, did it ring?' he asked, taking it out of her hand.

'It's loud,' she said, eyes wide, blood suddenly pulsing in her ears.

Jeremy flopped down in his seat. If he was concerned that she'd found something else in his pocket while fishing out his phone, then he didn't show it. 'I turned the volume up at the farm because I'd missed a couple of calls about the camping cabins. I must have forgotten to turn it back down again.'

'I need to go,' said Rebecca.

'Why? What's wrong? Is it the boys?' He pressed the button to bring his phone back to life and stared at the screen.

Rebecca shook her head. 'No. Don't worry. It's Elizabeth. A bowl of rancid mussels has made her sick. I just need to check on her.'

'Of course. I'll come with you,' said Jeremy. 'Just let me grab the bill.'

Rebecca shook her head. 'You should stay. Have your coffee. Make the most of having a child-free night.'

'But Elizabeth . . .'

'Needs someone to hold her hair back while she throws up. She doesn't need an audience.'

Jeremy got out of his seat, stepped forward, and brushed his lips against her cheek. 'Call me if I can do anything.'

'I will.' Rebecca snatched her coat off the back of her chair and dashed towards the door. Her relief at being able to leave the pub without grand gestures and awkward conversations masked her guilt. For now. She knew it would return, but that was a problem for later. The pub door slammed behind her, disturbing a bin-raking seagull in the alleyway. The bird glared at her and squawked. 'I don't need any judgement from you, thank you very much.'

Rebecca shoved her arms into the sleeves of her coat and

wrapped it tight around her body. She pulled her phone from her bag, dialled Elizabeth's number, and waited for her to answer. 'You home? And don't give me any of that nonsense about being at the movies with Ryan.'

'I'm home,' said Elizabeth.

'Can I come round?'

'Sure. Where are you?'

Rebecca marched out of the alleyway. 'Just leaving the pub.'

'Head straight here and I'll see you in ten minutes.'

16

Rebecca arrived at her sister's house to see Elizabeth hovering on her doorstep wearing a knee-length padded coat with red tartan pyjamas peeking out from the bottom. 'Cat's here, by the way.'

Rebecca looked past Elizabeth and into her hallway. 'Why didn't you tell me on the phone?' she asked in a hushed tone.

'Because I knew you wouldn't come if I told you, and,' Elizabeth pulled up her sleeve to look at the silver watch on her wrist, 'given that it's only eight, I'm thinking your date with Jeremy didn't go well and you need to talk.'

Rebecca followed Elizabeth into her living room and said hello to Cat. Elizabeth gestured to the wine glasses on the coffee table. 'Want a glass?'

'No, thanks. I'll make myself a coffee. I didn't have time to drink mine at the pub.'

'Coffee is good. That means whatever happened isn't critical.'

Rebecca turned to follow Elizabeth into the kitchen, but

stopped when Elizabeth pointed to the sofa. 'You sit. I'll get your coffee. Back in a flash.'

Rebecca sighed, dropped onto her sister's grey leather sofa at the opposite end from Cat, and wrapped herself in the cashmere throw she'd given Elizabeth for Christmas the previous year. 'Sorry to gatecrash your evening,' she said to Cat.

'You're not. We were just having a couple of drinks.'

Rebecca looked down at Skye, Nick's dog, curled around Cat's bare feet. 'Is Nick away?'

'No, he's at home. Well, he's at my home. Seashell Cottage. But Skye is my little buddy, aren't you?' Cat reached down and scratched the little spaniel on the head. 'I couldn't resist her little face when she saw me putting on my coat, and Elizabeth doesn't mind the dog hairs.'

Rebecca wondered how many times Cat and Skye had been visitors in Elizabeth's home. It dawned on Rebecca that she had never been inside Seashell Cottage. Cat had rented it from Mrs Dean, the owner, who was convalescing in a care home. She'd moved in a few weeks earlier, but Rebecca hadn't bothered to visit. Jeremy was right. She'd spent too much time trying to get Cat involved in the business, and had spent no time getting to know her as a person. Rebecca slumped back in the chair. What was wrong with her? How had she not been able to see that? Was it because to her business and family were the same? Cat was new to everything and getting her involved in the business without being open about the family side of things was what had caused some of the tension in the first place. Rebecca had to invite Cat into her family life in a way that was distinct from the business.

'You need to come round to my house for dinner sometime. Oliver and Liam would love to see more of you. So would I,' Rebecca quickly added. 'Skye is welcome, too, of course. The boys adore her.'

The little dog lifted her head at the mention of her name, scanned the room, and, deciding it was nothing that required her further attention, went back to sleep. Cat smiled. 'Dinner sounds good.'

'I'll send you some dates and I can work around whatever suits you.'

'Dates for what?' asked Elizabeth, returning to the room with a mug of steaming coffee in one hand and an open bottle of Pinot Noir in the other. She handed Rebecca the coffee and topped up the two glasses on the table.

'Dates for Cat to come and have dinner with me and the boys.'

Elizabeth flopped into the middle of the sofa. 'Count me in, too. Now, let's get down to business. What happened with Jeremy?'

Rebecca took a deep breath, followed by a gulp of her coffee. She winced as the hot, dark liquid scalded the inside of her mouth. She shifted herself around to lean back on the arm of the chair and see Elizabeth and Cat more easily. 'Jeremy's phone rang while he was in the bathroom and I went to answer it.'

With a theatrical flair, Elizabeth gasped and clasped a hand to her heart. 'It was another woman?'

Rebecca reached out and nipped her sister on the arm. 'Do you want to hear this story or not?'

'I do.' Elizabeth turned to Cat. 'That was a joke, in case you didn't realise. There's only one woman for Jeremy.'

Rebecca nipped her again.

'Ouch.' Elizabeth rubbed at her skin. 'That actually hurts.'

'Anyway, I had to grab his phone because he'd turned his

ringer up full blast and the noise was annoying everyone. Charlie Sinclair in particular.'

Cat leaned forward and reached down to stroke Skye, who had curled herself into a tight ball at Cat's feet. 'Oh dear. A grumpy Charlie can be pretty rotten, I hear.'

'Exactly. As I was scrabbling to find the damn phone, my hand touched something else in Jeremy's pocket.' Elizabeth let out a tiny squeal, and Rebecca gave her an irked glare. 'Talking to you when you've had a drink is like talking to you as a teenager again. It was a velvet box.'

This time, Elizabeth's sharp intake of breath wasn't staged. 'You're thinking it was a ring?'

'That was my first thought,' said Rebecca. 'Then I realised the box wasn't velvet, the lining of his pocket was. Jeremy came back before I got a chance to take a peek, so I don't know what it was.'

Elizabeth curled her legs underneath her on the sofa. 'And you're upset because...'

'What if he was going to propose?'

'And that would be terrible because...'

'I think we need to keep things strictly co-parenting.'

'And you think that's a good idea because...'

'Will you stop saying because and say something more helpful?'

'Because is the helpful part,' said Elizabeth. 'You know *what* you're doing; you're just not clear about *why*. Is it that you think it's best for the boys, or maybe you think it's best for the business now that Dad's retiring?'

Rebecca looked at Cat, who didn't appear to react at all to Elizabeth's statement. But then of course she wouldn't. Their father had said they'd discuss it when Megan came home. But that didn't mean he wouldn't tell Elizabeth in the meantime. And if he'd told Elizabeth, he would have told

Cat, too. Without intending to, Rebecca had still been thinking of Cat as an outsider. And if she'd been thinking that, Cat had no doubt picked up on that. No wonder their relationship was tense.

Elizabeth put her hand on Rebecca's leg. 'The boys and the business would benefit immensely from you being happy. There's no downside to you going after what you want.'

Ryan and their dad hadn't seemed concerned about Jeremy being home and the implications for Rebecca's new job. Now it appeared Elizabeth knew and she clearly didn't see it as a problem. Had Rebecca been using her new job as a convenient excuse to play it safe with Jeremy?

'There's no downside,' Elizabeth repeated.

'What if I screw it up?'

'Why would you screw it up?'

'Because nothing lasts forever. Certainly not relationships, and it always impacts the kids.'

'There are plenty of people who stay together forever and they still screw up their kids. Everyone carries some kind of childhood trauma.'

Rebecca stood and picked up a framed photograph from the top shelf of Elizabeth's bookcase. Her own white gloss bookcase would look so out of place in Jeremy's rustic farmhouse. Where had that thought come from? She ran her fingers along her eyebrows, stretching her skin as she went to smooth out the crease she knew had formed between her eyes. 'This is the last full family photograph.' Rebecca glanced at Cat and winced. 'Sorry, I didn't mean it like that.'

Cat took the photo and Rebecca watched her youngest sister studying it. Her eyes seemed drawn to the baby boy in the centre of the image. Ryan was only weeks old, swaddled in a fluffy lemon blanket in their father's arms where Cat should have been. Megan sat on their mother's knee, her cheeky grin a contrast to Elizabeth's gappy smile. Ten-year-old Rebecca stood just behind her mother's shoulder, her face lined with worry about what was causing her mum's haunted expression. Within a year of that photo being taken, her mother had been hospitalised, and despite years of treatment, she had never come home again. Rebecca's carefree childhood had morphed into one of worry and responsibility. She'd stopped playing with her siblings. Instead, she'd seen it as her role to look after them.

'I must have been about six here,' said Elizabeth.

Rebecca attempted to smile, but the ache in her chest was strong. 'Five. The same as Oliver and Liam.'

'You looked super cute with no front teeth,' said Cat.

'That's right,' said Elizabeth. 'One of them fell out while we were having dinner and Rebecca combed through my dinner until she found it. Do you remember?'

'I do.'

Elizabeth took the photo frame and placed it on the table beside the wine bottle. 'I know what else you're thinking,' she said.

Chaos had ensued seconds after they had taken the photograph when Alan had tried to get Catherine to hold Ryan. It had been the first time their mother had scared Elizabeth and Megan. 'I have the same photo in my living room and it's impossible not to think about it whenever I see it.'

'There's a simple solution to that,' said Elizabeth.

'What?'

'Get rid of the photo.'

'You sound like Jeremy.'

'I'm serious. Why keep something in your house that haunts you?'

Cat leaned back just a touch on the sofa. If Rebecca was going to do a better job of welcoming Cat into the family, perhaps Cat should see the good stuff and the bad. 'Mum had a bit of a breakdown right after this photo was taken,' Rebecca said. 'She started screaming. Dad was trying to calm her down, and he passed Ryan to me. Megan and Elizabeth were petrified and I couldn't do anything about it because Ryan had started screaming. Megan and Elizabeth were clinging to each other, tears streaming down their faces. I can't bear the thought of the boys ever being in that situation.'

Elizabeth turned and grabbed Rebecca by the shoulders. 'They will never be in that situation.'

'I would have thought the same with Mum and Dad. You know how much they loved each other and even they couldn't make it work.'

'That was very different. And just because you don't have many examples of successful marriages doesn't mean they don't exist.'

Rebecca plucked the bottle of wine off the table and poured a good glug into Elizabeth's glass. 'I'm sure your marriage would have been different.'

Elizabeth gazed dreamily at the space beyond Rebecca. It was a look Rebecca had seen many times. Just thinking about Steven had always made those big brown eyes of hers go all misty. The mist had turned to despair in the early months after Steven's sudden death. Now, three years on from the tragedy, Rebecca smiled, seeing tender memories written across her sister's face instead of dark trauma.

She didn't get the sense Elizabeth was open to love again. Not yet. Although she knew her sister would get there eventually. She was the romantic dreamer of the family. When Elizabeth fell for someone, she fell hard. She and

Steven had the kind of love that irritated everyone else. It had certainly irritated Rebecca. Steven was big into public displays of affection. He was the type who sprinted out of the car so he could open Elizabeth's door for her. Neither of them could commit to something until they'd checked with the other one. Rebecca had called it creepy. Considerate, her sister had insisted. Elizabeth had lapped it up. But Steven had, too. There was nothing about the man that suggested he was anything other than completely devoted to Elizabeth. But then life got in the way.

Cat didn't budge on the seat and Rebecca could have sworn she was even holding her breath.

'Sorry, Cat. You must hate these trips down memory lane.'

'No, it's fine. It's good to hear. But it also just reminds me of what I've missed out on.' Cat hadn't been around to witness any of Elizabeth's relationship.

'When you find love,' said Elizabeth, 'you have to grab it with both hands while you can.'

'Love isn't always enough,' said Rebecca. 'And if you know it won't last, why bother starting it when there's so much at stake? There's a slim chance I'll get my happily ever after, but there's a hell of a lot to lose if I don't.'

Cat placed her wine glass on the table and cleared her throat. 'Oh my God. This is all my fault,' she said.

'Don't be silly,' said Elizabeth. 'How could this possibly be your fault?'

'Jeremy and I were chatting about his business and he started talking about you two ending up together being fate, I guess, but that you weren't yet in the same place as he was. I made a comment about you having more to lose with him than you did with anyone else, then he said something about needing to give you certainty. Maybe he was trying to show you he's not going anywhere this time. I'm so sorry.'

Rebecca waved away Cat's concern. 'Honestly, this is not your fault.'

'I'm so sorry.' Cat squirmed in her seat. 'It's not my place to get involved in your love life. I should have just kept my opinions to myself.'

Rebecca forced a smile, hoping to give Cat some reassurance. 'Having an opinion on my love life is genetic, so please don't worry about it.' She turned to Elizabeth. 'Oh, and I should probably mention that he thinks you've eaten some bad mussels and you're currently throwing up.'

Elizabeth screwed up her face. 'Lovely.'

Rebecca drained her coffee and stood up. She'd hoped talking things through would bring her some clarity on what to do next. All it had done was throw mud on top of mud and she couldn't yet see what her next move was going to be.

'Where are you going?' asked Elizabeth.

Rebecca stalked out of the room. 'To get myself a wine glass,' she called back.

17

Jeremy was nearing the end of his morning run. He pounded the pavement, feeling the vibrations of each step through his body as he turned onto Main Street. The lights in the Thistle Bay Chocolate Shop flickered on and he stopped dead. He leaned forward and rested his hands on his thighs while he caught his breath. In the hour before the sun was to rise, his view into the shop was as clear as a television screen. Elizabeth was busying herself with a task obscured by the counter. Her hair was scraped back off her face, revealing rosy cheeks and no hint of an evening spent throwing up. He couldn't resist.

Jeremy shoved open the shop door, and Elizabeth's head shot up at the chime above the door.

'Hey, Lizzie. Feeling better?'

'Jeremy,' she said with wide eyes. 'What are you doing here?'

'Just out for a run and I saw your light on.' He let the door close behind him and made a show of appreciating the festive window display. Sprigs of holly and red berries were interspersed with chocolate snowmen, Santas, and beautifully decorated Christmas stockings. 'I didn't expect to see you at work today,' he said, walking towards Elizabeth and placing his forearms on the counter.

Elizabeth's hands went rigid and molten chocolate dripped from the edge of her pallet knife. 'Oh, well, I feel so much better.' Her eyes twitched as she glanced around the room. Elizabeth had always been a terrible liar. Whatever had happened last night, it had nothing to do with Elizabeth and a dodgy bowl of mussels. 'You're sweating all over my counter,' she said.

'Sorry.' Jeremy straightened up and Elizabeth spritzed a clear liquid onto the marbled worktop and wiped it clean with a square of blue paper towel. 'I guess you'll be avoiding lobster for a while,' he said.

Elizabeth smiled and scrunched up the now damp towel. 'Mussels, and no, I'm not in a hurry to eat another bowl.'

There was no point in pressing her further. Elizabeth may be a terrible liar, but she was also fiercely loyal to her family. If Rebecca didn't want him to know the real reason she'd scarpered the night before, then he wouldn't get answers by quizzing Elizabeth. 'Good to see you, Elizabeth.'

'You too, Jeremy.'

He left Elizabeth alone in the shop, knowing the poor woman's heart would be racing at the fib she had just told him.

He walked the rest of the way back to Gloria's, his head consumed by thoughts of one woman. If he hadn't been a Marine, he would have married Rebecca and had a very different life. She was the only woman he had ever fallen in love with, and he couldn't see a time when that would change. But when you're a Royal Marine, you have to be all in. He'd seen other guys get married, some happily, others creaking under the weight of military life. He'd prioritised his career over Rebecca, and she had never resented his decision. To a far lesser extent, she had done the same.

The pull of the Royal Marines was primal and that had overtaken everything else. He'd had to live up to the expectations that came with the green beret and he couldn't do that if he left a piece of himself in Thistle Bay. After the boys had been born, he'd stayed at Rebecca's house because it maximised the time he got to spend with Oliver and Liam. They were parents during the day and a couple in the evenings. Only he had put little effort into being a couple. Before last night, he hadn't picked her up for a date since they were teenagers, and he couldn't remember the last time he'd taken her out somewhere, just the two of them. He and Rebecca were meant to be together, but judging by her reaction last night, he was going to have to prove that to her all over again.

Jeremy had only just stepped inside the bed and breakfast when he spotted one of the Winterson twins tearing along the corridor towards the dining room, eyes wide and head twisting round like an owl. Her usually tightly wound hair hung around her shoulders. 'Everything OK, Mrs Winterson?'

'Oh dear, Jeremy, no, it's not. We've got a leak and there's water pouring all over our bedroom.'

Gloria appeared by his side, having seen or heard the commotion.

'I'll take a look. Do you have a toolbox, Gloria?'

'Yes, I'll fetch it.' Gloria hurried up the corridor, and Jeremy and Mrs Winterson followed.

Jeremy felt the water before he saw it. His trainers squelched on the cream carpet in the downstairs bedroom. The other Mrs Winterson was standing between their unmade beds. He glanced around the room. It wasn't immediately obvious where the water was coming from, but there was a clear tidemark on the carpet indicating it wasn't just a small leak. Jeremy ran his hands along the top and down the sides of the radiator behind the room's door, but it was dry.

Gloria bustled in with a metal toolbox. 'Oh good heavens,' she said, cupping her hand to her mouth. 'You poor things. Let's get your things moved to make sure nothing gets wet.' Gloria plucked a coat from the chair by the French doors that provided direct access to an enclosed garden at the back of the property and laid it on one of the two double beds. The other two women picked shoes up from the floor in front of the TV stand and moved them into the en suite bathroom.

'Can you see where the water is coming from, son?' asked Gloria.

Jeremy knelt down, and water soaked through his running leggings. He ran his hand along the bottom of the radiator and felt a gush of water. It wasn't coming from the radiator itself. It was spewing out from behind the skirting board. 'There's a leak behind this wall. I'm going to need to turn your water off. Where's your stopcock?'

Gloria fumbled with her phone in her hand. 'I, oh gosh, I'm not sure. I've never needed it before. There's something under the kitchen sink, but I don't know if that's what you're looking for.'

'I'll find it.' Jeremy left Gloria and her guests flapping in the bedroom while he trailed damp footprints to the kitchen.

Susie rushed from the other end of the dining room and followed him to the kitchen. 'What's happened?' she asked.

'A burst pipe behind the wall, I think.' Jeremy crouched down and peered under the sink. He pulled out a dozen different bottles of household cleaner, reached to the back of the cupboard, and turned the stopcock to the off position.

'Can you manage everything here with no water?' Jeremy asked.

Susie nodded. 'Of course, yes. I'll be fine.'

'Thanks, Susie.'

He returned to the bedroom to find the two Mrs Wintersons standing beside the beds, their packed suitcases sitting on top. Gloria's phone rang, and she glanced at her screen. 'Hopefully, this is Megan's plumber. Hello?' she said, answering. 'Yes, it is. Thanks for calling me so quickly. I really don't know what the problem is, but there's water coming out from behind a wall and there's a lot.' Jeremy touched the skirting board and was relieved that the gush had slowed to a trickle. 'Yes, I think so. Jeremy, did you turn the water off?'

Jeremy nodded. 'Do you want me to have a word?'

Gloria tossed him the phone, and he caught the look of relief on her face. While Jeremy filled the plumber in on what he knew, Gloria unplugged a floor lamp from the corner of the room and moved it into the bathroom. Jeremy kept his gaze locked on her to make sure she wasn't planning to plug the lamp in. He was pretty sure the water hadn't reached the corner where the lamp had been, but he wasn't going to take any chances.

'Where will we sleep tonight?' he heard one of the ladies ask. 'We can't sleep in a sopping bedroom.'

'Don't worry, I'm sure Mrs Murphy can just move us to another room.'

Gloria nodded and touched the panicking woman's arm. 'Yes. We'll figure something out.'

Jeremy could tell from the look on Gloria's face that she

didn't yet know what that solution was going to be. He'd never seen her flustered before. Instead of standing on the edge of a soggy carpet, she looked like she was teetering on the edge of a loch, expecting to be shoved in.

When the plumber arrived, Jeremy talked him through what he suspected the problem was and left him to get on with it. He grabbed a change of clothes, headed to Rebecca's and let himself in the front door.

'OK if I use your shower?' he asked, seeing Rebecca standing in her kitchen scrolling through emails on her laptop.

'Sure, but why?'

'The water's off at Gloria's. Mum's house only has one bathroom and I can't stop thinking about the naked man who was last in there.'

'That's ...'

'Sick, I know, but it's an image that several bottles of wine and a few beers haven't yet shifted.'

Rebecca laughed. 'Why is the water off at Gloria's?'

'Burst pipe in the one of the downstairs bedrooms.'

'Oh no.' Rebecca snatched her phone from the counter. 'I'd better call her and see if we can get something sorted out.'

'Relax, Bex. Megan sorted it. There's a plumber there now. That's why the water is off. He'll have her back up and running in no time.'

'How could Megan sort it from Majorca?'

'I'm thinking she used the phone. You're familiar with the phone, right?' He drew out his words and clasped her hand in his. 'It's this thing that you have glued to your hand far too often.' He prised the phone out of her hand and replaced it on the counter.

'Megan should be getting on a flight in the next couple of hours. I could have sorted it.'

'You could have, but the important thing is that it's sorted. Now, I'm going to grab a shower. Are you sticking around?'

She shook her head. 'Your mum just dropped the boys off. They're upstairs grabbing their bags for swimming lessons.'

'Will I see you guys later today?'

'I don't know. But we're all having dinner at Dad's tomorrow night. Can you make it?'

Oliver and Liam burst into the room with deafening roars and Jeremy's delayed terror-stricken reaction earned him an eyebrow raise from Liam.

'Right, boys, say bye to Daddy.' Rebecca huffed out a breath. 'And where are your swimming bags? That's what I sent you to collect.'

The boys hurled themselves into Jeremy's arms for a quick hug, then raced upstairs to fetch their backpacks. Jeremy followed behind them as they retreated. Oliver missed a step halfway up and stumbled forwards onto his elbows. Liam stopped and pulled his brother back to his feet, and the frenzied running continued. Jeremy grinned. It was the kind of view it was impossible to see on brief video calls.

18

Rebecca crawled her car along the farm track to minimise the loose pebbles pinging up against the black paintwork on her car. Jeremy knew there was something she wasn't telling him. According to Elizabeth, he'd quizzed her. Her sister had always been a hopeless liar, and if Jeremy hadn't been suspicious of Rebecca's premature departure last night, he certainly would be now. He'd looked ready to ask her when he'd used her shower that morning, but the boys had interrupted them, as usual. Children were a helpful buffer when trying to avoid uncomfortable conversations. She glanced in her rear-view mirror. Oliver had his forehead pressed against the window, no doubt hoping to glimpse his dad.

'Oliver, head off the glass, please,' she said. She was forever wiping fingerprints and forehead smears off the glass in both her car and her home.

Oliver sat back in his car seat. 'Do you know what the surprise is, Mummy?'

'What surprise?' asked Rebecca.

'Nana Gloria told me Daddy has a surprise for us up at the farm.'

'Hmm. Maybe she just meant you'll get to see Daddy.' Rebecca parked her car alongside Jeremy's in front of the house and switched off the ignition. She turned around to see the boys.

Liam was shaking his head. 'No. She told me there's a surprise, too, and Daddy's not the surprise, is he?'

'Let's find out, shall we?' Rebecca climbed out of the car and opened the rear passenger door for Oliver. Oliver jumped out, followed closely by Liam, who clambered over the seats and landed on his knees in the gravel. Rebecca looked up at the house for signs of Jeremy while the boys ran straight for the first field.

'I see Daddy,' yelled Liam.

Jeremy waved at them in the distance. Rebecca headed to the back of her car to swap her heels for the walking shoes stowed in her boot. There was no hope of getting Oliver and Liam to change their shoes. They had already reached Jeremy before she had her first shoe off. She shivered in the freezing temperature and hoped the grass was more crunchy than muddy.

She changed her footwear and caught up with the others, noting the deep line between Jeremy's eyes. 'What's this about a surprise?' he asked.

Rebecca shrugged. 'Don't look at me. Gloria said you were looking for us and apparently she told these two that you have a surprise for them.'

Jeremy crouched down between the boys. 'I'll need to speak to Nana tonight. I'm not sure what she's meaning. But I could use a hand if you two think you have the muscles for it.' Oliver and Liam flexed their tiny biceps in a very enthusiastic display of their respective strengths. 'Excellent. You'll have no problem helping me to move this wood. Let me pop up to the house and get you both some gloves.'

Jeremy headed back towards the house, and Rebecca marched alongside him. 'Were you actually looking for us?' she asked.

'Nope. It's lovely to see you all, but I've no idea what Gloria is talking about.' Jeremy grabbed a couple of sets of gloves. 'Did you see Gloria?'

'I did. I stopped by to see how I could help, but it seems Gloria has it all under control. The plumber was just tidying up. He's coming back with some blowers to help dry the floor.'

Oliver screeched. 'I see the surprise, Daddy!'

Several loud grunting noises rang out, and the boys bounced with excitement, eyes cast toward Jeremy's squatter sheep. Jeremy gripped Rebecca's arm. 'This wasn't about me looking for you. This was dear old Nana Gloria scheming.'

'No!' said Rebecca. 'She knows you're not keeping them, so she wouldn't want the boys to see them and then be disappointed . . .' Her words trailed off.

'She planned this, didn't she?'

'That minx. Boys, wait,' Rebecca called, but the boys were already sprinting towards the animals.

Rebecca and Jeremy jogged behind them to catch up. By the time they reached the boys, Oliver had his hand between the horizontal slats of the enclosure and was petting one of the sheep on the nose, while Liam had climbed onto the first rung of the fence and was stretching his arm out towards the other sheep, who remained a few steps back from the commotion. 'Here, sheepy.'

Jeremy moved to Oliver's side. 'Just be careful with this one. She's the grumpy one. I'm not sure if she bites.'

Oliver gently stroked the sheep, who stood motionless

with no sign of the grumpy nature Jeremy claimed she had. A distinctive oval-shaped black spot was the only blemish on the sheep's otherwise white face. Oliver touched a finger to the dark dot. 'She's a girl?' he asked.

'She is,' said Jeremy. He glanced at Rebecca with a helpless expression on his face.

Rebecca stepped forward and ran her hand across the top of Oliver's head. 'These sheep belong to Mr Henderson. He'll be taking them with him in a few days, but it's lovely that you got to see them before they left, isn't it?'

Oliver's head dropped. 'I thought they were ours,' he whispered.

'I'm sorry, buddy. They don't belong to us.'

Liam had successfully coaxed the other sheep to the fence and was leaning over to pet her fleecy coat. 'What's their names?' he asked, his tone much brighter than his brother's.

Jeremy looked at Rebecca, who shrugged. Hopefully, the boys wouldn't be clued up enough about cuts of meat to realise how inappropriate their names were.

'That one beside you, Liam, is Chop. And this one here is Rump,' said Jeremy. His eyes narrowed slightly, as if he were bracing himself for questions he didn't want to answer.

Rump took a step back from the fence and lunged forward on her front legs, sending a cloud of dust up. Oliver snatched his hand away from the sheep. 'I don't think my sheep likes the name Rump,' he said. Unfazed, he stuck his hand back through the fence, and the sheep once again put her nose forward to be petted. 'Don't worry, I'm going to think of a better name for you.'

'Buddy, they're not our sheep, so we can't name them.'

'I'm going to come up with a really cool name for my sheep,' said Liam.

Jeremy sighed and stepped back towards Rebecca. 'Gloria is in so much trouble when I see her tonight. I'm going to make *her* tell them the sheep are not staying.'

Rebecca laughed. 'It was a pretty sneaky plan of hers. It's not like her to play games and she would never normally involve the boys.' Apart from the occasional attempt at matchmaking, Gloria wasn't a schemer. She was one of those people who didn't hide her feelings and always got to the point. If she didn't agree with something you were doing, she wouldn't hesitate to tell you.

'The whole town is going crazy for these sheep. I haven't seen them so united since the MacAulays applied for planning permission to add a third storey to their house.'

'They'll get over it.'

Jeremy stared at Oliver patting the sheep. 'Last time I checked, the MacAulays were still in a two-storey.'

'Can we feed the sheep, Daddy?' asked Liam, still dangling over the fence. 'My one is hungry.'

'I've already fed them today,' said Jeremy. 'I haven't eaten, though, and I have some picnic food up at the house. Do you boys and Mummy want to hang around for some food?'

The boys could shovel food away any time of the day or night, but they glanced at Rebecca to see if they were allowed to stay. 'Sure. We can stay for some food.'

'Can we bring the food here so the sheep don't have to stay on their own?' asked Oliver.

'It's a bit cold to eat down here,' said Rebecca.

'And they're not on their own,' added Jeremy. 'They have each other. Why don't you two race to the house and see if you can beat me and Mummy?'

Liam jumped off the fence and sprinted away before Oliver could even take his hand out of the fence. 'See you later,' Oliver said to the sheep before darting after his brother.

Rebecca turned to head back up the field. She paused when Jeremy moved in the opposite direction. 'You coming?'

'I'll see you up there,' he said. 'I've got to feed the sheep.'

'But you said – '

'I know,' he interrupted her. 'I didn't want Oliver to get any more attached to these two than he already is.'

19

A full-family Friday night dinner at her dad's house meant two things: Rebecca didn't have to cook and Megan was home. She and Jeremy had been dancing around each other all week, coordinating childcare with their respective jobs and talking about little else except the boys. He knew something was on her mind, but she'd shut him down each time he'd asked.

Rebecca pushed open her dad's front door and headed straight for the roaring fire in the living room, seeking a welcome respite from the bitter December cold she hadn't been able to shake since leaving the office. Jeremy and the boys were already there. The flutter in her chest told her Jeremy was watching her. Their eyes locked as she moved towards the fire and she felt herself finally thawing out under his smouldering gaze.

Megan was sitting on the sofa between Oliver and Liam and she gave Rebecca a wave. Her long, wavy hair was twisted in a bun on top of her head and she was dressed in yoga pants and a black sleeveless vest despite the temperature outside.

Oliver oohed and aahed over a set of ceramic tiles Megan had just given him to paint. Oliver could happily spend hours with a paintbrush in his hand and had the patience to create some pretty elaborate artworks. Liam was less artistic and definitely less patient. He was clutching a dinosaur buried in a block of plaster and his obvious delight no doubt came from the thought of smashing it to smithereens to free the dinosaur rather than the careful excavation the manufacturer had likely intended.

Oliver thrust one of his tiles towards Rebecca. 'Maybe we can put them on the kitchen wall, Mummy?'

Rebecca ran her thumb across the grooves on the tile. Megan had a knack for finding kits that Rebecca considered modern-day equivalents of paint-by-numbers. Each one allowed Oliver to explore his creativity in a way that also produced a pretty decent outcome. 'Yeah, let's look at that once they're painted.'

'I have an idea,' said Jeremy, taking the tile from her. 'Since Mummy's kitchen is already tiled, we can put them on the walls in Daddy's house. What do you think, buddy?'

Megan stood up and put her arms out towards Rebecca. 'It's good to be home.' Rebecca hugged her sister back and Megan whispered in her ear, 'Mummy's house and Daddy's house. Seriously?'

Rebecca sighed. 'Why does everyone just presume Jeremy and I are going to shack up now that he's home for good?'

Megan smiled and arched one of her sun-kissed eyebrows. 'Seriously?'

Rebecca huffed out a quick breath. 'Forget it.' She held her hands out towards the fire. 'Thanks for sorting out the plumber for Gloria.'

'What do you mean?'

'The plumber for her leak. Gloria told Jeremy you organised him. Didn't you?'

'Nope. Didn't know she had a leak. I pulled together a list of useful contacts for her last time I was home and stored them all in her phone. She'll have called the number I gave her.'

Rebecca rolled her shoulders back and forth. 'Why didn't she just call me?'

'Probably because you aren't a plumber.'

'You know what I mean.'

'You don't need to be all things to all people. Haven't you got enough on your plate?'

'It smells like dinner is almost ready, boys.' Jeremy took the presents away from Oliver and Liam and placed them on a side table in the lounge. 'Go and wash your hands.'

The boys rushed to the downstairs bathroom, and Jeremy followed to supervise.

Megan stepped in front of Rebecca to block her move away from the fireplace. 'The sexual tension between you two is fizzing like the vinegar and baking soda I poured down Dad's sink this morning. It's a sin to let that go to waste.'

'I'm not sure that's the sinful part, but it's not happening.'

'Why not?'

'It's just not the right time.'

'You're too busy, right? And you're about to get busier. I spoke to Dad earlier.'

'So you see where I'm coming from?'

Megan nodded and leaned closer. 'I do, but I don't agree with you. You need something that's just for you, lovely. It can't be all about work.'

Rebecca sighed. 'Adding in a relationship means taking

time away from my business or my boys, and I'm not prepared to do either.'

Megan gripped Rebecca's arm. 'It's not just your business, though. You've built a very capable team around you. Let us help.'

'Us?'

'Fine. Them,' Megan conceded quickly, dashing Rebecca's hopes that her sister had perhaps come home for good this time. Rebecca knew better than to offer her opinion on where Megan should be living. Megan was the sister who jumped first and figured out a plan as she went along. She ignored anyone else's attempts to help her steer her life and drowned out well-meaning advice effortlessly. Megan released Rebecca's arm. 'It doesn't have to be work *or* love.'

Rebecca followed Megan to the kitchen, where the others had already taken their seats around the table. Alan sat on the bench that lined the back wall with Cat on one side and Elizabeth on the other. Gloria was on one of the chairs, and the boys' melamine plates with a rainforest print were laid at opposite ends of the built-in seating. Megan squeezed in beside Elizabeth and Jeremy scooted in beside Cat, leaving the other two chairs for Rebecca and Ryan.

Oliver and Liam flew into the room and made a beeline for their usual spaces around the table. Ryan brought over the large oval platter that had become an essential kitchen item when feeding such a large brood.

'Dinner is served,' Ryan said as he lowered the platter onto the middle of the table.

'I love it when Uncle Ryan cooks,' said Liam, almost drooling at the sight of juicy sausages and hot dog buns.

Ryan pointed to the various batches of sausages. 'These are spicy. Then we have caramelised onion, and pork and apple.' He spun back to the kitchen island and plucked a smaller platter off the worktop. 'And these are the vegetarian ones for Megan. Black beans and other random things that don't sound as though they belong in a sausage.'

Megan shot Ryan a playful look and reached over to grab the platter. 'Oh, how I've missed you, little brother.'

'Can I share your sausages, Auntie Megan?' asked Oliver.

'Of course you can. Do you like veggie sausages?'

'I'm a vegetarian,' announced Oliver, with his shoulders pushed back and chin slightly protruding.

'Are you now?' Megan asked, glancing Rebecca's way. 'And why is that?'

'Because the stegosaurus was a vegetarian, and I want to be a stegosaurus when I grow up.'

Rebecca's skin tingled, and she drowned out the conversation between Megan and Oliver about black beans. Jeremy's gaze roamed over her body, and she knew the fieriness in his eyes had nothing to do with their son's sudden vegetarianism. She only had to get through this one night. Now Megan was home and Alan had shared his retirement plans with all of his children, she could tell Jeremy. He would understand why, yet again, now wasn't their time.

20

The following day, Rebecca strolled from her office through to the shop, finding Elizabeth perched on a stool and cramming a sandwich into her mouth. There were no customers and a quick glance up Main Street from the shop windows revealed very few potential customers. That morning's weather forecast had predicted a snowstorm, and heavy snowflakes were now blanketing the town in white.

Elizabeth gave her a wave and swallowed her mouthful of food. 'Hey, what's up?'

'Just checking in,' said Rebecca, dawdling out from behind the counter and repositioning some of the stock on the shelves to cover up gaps. Their new mulled wine truffles packaged in bright-red Christmas crackers were a big hit.

'Checking in or checking up?'

'In,' said Rebecca, keeping her tone light. She rearranged the boxes of Christmas truffles, with their white icing and holly and berry designs. 'I just want to make sure everything goes smoothly for Dad's party.'

Elizabeth smirked, dug her phone out of the back pocket of her jeans, and scanned notes that Rebecca could see she had typed into the party plan spreadsheet. 'Meena is arriving at the house at four. Most of the prep will be done, but she'll need in to set up and she'll cook the hot food onsite.'

'I can be there.'

Elizabeth shook her head. 'Megan will be there anyway, so just leave it to her.'

'It's no hassle for me to go.'

'And drag the boys there two hours before they need to be there? Leave it to Megan. It'll make her feel useful. She's feeling guilty that she hasn't helped.'

'That's ridiculous.'

'Not to her. Your spreadsheet has twenty items on it and the only thing with her name against it is decorations. Let her help Meena. It'll give her something to contribute that's more than just lighting a few candles.'

Decorations had been a last-minute addition thanks to Ryan when he'd seen the printout of the party plan on Rebecca's desk and had spotted her glaring mistake. Megan's name wasn't on it. It wasn't like Rebecca had purposely excluded her. It was geography that prevented her from getting more involved. What could her sister have realistically contributed from Majorca? Rebecca had substituted Megan's name in place of her own and tweaked the line item to *decorations – not Christmas* before sending the plan to her siblings at the beginning of the month. 'Fine. Megan can deal with Meena and I'll check in with her when I get there. I'm going to aim for about five so I can give Ryan a hand setting up the drinks.'

Elizabeth shook her head. 'He won't need a hand. And if he does, Megan can help. I'm arriving at six, guests at six thirty.'

'I'll suggest to Cat that she gets there about six, too, so

she feels part of it.' Cat was family and, taking Jeremy's advice, Rebecca wanted her to feel like part of the sibling crowd rather than one of the invited guests.

'Already done. Cat and Nick are picking me up on their way.'

'It's all in hand, then.' Rebecca opened the spreadsheet on her phone. The only task assigned to her that she hadn't yet marked off was the cleaning. She'd arranged for Alan's cleaners to come a day early to make sure the house was spotless. She highlighted the row and marked it complete. The comfort she expected to feel at knowing everything on her plan was assigned to someone and on track didn't come. 'Any idea how Megan plans to decorate?'

'No clue. I suggested she keep it simple with a few fancy candles, but you know Megan.' Elizabeth shrugged. 'Maybe balloons and banners?'

Rebecca winced. Balloons and banners were for children's birthday parties. They weren't for sixty-fourth birthday parties serving fillet of lamb canapés with balsamic-glazed baby beetroot and champagne mojitos.

The bell tinged above the shop door and Elizabeth greeted a couple of rather soggy customers.

'Leave her to get on with it, Rebecca,' whispered Elizabeth. 'Whatever she does might not be to your liking, but Dad will love it.' With that she strolled out from behind the counter, leaving Rebecca to retreat out the back door.

Rebecca arrived at her father's house promptly at five, with Oliver and Liam in tow. Much of the snow had already melted, but someone had scraped the path clear and sprinkled salt down to stop the walkway from icing over.

Liam tugged at his shirt collar and Oliver smacked his brother's hand away from his neck. 'Leave it alone or it'll get messed up.'

'I don't care. It's itchy,' Liam complained.

Rebecca sighed and ran her hands around her son's collar. 'It's not itchy. You're just not used to wearing a smart shirt. Once I get your photo taken with Grandpa, you can get as messy as you like, but please stay tidy until then.' Liam wore soft-necked polo shirts to school and lived in T-shirts and football strips for the rest of the time. Seeing her children dressed up in smart trousers and shirts was a rarity, and she was determined to get at least one good photo before they stripped off. She made a mental note to grab Nick as soon as he arrived with his camera.

'Mummy, look at the lights,' said Oliver.

Rebecca turned to see the two-storey grey-brick house that had been her childhood home lit up by what seemed to be a thousand fairy lights. A dusting of snow clung to the roof, giving the house the festive-vibe that Rebecca had hoped to avoid. She cleared her throat and reminded herself that she and Megan had opposing styles and what mattered most was their dad's happiness.

Alan had moved the family to Thistle Bay, her mother's hometown, from the Philippines when Rebecca was ten. She had a clear memory of the day they arrived at this very house. The carefree childhood that she hadn't fully appreciated at the time was gone. Evenings snuggled into her mother reading cosy mystery novels together had never happened again. Catherine Knight had left the Philippines uncomfortably pregnant yet happy, as far as Rebecca had known at the time. By the time Rebecca and her siblings had arrived in Scotland, her baby brother was already a month old and her mother had morphed into a person

Rebecca barely recognised. She cried when the baby cried and she was short-tempered with Elizabeth and Megan. While her father busied himself starting Thistle Bay Chocolate Company, Rebecca did what she could to look after her younger sisters. She fixed them breakfast and snacks, she encouraged them to play quieter activities on their mother's bad days, and she shielded them as much as she could from the increasingly strained conversations between their parents.

The happy home, this home, that she and her siblings still flocked to most Sunday afternoons held bittersweet memories for Rebecca. Less than a year after the family had moved, Catherine had been transferred to full-time hospital care. The relief Rebecca had felt at not having to tiptoe around the house was to this day tinged with guilt that they could not care for her mother at home. Her father had invested in a complete refurbishment that had transformed the building from a cold, dreary house into their family home. Rebecca had helped her sisters to choose everything from the colour of paint on their walls to the bedspreads and light fixtures. She had tried to rein in Megan's grand plans for a safari-themed bedroom. Always wildly creative, Megan, who had barely turned four, had drawn a picture of what she wanted in her room. There was an elephant, a giraffe, a snake coiled around a tree, and a zebra. Alan had hired a mural painter to give Megan exactly what she wanted. It was only later that Rebecca realised Alan had been trying to create a space his children loved to be in to compensate for them being dragged away from familiarity, and having to cope not only with new schools and new friends but also with the loss of their mother.

Alan's plan had worked and the younger children settled quickly. It had taken Rebecca longer, but she had got there.

Mostly. Special occasions were when she felt the weight of her mother's absence.

Shepherding the boys into the house, Rebecca prepared for a Christmas decor explosion, but there wasn't a tree or ornament in sight. Instead, candles filled the air with winter scents of cinnamon and cloves and citrusy notes of freshly cut oranges. An enormous bouquet of cream roses with snow-white chrysanthemums and sprigs of eucalyptus and blue sea thistles had overtaken the hallway table.

The boys spotted a rustic wooden crate loaded with bags of Thistle Bay Chocolate Company truffles. Stuffing their hands in, they rummaged around for their favourites. They grabbed a bag each and ran ahead through the living room and into the large family kitchen. Rebecca straightened up the crate's contents and followed them.

Megan's tasteful decoration continued throughout the ground floor of the house, with lighting from the lamps brightened further by more candles and bowls of fairy lights casting a soft glow around the room. The quiet hum of jazz came from speakers above the fireplace. Glass vases held stems of red berries and black cocktail napkins were dotted around the room for guests to use for catching stray crumbs.

The savoury aromas drifting from the kitchen made Rebecca's mouth water. Megan was in front of the French patio doors, sandwiched between Oliver and Liam, and Ryan was hovering at the cooker beside Meena Patel, no doubt trying to steal a few tasters of what was to come later. Meena was a Thistle Bay resident and the owner of the best catering business on the east coast. She'd moved to bigger premises out of town earlier in the year and home events were no longer a normal part of her business model, but she was a good friend of Alan's and had offered to cater the party.

'Megan, the place looks just wow,' said Rebecca. 'You've really done a great job.'

'Thanks,' said Megan, a broad smile spreading across her face. 'Do you boys want to see the best part?'

'Yes,' said Liam, relaxing his grip on his auntie.

'Me too,' shrieked Oliver, slipping his hand into Megan's.

She led them to the low table usually found in the bedroom Alan had converted into the boys' room for sleepovers. 'This puzzle is for you to do together. I bet you're good at jigsaws.'

'I am,' said Oliver confidently. Liam looked a little less sure, but nodded his head anyway.

Megan flipped over the box to show them the image. 'This is what you're tasked with making.'

'It's us,' screeched Liam.

'And Santa,' yelled Oliver. 'Mummy, look. It's us and Santa.'

'That's so cool, isn't it?' said Rebecca. 'I can't wait to see it completed.' Liam shook the lid of the box free and tipped the pieces onto the table. 'Just be careful you don't drop any of the pieces. You don't want one of you to be missing a nose when you're finished.'

'Or Santa missing his belly,' said Oliver, giggling at his own joke.

'It's two hundred and fifty pieces,' Megan said to Rebecca, leaving the boys to get to work. 'I'm hoping it'll keep them out of mischief until the party properly kicks off.'

'That was a great idea.'

'My first thought was painting, but then I figured no one would appreciate multi-coloured fingerprints on their party clothes, even if it was water-based paint.'

Rebecca laughed. 'Good thinking!'

Megan pulled Rebecca in for a hug. 'I also suspected you

would be early and would need something to keep the boys occupied until we could feed them.'

'I like being early.'

Megan squeezed Rebecca tighter. 'No, you like checking up on people.'

Her sister wasn't wrong, but Rebecca had to hand it to Megan, her decorations were plentiful yet elegant. She realised then that the last time she'd seen her sister decorate was when Megan took charge of the decorations for her own thirteenth birthday party. The nineties had thrown up over every inch of their father's kitchen and had put Rebecca off neon for life. It shouldn't have surprised her that her sister's sense of style had grown through the years, but somehow it had. She'd worried about Megan more than the others.

Megan had shown no interest in getting involved in the family business. Rebecca had worked in the chocolate business since she was a teenager and she couldn't fathom a career outside of that. And more than that, she couldn't see how her sister was going to make a living from being an artist. Megan had unbelievable talent, but that was rarely enough in the art world as far as Rebecca could see. The most talented people weren't often the ones who made it. However, Megan had proven her wrong at every turn, and Rebecca had to stop thinking of Megan as her baby sister. Megan had made it to the age of thirty-two by doing things her own way, and she was happy.

The party was in full swing by the time Rebecca spotted Jeremy in the kitchen with Gloria, who was huddled over the boys. Everyone at the party had a glass in his or her hand, and Meena's hors d'oeuvres had proven to be so irresistible the woman was squirrelled away in the kitchen whipping up another round. Jeremy had somehow procured for himself a plate of desserts, including a custard tart and a generous slice of carrot cake.

'This party is marvellous,' said Gloria when Rebecca joined her and Jeremy beside the boys, who were captivated by their last dozen jigsaw pieces. 'You've done your dad proud.'

'Thanks, Gloria.'

Jeremy slid his hands around Rebecca's waist and she felt a rush of heat within her. Gloria was right. In twenty-five years, they'd never lost their spark. She sank into his side. 'This has been the perfect homecoming,' he whispered in her ear.

'What about the bit when you saw your potential stepfather naked?'

Jeremy shuddered. 'OK, almost perfect.' Rebecca laughed, snatched Jeremy's spoon, and stole a corner of his carrot cake. 'It can be like this all the time, Bex.'

Rebecca straightened up and looked at Jeremy, her heart sinking at the glimmer of hope in his eyes that she might still change her mind.

Oliver and Liam slotted in their last jigsaw piece and squealed with excitement, drawing their parents' gaze away from each other and onto them. 'Well done, boys. You've worked so hard on that and it looks perfect,' said Rebecca.

Jeremy and Gloria continued to heap praise on the satisfied duo while Megan slid the completed puzzle onto a piece of cardboard. 'I'm going to move this to Grandpa's office so it doesn't get broken while you're eating.'

'Here, I'll take it.' Jeremy released his grip on Rebecca, handed her his plate of sweet treats, and disappeared with the jigsaw.

'Right, boys,' said Megan. 'Who wants a fancy-pants

drink to go with their dinner? We need some mint leaves, a lime, pineapple juice, and ginger beer.'

Rebecca smiled at her boys' delighted faces as they scampered to the fridge. 'Are you going to get them hyper?'

Megan pressed her hands to Rebecca's cheeks. 'They're already hyper, lovely, and it was nothing to do with me. Dad's going to say a few words soon, so I thought it best to get the boys settled with some food and drinks before he starts.'

Rebecca filled two plates with curry puffs, vegetable samosas, mini steak pies for Liam, and sweet potato and coconut curry pies for Oliver, while Megan kept the boys occupied mixing drinks.

'Auntie Megan, did you hear we've got pet sheep?' asked Oliver.

'Now I heard something about that,' said Megan, squeezing fresh lime juice into the glasses in front of her. 'I didn't think they were pet sheep, though.'

'They're not pets,' said Liam. 'We can't take them home with us. But they live on Daddy's farm, so they're just like pets. I want to call my sheep Sharon.'

'That's a great name,' said Megan, giving Rebecca a mischievous grin. 'Maybe not very sheep-like, though, is it?'

Liam pouted. 'Sharon the sheep. I like it.'

Rebecca glared at Megan, hoping she would understand that encouraging the boys to name the sheep wasn't the best idea. Megan smiled, dropped a spoon into one of the glasses, and stirred. 'What are your ideas, Oliver?'

'I want to call my sheep Olive because it's like my name.'

Megan stirred the other drink. 'Well, that's just perfect, isn't it?'

'Marmalade!' yelled Liam.

Jeremy returned, having snaffled another plate of food for himself. 'What kind of cocktail needs marmalade?'

'No, Daddy. That's what I want to name my sheep. We're calling them Olive and Marmalade.'

Jeremy stared open-mouthed between his children and Rebecca, then turned to glare at Megan. 'This was you, wasn't it?'

'I don't know what you're talking about,' Megan said, winking at Jeremy. 'I'm just the bartender.'

'Right, boys,' said Rebecca, intervening. 'Let's get you settled with your food. Grandpa looks ready to make his speech.' The boys sat at their small table and Rebecca gripped Jeremy's arm, steering him into the living room. Her stomach was in knots. Alan had said he would announce his retirement in the New Year, but when he made a decision, he acted quickly. He'd already stepped away from some of the day-to-day running of the business, and with Megan home, he'd now told all of his children about his plans. The only other person affected was Jeremy, and Rebecca hadn't told him yet. She should have and could have. She wasn't sure why she was dallying. Perhaps because telling him made everything final.

Alan tapped a spoon on his glass and a hush spread through the room. Ryan turned the volume down on the music, and Alan stood at the fire in front of his family and closest friends. 'Someone asked me tonight what I'm most proud of,' he started. 'I feel pretty fortunate that it took me quite some time to think through all the wonderful things I have in my life. I have a successful business that provides both jobs and top-quality chocolate for the community in which I live.'

'Here, here,' someone yelled from the back of the room, making an exaggerated rustling noise with what

Rebecca presumed was a bag of truffles from Megan's decorations.

'That business has gone from strength to strength thanks to the hard work and dedication of my children. Each of them has played a part in keeping Thistle Bay Chocolate Company secure for the next generation, and I thank them for that.' Alan shifted to the side and picked up a frame holding an image of his wife. 'It pains me every day that my wife, Catherine, was taken from us far too early. But then I remember how lucky I was to have found someone to love as much as I loved my wife. That kind of love doesn't come around too often and I remain forever grateful that I got to experience it.' Jeremy enclosed Rebecca's hand in his and it was only then that she realised she still had her arm looped through his.

Alan put the photograph down and picked up a glass of champagne. 'Back to the question. What I'm most proud of is having all five of my children here with me tonight. You all know how long my family has waited for this. The years we spent apart weren't easy for any of us, but I trusted we would be together again and now we are. My children make me feel a level of pride I didn't know existed until now and they are what I am most proud of.' Alan raised his glass. 'To family,' he said.

'To family,' everyone repeated.

A few people clapped their hands and Alan waved away the applause. 'Let's get some more food, shall we? Meena Patel has prepared another round of sumptuous bites and decadent desserts and I can't wait to dig in. Thank you, Meena.'

Meena, who had swapped out her chef's whites for a fuchsia sari, gave a timid smile. Her long dark hair was styled in loose waves with no kinks from whatever she'd used to tie it back in the kitchen. She made her way across the room offering nibbles from the silver platter she held and accepted the many compliments about her food.

'Nice speech,' said Jeremy, still holding Rebecca's hand. 'You look a little on edge. Is everything OK?'

Rebecca nodded. She had to tell Jeremy about her father's plans to retire and hand over to her. It was the only way he would understand why they couldn't be together. Not yet, anyway. He squeezed her hand tighter and her traitorous body tingled as it did every time Jeremy was near her. She wriggled her hand free and pushed her shoulders back. It was back to business. Her head was calling the shots now. 'I have to talk to you about something,' she said.

21

Before Rebecca had time to say whatever was on her mind, Ryan whisked her away for a family photo. Nick Bell was standing by, camera in hand, and Jeremy was pleased to see Cat looking relaxed and happy. Photographs taken, the family dispersed, with Rebecca being led to the kitchen by Oliver. Jeremy picked up a lamb stew that Meena had presented on a black ceramic spoon and decorated with cubes of candied apricot. He put the entire scoop of sumptuous meat in his mouth. A weight pressed on his shoulder and he turned his gaze to see Megan behind him and resting her chin on him. 'Is that good?' she asked.

'Uh-huh,' he replied as he chewed.

'That's from one of Mitch Adams' sheep. As tasty as it is, it wouldn't be so nice if you knew it was from a sheep who had run for her life, been gifted a name by your son, then made into a stew by Meena, would it?'

Jeremy swallowed his mouthful of food. He raised his hand to his chest, feeling chunks of meat work their way down beyond his throat. Megan stepped in front of him with a smug look on her face.

'Don't let the kids hear you talking like that. And while we're discussing stew, does my son wanting to be a vegetarian have anything to do with you?' Jeremy's tone was snarkier than he had intended.

Megan held up her hands. 'Not guilty. And also, calm down. He wants to be a stegosaurus, so I'm guessing it's a phase. Don't make a big deal of it and you'll find he's tucking into his turkey dinner at Christmas along with the rest of you.' Megan looked around her. 'Olive and Marmalade, however, don't seem to be a phase. But don't worry, I know you'll do the right thing. I have every faith in you. Your sons never need to know that you considered cooking and eating their new best friends.'

'Manipulation doesn't work on me, Megan. You should know that by now.'

'No one needs to manipulate you, Jer. You're a good man and everyone knows it.' Megan fluttered away from him to mingle with some other guests.

Jeremy reached for another spoon of stew and clocked Rebecca coming back. 'Bex, you've got to keep your sister away from me. She's on a mission to get me to keep those sheep.'

Rebecca laughed. 'Stay strong. You don't need sheep in your life. Just lamb.' She snatched the spoon of lamb and tipped it into her mouth.

Jeremy touched his chest again. 'Do you have any antacids?'

'Really?'

He nodded.

'They're upstairs. We can talk up there, too.'

He followed Rebecca to the door, but just then someone tapped a spoon against the side of a glass and a hush once again spread through the room. Alan Knight stood in the same spot beside the fireplace and everyone turned their attention to their host. 'While I have you all in the same place, there's one more thing I want to say.'

'Oh no.' Rebecca clutched her hand to her neck and turned to Jeremy with a pained look on her face. 'I'm so sorry,' she said, her gaze drifting towards her father.

'This birthday party is also doubling as my retirement party,' said Alan, getting straight to the point. 'I've decided to step down from Thistle Bay Chocolate Company. My daughter Rebecca will assume the role of chief executive officer. My son Ryan will take on the position of chief operating officer and together with Elizabeth, Megan, and Cat will support Rebecca as she formally takes the reins early next year.'

The excited chatter in the room drowned out whatever else Alan had said. Rebecca turned to face Jeremy, and from the anguished look on her face, he knew Alan had gone off script by announcing the news. People clustered around her, shaking her hand and kissing her cheek. The kind of attention Rebecca hated. Jeremy could only watch as she was coaxed the length of the room until she was beside her father. The room fell silent again as everyone waited to hear what she had to say.

'I don't want to spend too much time talking about work tonight, so I'll keep it brief. Thank you all so much for your good wishes. My brother and sisters and I are excited to have this opportunity. We love Thistle Bay Chocolate Company and we will work hard to make sure the business continues to thrive. And don't worry, this is not really Dad's retirement party. We'll have another gathering and do it properly in the spring.' Rebecca raised her glass. 'Cheers.'

Jeremy dutifully raised his glass. He caught Rebecca's eye and her smile slipped momentarily. Everything fell into place. If Alan was retiring, and retiring soon, Rebecca would feel the pressure like never before. She wasn't thinking about her job when she said she didn't have space for a relationship. She was thinking about her *new* job.

In Rebecca's mind, Jeremy was a distraction, and she needed complete focus. He knew that because he had said the same to her at one time. If he continued to push her, she would only dig her heels in harder and push him away further. He had expected to come back into town and start again with Rebecca and the boys. He could see now that wasn't happening. Rebecca would not start a relationship with him and take on the CEO job at the same time. It went against his instincts, but he had to back off.

22

The following morning, Jeremy left the bed and breakfast after eating only a slice of toast. He headed to the farm, having woken up with the overwhelming desire to smash things to smithereens. Today was the perfect day to say goodbye to Archie Henderson's avocado bathroom suite. He'd left the party before he and Rebecca could talk. She had been desperate to speak to him, but her attempts to shuffle her way across the living room were slow going thanks to what seemed like an endless queue of people stepping up to tell her how excited they were for her. A quick kiss on the cheek and whispered words to say he understood were all he had managed.

And he did understand. When Rebecca had been completing university applications, Jeremy had been preparing his mind and body for what he knew would be one of the most gruelling experiences of his life. He'd run every day, going out in all weathers, spent hours in the gym doing strength and conditioning exercises, and swum in the pool. He'd tried open-water swimming in the sea a few mornings a week before school until someone told his mum, who went ballistic and made him promise to swim in the sea only at weekends, when she could be there to monitor him.

When Jeremy had passed the initial recruitment process, it was Rebecca who had taken him out to celebrate. They were supportive of each other's ambitions, yet very aware that they were on entirely different paths.

He had left town two months before she did. Day one of the Royal Marines training process ended with more than a dozen hopeful recruits packing their bags and heading home. The lad in the bed next to Jeremy had beaten Jeremy's best run time by a full minute. When he had packed his things, Jeremy realised he needed more than the physical stamina and strength he'd spent the last year building. His days had been marred by physical fatigue and mental exhaustion, his physical environment had been stripped bare of anything that reminded him of home, and his single focus for the next nine months had to be making it through each day.

Rebecca had understood. She had always been just as focused. She set her sights on some far-off goal and she never wavered from that course. It didn't matter if that goal was getting her siblings through their school years unscathed by the death of their mother or making their family business so successful it could support not only her family but the families of scores of other people in the town, too. Jeremy understood responsibility far more than most. He'd shouldered responsibility for other people's lives. His children had been the catalyst for him to leave that level of responsibility behind. For Rebecca, becoming a mother had only added to her responsibilities.

Rebecca becoming CEO wasn't a surprise, but the timing of Alan's public announcement had caught her off guard.

The only question Jeremy had was whether their relationship was paused or permanently limited to parenting their two children.

Jeremy pushed the likely answer to the back of his mind, dug a hammer and crowbar out of his toolbox, and set to work ripping out the putrid-coloured bathtub.

After four straight hours of tearing the inside of the house to bits and heaving debris down the stairs and into the skip in front of the house, Jeremy looked down at his filthy, sodden clothes. His boots were coated in mud up to his ankles, and he moved to the edge of his driveway with a squelching sound. Did he really want groups of lads who looked like they'd just come out of the sheep dip on the commando endurance course peeling off their manky clothes in his brand-new camping cabins?

Hearing footsteps, he turned and saw Susie inching her way towards him.

'Hi, Susie,' Jeremy called out cheerfully, which seemed to loosen the nervous expression on her face.

'Hi. I'm sorry to come up unannounced.' She handed Jeremy a clear plastic box and a takeaway coffee cup. 'Gloria made you something to eat in case you were hungry. She said you planned to be here all day and probably wouldn't have thought to bring some lunch with you. I hope you don't mind me bringing it up.' Susie's gaze drifted behind him and he suspected her visit had a dual purpose: feeding him and checking out his sheep. *His sheep.* When did that happen?

Jeremy gratefully took the tub and coffee and tipped the cup back for a drink. The journey between the bed and breakfast and the farm was only a few minutes by car. Given the tepid coffee, he suspected Susie had walked up. 'I don't mind at all. Gloria was right. That's very kind of you both.

Thank you. I'm off to see the troublesome duo. Want to come?'

Susie rocked forwards on her toes with a grin on her face. 'If you don't mind.'

'Not at all. They seem to behave better when they have an audience, so you'd be doing me a favour. Tell me about your grandparents' smallholding.'

Susie chatted away about school holidays spent on the farm as she and Jeremy headed towards Chop and Rump. 'My favourite holiday was the Easter holiday. I headed down to the Borders for two weeks and helped with lambing. The lambs pop out, then get on their feet and feed within an hour. It's just amazing to witness. Sometimes lambs got stuck, and I had to help the mother birth them. I'd seen my granddad do it loads, so I knew what to do. As long as the feet were sticking out, all I had to do was pull hard and clear away the gunk from their faces and tickle their noses with straw to make them sneeze and take a breath.'

'Wow, you really sound like you know what you're doing,' said Jeremy.

'I know it's just sheep, but helping a lifeless lamb to take its first breath is just incredible.'

'Are you a vegetarian?'

Susie's cheeks flushed pink. 'No,' she said, her eyes dropping to the ground as they picked their way down the field. 'But I only eat meat that comes from the Sunday farmers' market. I like to know the animals are local and well taken care of in life. It's expensive and some people don't think it's any better because I'm still eating the meat, but it feels better to me.'

'I get that,' said Jeremy. They arrived at the sheep enclosure, where Chop and Rump were busy attempting to chomp on the frosted grass. 'Here they are.'

'They're magnificent,' said Susie, leaning on the fence. 'I've never seen them. I only heard the stories about these two escapees running amok in town. At the time I was busy on Mitch Adams' land, helping to herd the rest of them back into his fields.'

Jeremy led Susie to the gate and placed his hand on the latch. 'That one there with the black patch above her eye, that's Rump. Watch out for her. She's prone to head-butting.'

'Noted. A head-butt from a sheep can leave a pretty spectacular bruise.'

Jeremy laughed. 'Ah. It's not just me that sheep hate then.' He unlatched the gate, and Susie strode into the enclosure ahead of him.

'Have you seen them head-butt each other?' she asked.

Jeremy shook his head. 'No. Are they likely to do that?'

'They're usually establishing dominance. Maybe they've already established their pecking order.'

'I think so. Rump is in charge. She's remarkably calm around the boys, though.'

'She probably senses their gentle natures and knows they're not a threat.'

'I'm not a threat,' Jeremy insisted.

Susie gave a little smile. 'Your first thought on meeting them was carting them back off to Mitch Adams for you know what.'

'Yeah, but they don't know that.'

'You'd be surprised.' Susie grabbed the shovel and scooped up the damp patches of the hay bedding Jeremy had spread around the sheltered area of the barn.

'No, Susie. Leave that.'

'I don't mind. Drink your coffee before it gets cold, if it isn't already.'

Jeremy wrapped his hand around the paper cup. 'It's still warm. I'll drink as long as you stop shovelling.'

'Deal.' Susie, blatantly ignoring their deal, scooped up two more shovelfuls of hay, then propped the shovel up against the fence. Jeremy watched as Rump inspected the newcomer in the pasture. Chop was a bit more skittish and made it a couple of feet from Susie before bolting backwards and turning away. Susie held out her hand and allowed a curious Rump to come towards her.

Jeremy's body tensed as he prepared himself for the sheep giving the visitor a hard time or a taste of her hard head. 'Now why can't she be as calm as that around me?'

As if to rub it in further, Rump bent her legs, dropped to the ground at Susie's feet, and gave a quiet bleat. 'There's something special about animals that aren't being raised for food. They seem to know.'

The only thing he thought Rump knew was how to be belligerent around him and sweet as chocolate when anyone else was watching. The other sheep approached him. Jeremy allowed the animal to nuzzle his hand while he scratched the top of her head with his other hand. 'Chop here has a calmer temperament, don't you, darling?' He flicked his eyes towards Susie, who smiled. 'Don't tell anyone I just called a sheep darling.'

'Your secret is safe with me.'

After working for another few hours and cleaning himself up as best he could with only the farmhouse's kitchen sink available to him, Jeremy arrived at Rebecca's cottage to see his children with their faces pressed against the glass of the dining room window. When they spotted him, he gave them a wave and smiled as they bounced up and down, their screeching audible from the driveway. The front door was locked, so he used the key Rebecca had given him.

Two excitable children firing a random rabble of words in his direction met him in the hallway. Jeremy put his finger to his lips and the boys quietened down. 'Where's Mummy?' he asked.

'She's on a work call,' said Oliver.

'Then let's make sure we're extra quiet so Mummy can concentrate on her call,' Jeremy whispered, hoping the boys would follow his lead. 'Using only your hands, who wants to go to the park?'

'Me!' Oliver screeched, earning a smack on the arm from his brother. 'Ouch!' he squealed.

'Liam, you don't hit your brother,' Jeremy reprimanded, making his unhappy tone clear but keeping his voice low. 'Apologise right now.'

'But he used his words, and you said we had to only use our hands,' Liam protested.

'Everyone makes mistakes. Nothing justifies hitting another person,' said Jeremy.

'Can we still go to the park?' asked Liam, his lips curled down.

'Well, you've made a mistake, but you haven't yet tried to fix it, have you?'

Liam shook his head and turned to his brother. 'I'm sorry for hitting you,' he said.

Oliver shrugged. 'It's OK. Can we still go to the park, Daddy?'

'It's freezing outside, so you can go to the park if you can find your hats, scarves, gloves, coats, and shoes without making a noise.' The boys turned to each other and grinned. 'What?' asked Jeremy.

They pointed to the coat stand behind him. 'Mummy has everything ready for us,' whispered Oliver.

'Clever Mummy,' said Jeremy. He unhooked the coats and passed them over. Gloves poked out from each coat pocket, and there were scarves and woollen hats stuffed into each sleeve. As the boys dressed, Jeremy wandered to the kitchen at the back of the house. Rebecca was perched on a barstool at the worktop. She'd moved the seat from the family room to the kitchen side of the worktop, presumably to catch the boys if they came into the room and prevent them from making an unexpected appearance on her video call. She had headphones on and he could hear the faint buzz of someone else speaking from them. Rebecca glanced up, stretched her hand to one edge of her laptop, and flashed her hand twice in a gesture that he understood to mean she would be another ten minutes.

Jeremy dangled his key to her house and pointed back down the corridor in a move he hoped would tell her he was taking the kids to the park. She gave him a thumbs-up and averted her eyes back to her laptop screen.

Jeremy and the boys crossed the road and headed into the park at the same time as Megan arrived, her woolly hat pulled low on her head. A matching scarf obscured half of her face, and the buttons on her coat were straining at the layers underneath.

'You feeling the cold?' Jeremy asked.

'A few years in hot climates will do that to you.'

Jeremy nodded. It didn't take long for the body to acclimatise to warm weather, but it took more than just a few days to get used to a Scottish winter again.

'I've just come from Gloria's. I had afternoon tea with the Winterson twins before they leave tomorrow.'

'They're quite the characters, aren't they?'

'Oh yes, although they've been sweet about the leak in their bedroom. They're been fawning all over me because they're helping me to design a mural for the room when it gets redecorated. Well, that and they have a grandson they're desperate to introduce me to.'

Jeremy watched the boys clamber up the climbing frame. 'Did they have a photograph of him in their album?'

'They did. But it looked more like a mug shot than a photo. He has these menacing eyes and a lopsided goatee.'

Jeremy laughed. 'Sounds like you should steer clear of him.'

'I plan to.'

'So a mural, huh? Aren't you leaving tomorrow, too?'

'I am. There aren't many tourists kicking about, though, so Gloria doesn't need the room until Easter. I'll be back to do the mural before then. We're going for greenery draping down from the ceiling to bring the outdoors in and make the room an extension of the garden. Just don't tell the Wintersons. They wanted a full-on underwater scene with tropical fish and a pod of dolphins.'

'Don't be surprised if they book another stay at Easter to check out your work.'

Megan shrugged. 'I'll have thought of an excuse by then. And if not, I might just have to go on that date with their villainous grandson.' She called over to the boys. 'Auntie Megan has to go back to Grandpa's to pack. Bring it in for a hug, boys.'

Oliver and Liam ran towards them and flung themselves at their auntie. Megan gave them a bear hug.

'You coming in for a drink?' Jeremy asked.

Megan shook her head. 'Nope. I saw Rebecca earlier, and I don't want to intrude on family time. See you next time, Jer.'

'Safe flight.'

Jeremy and the boys stayed at the park until the last sliver of daylight disappeared and Jeremy insisted, to much grumbling, that it was time to go inside.

After they removed their coats and shoes and joined Rebecca in the kitchen, Liam asked, 'Is Daddy staying for dinner?'

Jeremy leaned down and kissed his son on the top of his head. Rebecca would never admit to being tired, but a full-time job and five-year-old twins was enough to exhaust even the most energetic of people. 'Daddy is going to make dinner to give Mummy a break.'

'No need,' said Rebecca, looking Jeremy up and down. 'Alex is making us a moussaka. I'll collect it from the pub while you're showering.'

'Yeah, sorry. I would have stopped off at Gloria's for a shower first, but I was running late and your phone was busy, so I thought it best to come straight here.' Jeremy hauled his T-shirt off over his head as the boys scampered off upstairs and Rebecca headed for the front door.

'Oh,' said Rebecca, turning back to him, 'just don't mention the L-word to Oliver while we're eating.'

'The L-word?'

'Lamb.'

He smiled, but the crease between Rebecca's eyes told him their meat-based meal wasn't the only thing she was anxious about. 'I'm also not going to mention what happened at your dad's party. I understand, Bex. This just isn't our time.'

She no doubt expected him to try to persuade her otherwise, but what was the point? He would only push her away further. The crease between her eyes seemed to deepen and the relief he'd expected to see on her face didn't come.

Instead, she spun around and marched towards the door, the coat rack clanging against the wall as she grabbed her coat. The fact that Rebecca wasn't happy about how things had turned out either brought him no comfort. He scrunched his T-shirt into a ball and launched it at the wall.

23

The first morning of the new week was done and Rebecca hung up her white coat and whipped off her hairnet following her daily walkabout on the factory floor. The Thistle Bay factory was one place that kept her connected to why she loved this business. Edinburgh's facility had a constant thrum of machinery as identical products whizzed along the production lines. Thistle Bay was different. It was often quiet enough to hold a conversation without the need to yell, and the lines were staffed by locals who spent their time hand-decorating chocolates ready to be gifted to other people's loved ones. Her family business brought employment, friendships, and joy to other families, and she loved playing her part in that.

She pulled open the door that led into the back of the shop. Her sister stood there with her head in her hands and Ben, Elizabeth's co-master chocolatier, had his hands on her shoulders.

'Oh good, Rebecca, maybe you can talk some sense into her,' said Ben.

Elizabeth straightened up and turned to face Rebecca.

'I'm fine. We just had twenty four-year-olds in here for cookie decorating.'

'*You* just had twenty four-year-olds,' Ben corrected. 'I was in here keeping well out of it.'

Rebecca laughed. 'The nursery party. I wondered how that would go.'

'It was loud,' said Ben. 'I'm trying to persuade Elizabeth to go out for lunch to get her energy back.'

Elizabeth massaged her temples with her fingers. 'I don't need lunch. I need quiet, and look,' she swept her hand around the shop, 'it's all quiet now.'

'Do you fancy combining the two?' asked Rebecca. 'Lunch and quiet. I need to grab Jeremy some food from Mystic's and drop it off to him at the farm. I came to ask for your help to make sure the coffees didn't spill all over my car on the way. It's pretty bumpy terrain up there.' Elizabeth had never said no to a request for help.

Ben put his hands on Elizabeth's shoulders again and nudged her towards Rebecca. 'Marvellous. Elizabeth would love to help you.'

'Great.' Now Rebecca just needed to cross her fingers that Jeremy was actually at the farm.

After picking up coffees and takeaway toasted sandwiches at Mystic's, Rebecca crawled her car up the driveway, successfully circumventing all the potholes.

'This is a pleasant surprise,' said Jeremy as they exited the car.

Rebecca felt her sister's glare. 'He means you. He obviously knew I was coming.'

'Yep. That's why I'm hanging about in the driveway.' Jeremy seemed to sense Rebecca's fib and played along without hesitation. He reached for the coffee Rebecca held out. 'I was waiting for this little beauty. So how's things?'

'Good. Elizabeth has been running a Christmas cookie decorating party for twenty nursery kids.'

'Ah, was it painful?'

Elizabeth squeezed the skin between her eyebrows. 'Now it is. It was actually a lot of fun. The kids loved it and it was only an hour. The teachers now have a class of kids caked in melted chocolate with enough sugar in their system to see them through to Christmas Day.'

They tucked into their toasted sandwiches listening to Elizabeth telling stories that to Rebecca sounded like scenes from a comedy sketch show rather than a kids' party. 'Oh, and it turned out one kid had a phobia of Santa Claus, so Ben and I had to pull down all the Santa decorations because the kid would not stop screaming. I thought we'd got them all until another kid passed him a Santa cookie to decorate and he went ballistic.'

Jeremy laughed. 'How does someone develop a phobia of Santa?'

Elizabeth shrugged. 'Who knows?'

'December must be a nightmare for his parents.' Rebecca rubbed her gloved hands together to warm them up as Elizabeth shivered beside her. The farmhouse behind them wasn't doing much to protect them from the biting December wind.

'I think this might be the quickest lunch break I've ever taken,' said Elizabeth. 'It's freezing. No offence, Jeremy, but I'm ready to leave any time you are, Rebecca.'

'Before you go,' Jeremy said to Elizabeth. 'This is probably not the best time to ask, given your thumping headache, but how would one go about arranging a Christmas cookie decorating party? I think the boys would love that.'

'I'll pick up some cookies at the supermarket,' said Rebecca. 'You can decorate them whenever you're free.'

Jeremy shook his head. 'No, I'm thinking about one in the shop. We'll invite the grandparents, the aunties, and whoever else fancies it. I want this Christmas to feel special for the boys.'

Rebecca grabbed the collar of Jeremy's coat and yanked it up around his neck. 'Their dad's home. It's already special for them.'

They heard a vehicle approaching on the driveway and Rebecca turned to see a white American-style pickup hurtling towards them, making no attempt to avoid the divots in the road. The car lurched to a stop and a woman with sleek blonde hair, long legs, and already grubby working boots hopped out of the driver's door.

'Mr Lewis, I presume,' she said, thrusting her hand towards Jeremy.

Jeremy moved closer and extended his hand. 'Yes, but call me Jeremy.'

'Great, I'm Serena.' She shook his hand and marched straight past him and onto the grass. 'Is this the site?' She pulled a piece of paper from a deep pocket in her high-visibility coat and unfolded it. Jeremy peered over her shoulder and Rebecca recognised the site plans he'd had had drawn up. 'This is going to be brilliant,' Serena said. 'What a view you have up here!'

'It's good, isn't it? It doesn't feel like too much of an incline to get up here, but we're still elevated enough to see above the rooftops and out to the water.'

'I'm excited to see the barbecue hut once constructed. I've only ever seen our show one, which is not the same as seeing it in situ.'

'Same here. I think it's going to be spectacular once it's

finished. Just give me a minute and I'll show you around,' said Jeremy. He downed his coffee and disappeared into the house.

The woman turned back to Rebecca and Elizabeth. 'Hi, I'm Serena from Cosy Cabins.'

'I'm Rebecca. This is my sister Elizabeth.'

'Good to meet you both. I'm just here to look at the foundations and make sure we have what we need for next week,' said Serena. 'With the rise of these websites where people can manage their own holiday rentals, we had a wave of people earlier in the year looking to install cabins in what was essentially their back gardens. They tried to shave a few quid off the bill by laying their own foundations. Unfortunately, what usually happened was they tried to cut the bill by cutting corners and we'd turn up onsite unable to complete the installation because all they'd done was mow the lawn.'

'There's been no corner cutting here.' Rebecca looked out over what Jeremy had called his camping field and surveyed the groundwork that she had overseen. During the summer, what had been a flawless field of green grass had resembled an archaeological dig as five craters were dug into the ground, utilities laid, and ground-level concrete plinths installed to the exact specification Cosy Cabins had provided. 'We stuck rigidly to the plans your company sent Jeremy, so you shouldn't have any problems.'

Serena turned to Rebecca. A breeze messed up her blonde hair, and she tucked it behind her ears. 'Are you Mrs Lewis?'

'No.'

Serena looked towards the house. 'Does that mean he's single?'

Rebecca shoved the last corner of her sandwich in her mouth and mumbled, 'I guess so.'

'Interesting,' said Serena, flashing a wide smile as Jeremy came back. Rebecca squinted at the sheen coming from Serena's porcelain veneers, which were definitely too big for her dainty mouth.

'Ready?' asked Jeremy.

'Sure am,' said an even perkier Serena. 'Just let me grab a few things from the truck.' She bounced over to the rear of her vehicle and pulled out a giant tool bag. Rebecca wasn't sure what tools the woman thought she might need to inspect a field. 'Lead the way,' Serena said, hoisting the bag over her shoulder.

'Can I take that for you?' Jeremy asked.

'No, thanks. I've got it.'

Jeremy turned to Elizabeth. 'I'll catch you later about the party.' He nodded towards Rebecca. 'I'll twist her arm.'

Rebecca watched Jeremy and Serena head off into the middle of the field. 'I don't want to be judgemental, but she's a bit too keen, isn't she?'

Elizabeth elbowed Rebecca in the side. 'Next time someone asks if you're Mrs Lewis, just say yes.'

'Hey,' said Rebecca, rubbing the dull ache she now had in her side. 'I'm not, though, am I?'

'And whose fault is that?'

Rebecca looked out into the field. Serena tossed her head back, her long blonde hair bouncing against the fabric of her worker's coat, which somehow managed to make her look slender even in the bulk of the padding. She laughed at something Jeremy had said. Rebecca's skin prickled as though she had just run through a field of nettles. She turned to Elizabeth. 'She's too short for him, right?'

Her sister raised her eyebrows.

'Never mind,' said Rebecca before Elizabeth had time to answer. She didn't need another lecture about her romantic life choices. She'd taken Elizabeth up to the farm to get her fresh air away from work and it had somehow backfired. It had given Jeremy the idea for a Christmas cookie decorating party that she knew he'd force her to attend, and she'd given a gorgeous blonde the go-ahead to go after her . . . her what?

Rebecca turned and stalked back to her car.

24

Rebecca buried herself in work for the rest of the week and allowed Jeremy to spend a lot of time with her and the boys. He picked them up from school a few times and cooked dinner most nights. They'd have to agree a more formal arrangement at some point, but December didn't seem like the right month to think about that. Besides, Jeremy needed to get his business off the ground before he would know his future schedule.

By Friday night, Rebecca was fighting exhaustion as she strolled around the back of her father's home, pulling her long coat tighter around her body, bracing herself against the chill in the air. The squeals of laughter from her children reached her before she had even unlocked the blue iron gate. She shoved the gate open and winced at the groaning of rusting metal. The hinges needed oiled, and the paintwork freshened up. She pulled her phone from the front pocket of her bag and made a note to check out some paint samples and speak to Arthur. He would know someone for the job. She tucked her phone into the back pocket of her trousers.

The boys were in the garden on their hands and knees in front of one of her father's flowerbeds. Neither of them was wearing a coat, despite the frigid temperature. She glanced down at the spike heels on her shoes and decided against walking across the grass to see what they were up to. 'Hi, boys,' she yelled from the patio.

'Hi, Mummy,' Liam replied, not even bothering to look up.

Oliver gave her a wave, metal glinting from the trowel in his hand.

She pushed open the back door and stepped into the welcoming warmth of her father's kitchen. The mouth-watering spiciness of sautéed onions and fragrant Indian spices escaped from the pot her father was stirring at the stovetop.

'Can I interest you in some chana masala?' Alan asked.

'If it tastes as good as it smells, absolutely,' replied Rebecca. She removed her coat and hung it on the coat stand tucked in the corner. She'd given up arguing about food. When the boys had started school after the summer, Friday nights had unofficially become the day Grandpa picked them up from school to give Rebecca an extra couple of hours in the office. Despite her insistence that she would give the boys dinner after she picked them up, her father always prepared a meal for them, and Rebecca joined them, or if she was late, she was handed a tin-foil-covered plate to take home with her. 'The boys appear to be digging out there. Please tell me you know about that and they've not gone rogue and dug up your flowerbeds.'

Alan laughed and turned the heat off under his pan of curry.

'They're digging for worms. In their school bags there's a list of bugs to find and the only thing they've yet to check off is a worm. I told them they had until next week to complete it, but they insisted on doing it tonight.'

Rebecca pulled some bowls out of a cupboard and laid them across the kitchen island. 'Well, I hope they find one. It's one less piece of homework for me to help them with this weekend.'

'Some of your parcels arrived this week. I've stashed them in Megan's room if you want a peek before I call the boys in.'

'I will, thanks.'

Alan sprinkled a handful of chopped coriander leaves over the chana masala and placed the lid on. 'I bumped into Jeremy today.' Rebecca waited for the inevitable lecture about the state of her love life. 'He seemed very matter of fact about the two of you not being a couple,' Alan continued.

'We're not a couple.'

'Yes, I hear that from you often, but Jeremy is usually less definite. Did something happen between you two?'

Rebecca shook her head. 'Nothing happened.'

Alan stirred the pan of rice simmering away on top of the cooker. 'The last I heard, you were going to be taking it slowly. It appears things have now ground to a halt. Is that because I'm retiring?'

Rebecca shook her head. 'It's not about that. Well, it's a little about that. I want to take over from you and continue to see the business thriving. For that, I need to be focused.'

'You always tried to take on too much, Rebecca. Even as a child, you thought you had to become a mother to the others. I hoped Gloria coming to look after you all full time would allow you to be a child again, but you stayed so serious. You're allowed to love, Rebecca.'

'Love isn't enough to keep people together.' She cast her

eyes towards the French doors leading to the garden. 'And there's too much at stake for me right now.'

Alan came out from behind the cooker and stepped towards her. 'Love is always enough.'

'It wasn't enough to keep you and Mum together.'

Alan gripped Rebecca's hands tightly. 'I loved your mother very much and I know she loved me. Our separation was physical, but our marriage was very much intact. Your mother being sick and hospitalised was the only reason we weren't together.'

'You don't know what would have happened if she hadn't been sick.'

'I don't know. But I know that I've never found anyone I could love as much as I loved your mother, and that's proof enough for me that our marriage was a success. Don't allow your new job to limit your future.' He squeezed her hands once more, then released them. 'You peek at the presents. I'll plate up, then get the dynamic duo in.'

'Thanks, Dad.' Rebecca slipped her shoes off and headed straight for her sister's childhood bedroom. Pushing open the door, she reflected on her father's words. Her life didn't feel limited. Like Megan's bedroom, it was bursting at the seams.

Megan's paint-splashed wooden easel in front of the wide corner window held a blank canvas. The walls were lined with paintings that showcased Megan's progression as an artist. She had turned her hand to everything from vibrant abstract pieces to intricate paintings of their hometown, with every detail captured and beautifully presented. A painting of a little black dog with soulful eyes and a glistening wet nose was so realistic that it looked like a photograph. Rebecca plucked her phone out of her pocket, switched on her camera, and snapped a picture of the dog's portrait.

The far corner of the room was packed tight with plain cardboard boxes. Megan had stayed at home longer than any of the other Knight children. At age thirty-two, she was the only one who had yet to formally move out. She had lived something of a nomadic existence since she'd graduated and had regularly returned to their father's house between countries. Alan appeared relaxed about Megan's travelling. He said she needed to find herself and she would do that soon enough. Rebecca had been content to go along with that until Megan had crossed the threshold into her thirties. It was now almost a decade since Megan had graduated art school and Rebecca thought she ought to have found herself by now. She understood Megan didn't want to join the family business. The corporate life just wasn't for her. But travelling the globe picking up odd jobs here and there wasn't a sustainable life choice.

Rebecca opened the flaps on a cardboard box and peered inside. It contained a stack of Megan's books. Her reading material was as eclectic as her painting had been over the years. Rebecca flicked through the books, seeing Scottish crime fiction, small-town romances, art guides, World War Two true stories, and multiple travel companions. The surrounding boxes were packed full of Megan's clothes and random art supplies. Rebecca heaved the box of books off its top spot and dumped it on the bed. The box underneath held more books, only this time there was a running theme of gratitude journals, the law of attraction, and signs from the universe. Rebecca suspected if she kept digging she'd find a pile of crystals and candles that high school Megan had used to build what she had called her altar. Rebecca had dismissed her sister's interest in spirituality at the time, telling her to leave the witchcraft for Halloween and watch she didn't burn the house down with her open flames. It was a response she would still give her sister if she recreated her altar when she was home.

She closed the box and spotted the end of another cardboard box still sealed with parcel tape. She picked up the box of clothes on top, added it to another pile, and dragged the sealed box forwards. Alan had buried her boxes in amongst Megan's, concealing them with the heavy boxes of books so little wandering hands wouldn't discover them. Rebecca quickly counted the packages that looked like hers and replaced Megan's possessions to bury the presents again. She'd leave the boys with Jeremy one day and come and wrap everything up before smuggling the gifts into her own home nearer Christmas Day.

Rebecca returned to her father's cosy kitchen to see her sons with glum looks on their faces. 'What's wrong?' she asked.

'We didn't find any worms,' said Oliver.

'You've got the entire weekend to find a worm, so you don't need to worry about that right now.'

'I've tried telling them that,' said Alan.

Her children were impatient. A trait common in five-year-olds, she suspected. If they wanted to do something, they wanted to do it right there and then. To add more fuel to the fire, Oliver was already the type of child who had to at least start, if not complete, his homework on the same day the teacher issued it. Both of his parents were quick-starts, so it was hardly surprising, but it sometimes felt as though he worried too much at such a young age. She took her seat at the table. 'I know where you'll definitely find a worm,' she said.

Oliver immediately brightened at the thought. 'Where?'

'Daddy's farm.'

'Yes!' said Liam. 'Can we go there after dinner?'

'It's too late tonight; the worms will all be sleeping. But we can head up there early tomorrow morning.'

'The early bird catches the worm,' declared Oliver. He shoved a forkful of food into his mouth, looking pleased with his turn of phrase and Rebecca's plan for him to finish his homework.

25

On Saturday morning, Jeremy was up at the farm so early that bats were swerving to avoid him as he crossed his driveway towards the small outhouse hidden behind the hedges. Rebecca had given him the challenge of finding a worm for Oliver and Liam's school project. He'd spent the evening before learning more about earthworms than he ever thought he'd need to know. Rebecca had assumed finding a worm on a farm was a simple task. In December's frozen soil, Jeremy didn't have the same confidence given that he'd read some worms can burrow six feet underground to stay warm and alive in the winter months.

His first task that morning had been to drive five miles out of town to meet a friend of Gloria's who was a keen fisherman and was happy to supply Jeremy with a box of the worms he used as bait. He'd then texted Arthur to give him the heads-up that he'd stolen soil from one of his greenhouses rather than try to dig up some of the ice-packed ground on the farm.

The dark sky quickly became a fiery orange as Jeremy worked on his construction. Using planks of wood he'd found discarded in the utility room of the farmhouse and his power drill, he knocked up a small square planter. He lined it with sheets of plastic to keep the worms from escaping to their certain icy deaths and tipped in Arthur's potting soil. The dirt stopped an inch short of the top, but it would do the job.

His phoned vibrated in his pocket and he pulled it out to read the message. Rebecca and the boys were on their way. Jeremy scooped a couple of holes into the soil, tipped the long brown worms in, and patted the soil back into place.

After stashing his tools in the hallway, he cleared a pile of post from behind the door in the kitchen, dumping it on the worktop to be dealt with later. A brochure for archery equipment caught his eye, and he scrubbed the dirt off his hands with more force than was necessary. He hated the feeling of uncertainty. He could never work a nine-to-five job where he shuffled a tidal wave of paperwork all day. Buying the land had been the right thing to do, and he was certain that building a business here was the way to go, but something was stopping him from ordering the kit he needed to build his adventure experience. He could never replicate Marine training on his land. He wasn't trying to. But he worried he was sticking too closely to what he knew when he had an opportunity to build something from nothing. The bare fields were almost so much of a blank canvas that they were keeping him stuck. He wasn't unique in his uncertainty. He'd witnessed many Marines before him struggling to carve out alternative career paths when their military service ended. That didn't make it any less frustrating.

Rebecca's tyres crunched the gravel on his driveway. Jeremy snatched two coffee-stained spoons from the worktop and headed out to get the boys from the car.

Liam launched himself into Jeremy's arms and squeezed his little arms around Jeremy's neck. Oliver climbed out of the car, holding a piece of paper and a pencil. 'We need to find a worm, Daddy,' he said, thrusting his paper at Jeremy.

Jeremy looked down at the checklist, his eyes scanning the tick boxes and the glaring space beside *worm*. 'It's freezing on the farm, so the worms will be deep in the earth to keep warm. But I think you might find some in the planter on the driveway over there.' Jeremy pointed to the planter that had existed for all of ten minutes. The boys dashed over, with Liam ready to shove his hands into the dirt until Rebecca dragged him back.

'Daddy will have something you can dig with,' she said. Jeremy handed a spoon to each child. Rebecca laughed. 'Seriously? You're expecting them to dig with teaspoons?'

'What?' said Jeremy. 'Worms are very delicate. If they pummel the soil with a shovel, they'll end up slicing the poor things in half.'

'They're worms,' said Rebecca.

'What's your point?' asked Jeremy. The boys shifted the soil around with their spoons, Oliver being a bit more precise with his digging than Liam. Jeremy scanned the list again and leaned closer to Rebecca. 'Where did they find a ladybird in December?'

'On Dad's shed. The fact it was a glass ladybird didn't seem to register.'

'And a butterfly?'

'A moth.'

'I found one,' yelled Oliver.

Liam dropped his spoon and shuffled on his knees to Oliver's side of the planter. He shoved his bare hand in the hole Oliver had carefully crafted and picked the worm up. 'It's so cool.'

Rebecca shuddered. 'Well done. Can we check worm off the list now and head somewhere inside?'

'I want to find another one,' said Oliver.

'I actually thought it might be fun to build a worm farm. Do you boys want to help?' Jeremy asked.

The boys nodded their heads enthusiastically.

'What on earth is a worm farm?' asked Rebecca.

Jeremy produced the box that Gloria's fisherman friend had given him. 'Let's find as many worms as we can and put them in here. Once the pet shop is open, we can buy the things we need to give the worms a really cosy home to keep them safe until the spring.'

'Are you kidding me?' asked Rebecca.

'It's going to be so cool, Mummy,' said Oliver. 'We'll finally have pets. I don't think anyone else at school has sheep and worms for pets.'

'There's a reason for that, darling. Sheep and worms are not really pets. They belong on a farm.'

'This *is* a farm, Mummy,' said Liam, rolling his little eyes back in his head.

Jeremy wrapped an arm around Rebecca's shoulders and gave her a squeeze. 'It'll be fine.'

'It's all on you. They better not expect to bring those worms home at any point.'

Eighteen worms later and the boys had to leave to go to football practice. Jeremy promised them he would keep looking for worms and they could help him build the worm farm as soon as they were finished at football. Jeremy waved his children off with their mother and lowered his hands into the soil. He found the nineteenth worm quickly, then spent a frustrating twenty minutes finding number twenty. With all the worms safely back in their box, Jeremy scrubbed his hands again, grabbed his laptop, and headed into town with a head-splitting need for caffeine.

'Morning, Jeremy,' said a bright and cheery Mystic. 'How's life as a sheep farmer?'

'Before you crack jokes at my expense, I should tell you I've had no coffee this morning.'

'Warning noted,' said Mystic with a smile. 'What can I get you?'

'A latte, please.' Jeremy waved at Susie, who was in front of the coffee machine and already at work steaming his milk. 'Any chance you can rustle me up a couple of packed lunches for the boys? I'm taking them up to the farm later and I have little in the way of food at the house.'

'Sure. Anything in particular?'

'Just whatever you have. Some sandwiches. Maybe a little cookie or cake for later.'

'And something for yourself?' Mystic asked.

Jeremy nodded. 'Just a sandwich would be good.'

'I'll get right on it.'

'Thanks.' Jeremy moved to the end of the counter to collect his steaming-hot latte. 'Oh, and it needs to be vegetarian for Oliver.' He caught Mystic's look of confusion. 'It's a long story,' he said. 'Thanks, Susie.'

He sat at a table for two, opened his laptop, and typed *building a worm farm* into his search engine.

'Why do you have worms on your screen?'

Jeremy turned to see Cat standing behind him, her arms full with her laptop and a couple of folders containing what he presumed were her tasks for the day ahead. 'Pull up a pew and I'll tell you.'

Jeremy rattled off how he'd spent his evening and the earliest part of the day, much to Cat's amusement.

'Why don't you just give the worms back to the fisherman?' she asked.

'That's a perfectly logical question with no logical answer.'

'Is it because you know he'll just feed them to the fish and you think you can save them the way you're saving the sheep?'

Jeremy shook his head. 'I'm not saving the sheep. They're going somewhere else.'

'Oh really? So you have a plan for them that's better than mine?'

'Not yet. But something will come to me. I feel like the worms will look after themselves. The sheep won't. They're a big commitment and definitely not one that I see fitting into my business model.' He raised his hand to shush her before she reiterated her family farm sales pitch.

The excitable chatter of his children arriving drowned out the chime above the door to Mystic's coffee shop. Jeremy turned to see Oliver and Liam with little red faces and unzipped coats revealing muddy football tops. 'You two look like you've had fun,' said Jeremy.

Rebecca stood behind the boys, her cheeks also slightly pink, but from the cold rather than the exertion that his two football players had expended. 'I didn't see the point in taking them home to change, given your plan to have them playing in the mud again shortly.'

'Auntie Cat, have you heard we're getting pet worms?' asked Liam.

'I did. How exciting.'

'You can come up to Daddy's farm and see them if you want to,' said Liam.

'You could also meet Olive and Marmalade,' said Oliver.

Cat gave Jeremy a look at the mention of the sheep, or

perhaps it was the fact that they now appeared to have new names that caused her to smirk. 'I would love that, thank you.'

Oliver slid onto the chair beside Cat and Jeremy noticed Cat putting her arm around Oliver and kissing him on his sweaty little head. The relationship between Cat and Rebecca was still a little tense, but his children seemed to have already accepted their new aunt and doled out the same love and affection he'd seen them show Elizabeth and Megan.

Jeremy caught Rebecca glancing at his laptop screen, which was still displaying a close-up image of earthworms. 'They've told everyone at football they're getting pet worms,' she said, her voice almost a whisper.

'They are,' Jeremy whispered back. He closed his laptop and pushed his chair back. 'Would either of you ladies like to join us for worm farm shopping?'

Rebecca laughed and shook her head. 'No, thank you. I think I'll use the time to grab a coffee and catch up on some work.'

'Cat?' asked Jeremy. 'Want to help rehome some worms?'

Cat tapped her hand on the folders on the table in front of her. 'Sorry. I've got some work to catch up on, too.'

Jeremy collected and paid for the packed lunches. As he led the boys out of Mystic's, he heard Rebecca asking Cat if Ryan had sent her through some snapshots of the new machinery in Edinburgh and whether there was anything she could use for social media posts. He wished she would use some of her child-free time for something that wasn't work. The only way that was going to happen, though, was if he forced her.

Two hours and a roughly constructed worm farm later, Jeremy rubbed his gloved hands over his face before he remembered they were covered in mud, which was now smeared across his sweaty skin. The freezing temperatures and damp outdoor air, the mud, and the physical activity – it suited him. Sitting at a desk with a computer screen and nothing but a bunch of numbers or letters wasn't for him. It never had been. He watched his children dangling over the fence to pet the sheep. Seeing their joy at not only spending time with him but also spending time outdoors getting dirty, and seeing that sense of accomplishment on their faces with each small task completed, that was what his business should be about. This wasn't a place for stag dos and corporate stiffs; it was a place for families to come together and have a shared experience. For exhausted parents to relax and kids to be challenged and proud of themselves when they rose to meet that challenge.

This, he realised, was why he hadn't ordered any kit or built up anything other than the accommodation. Something had been missing from his plans and he'd finally found it. He'd thought about families coming to stay, too, but he'd never been able to envision what that would look like. Being here, using the space with his children, had opened up his eyes to a new possibility, and the flutter in his gut told him he was on the right path.

Footsteps squelched in the mud behind him and he turned to see Rebecca teetering towards him, carrying two takeaway coffees. 'Thought you could probably do with a break,' she said.

He took his cup, feeling the warmth in his hand, and gratefully sipped the hot liquid. 'What do you think about making this place a family adventure park?'

'Meaning what?'

'I was still in single digits when Mum would toss me out of the door and I would head into nature. I played commandoes with other kids and we'd climb trees, build dens, collect conkers, and forage for wild berries. Our imaginations kept us entertained all day, and we all headed back at dinnertime tired and filthy. There are so few opportunities for kids these days to get that experience.'

For once, Rebecca's face gave nothing away.

'I've got the space here to give families a memorable outdoor break. We can do archery. I'll run bush craft workshops for kids and create scavenger hunts. It sounds like that checklist of bugs kept the boys amused for a good chunk of time. I can stock bikes for family cycles around the country lanes, and I might even plant some veggies for them to harvest. What do you think?'

'I think you should sleep on it. Working with kids is quite the departure from what you've been planning so far.'

It didn't feel like a big change to Jeremy. It had been the flexibility of his adventure experience idea that had appealed to him. The ability to invite people into his world when he chose to or decline bookings whenever he craved solitude was a level of control over his days he'd never had before. Catering for families didn't change that. He smiled, not caring that he was caked in mud and frozen to the core. It didn't even matter that the house he planned to make his home was uninhabitable. To the outsider, the farm currently looked like chaos incarnate. But Jeremy now had a vivid picture of every aspect of his business, and it was exhilarating.

It was just his love life that was foggier than the fancy crystal glasses Rebecca had once scolded him for putting in the dishwasher.

26

On Sunday, Rebecca found herself on the anniversary of her mother's death with two tasks that couldn't have been more different: visiting her mother's grave and making an appearance at Jeremy's Christmas cookie decorating party.

She collected the flowers she'd ordered and headed straight for the cemetery. Over the years, her siblings had begun to do their own things on this date. That was normal, she supposed, after so many years had passed. And the harsh reality was that they each had different experiences and different memories of their mother. Being the eldest, Rebecca had had more years with her mother when she was well. Elizabeth had only been five years old when the family had moved back to Thistle Bay and Catherine hadn't been well before the move. Megan and Ryan had few memories of their mother, and they probably weren't the happiest despite Rebecca's efforts to shield them from Catherine's worst days. Then there was Cat. She had no memories of their mother at all.

Rebecca wrapped her scarf tighter around her neck and pushed open the gate to the deserted cemetery. The small church provided no shelter from the icy wind. She clutched the bouquet of flowers close to her body as she walked.

The grey marble headstone bearing her mum's name came into view. Fresh flowers rested against the marble. Rebecca wasn't the first person to visit this year. She glanced around her, then bent down to the flowers. She moved a white rose to read the card hidden behind, recognising the handwriting immediately. It read simply, *With love, from Jeremy*.

She couldn't believe Jeremy had remembered. He hadn't mentioned anything when he'd collected the boys that morning. He'd only reminded her not to be late for the party.

Rebecca's hand trembled as she laid her own floral tribute. She ran her fingertips along the glossy surface of the marble, feeling the coolness beneath her touch. Life was so unfair. She closed her eyes, and the sound of her mother's laughter seemed to echo around her, bringing back bittersweet memories. Catherine had loved to dance. Music was always on, and sometimes Catherine would reach for Rebecca and spin her around as though they were on a dance floor. She wouldn't stop until Rebecca was pink cheeked, puffed out, and giggling. In their quieter moments, they would snuggle together, tell stories or read books, and eat red velvet cupcakes that they'd baked themselves.

Rebecca brushed away the tear that had trickled down her cheek. 'I miss you, Mum,' she whispered, her heart aching. She hoped, somewhere, her mother could hear her.

Rebecca went straight from the cemetery to her family's chocolate shop. Decorating cookies was the last thing she wanted to do today, but it had seemed important to Jeremy, and the boys were looking forward to it. It wasn't her idea of fun, but it was probably a helpful distraction to get her through the day. That was what December was about for her – a series of distractions, initially from her mother's illness, and later her mother's absence. By her late teens, increased chocolate production and shipping orders had taken the place of Santa and presents at Christmas. These days, drinking mulled wine was the only festive activity she appreciated.

She went through the motions for the boys, of course, and today that meant decorating festive-themed cookies with colourful icing that she knew she would later regret allowing them to eat.

Elizabeth had decorated the party room attached to the shop with far too many fairy lights. A headache from the twinkling would surely be inevitable. Jeremy, Oliver, Liam, and Cat were already in the room, and Elizabeth appeared from behind Rebecca with an apron in one hand and a cheeky grin on her face. 'You ready for this?' she asked, handing Rebecca the apron.

'Of course,' said Rebecca with as much enthusiasm as she could muster.

Elizabeth laughed. 'Don't worry, the kids are calm.'

'So far. Just you wait until Liam eats that first cookie.' Rebecca slipped her apron over her head and Elizabeth stepped behind her to tie it.

'Jeremy is looking particularly fine today,' Elizabeth whispered in her ear.

'Let's just get this over with,' grumbled Rebecca.

'Mummy!' yelled the boys. Oliver ran towards her and squeezed his arms around her waist. 'Daddy says he'll take us to get a Christmas tree after this.'

'Is that so?' Rebecca joined the others at the large square table. 'We have a tree, though. Maybe Daddy can come round and help me take it out of the attic.'

Jeremy rolled his eyes. He hated her tree. He leaned towards her. 'I thought having fun as a family would be a good way to honour your mum's memory.'

Rebecca swallowed. 'It is. Thank you for Mum's flowers.'

Elizabeth squeezed Rebecca's forearm and smiled. Even though the Knight siblings didn't come together as they used to on this day, Catherine was still in their thoughts. That's what mattered most.

'The Santas are over there,' said Elizabeth, pointing to a table in the corner. 'They're still too warm to ice.'

The wooden board in the centre of the main table was piled high with gingerbread teddy bears, Christmas trees, and stockings just waiting to be smothered in icing and sprinkles.

'I don't know how you do it all,' said Rebecca. 'This must have taken you hours.'

Elizabeth bumped up against Cat, who was busy emptying tubes of sugar snowflakes and gold stars onto plates. 'I had a little help this year.'

'Thanks,' Rebecca said to Cat. 'This looks amazing. And bright.'

'Happy to help,' said Cat. Rebecca sensed the cheer in her voice was forced. She hadn't known Cat would be here, but she was glad that she was. This was an opportunity to get Cat involved in her family life. Rebecca would focus on making sure the boys had a good time and Cat felt welcome. That was another way to honour her mother's memory.

Elizabeth reached forward and plucked a gingerbread tree from the top of the stack. 'Who wants to decorate the first one?' Oliver and Liam's hands shot up as they bounced around at the end of the table. Elizabeth scooped up another tree and placed them on the rubber mats in front of the boys. 'Get stuck in then.'

As the children spurted icing on everything but the cookies and giggled at Jeremy, who had somehow got icing on his chin only seconds into their decorating stint, Rebecca moved to the opposite side of the table. Cat still had an empty mat in front of her. Rebecca picked up two cookies and held them out towards Cat. 'Do you want the bear or the stocking?'

The corners of Cat's lips twitched and she pressed her lips together. 'The stocking, please. Bears don't seem very Christmassy.'

Rebecca passed the gingerbread stocking to Cat. 'They are when you have children. Oliver is much more into cuddly toys than Liam is, but they both love it when Santa puts a teddy bear in their stockings.'

Cat scooped up three tubes of icing. 'I guess. I've not been around many young kids.'

'And now you've suddenly got two five-year-olds in your life. They'll give you a crash course in Christmas with kids. It's very different.'

Rebecca painted red icing across her bear's body, leaving only the paws, which she planned to paint white. She glanced at Cat and smiled at the artistic flair with which she was decorating. Her stocking had stripes using coordinating colours and varying patterns. She dabbed green dots just below the white cuff of the stocking and picked up the tube of red icing. Using a wooden cocktail stick and a steady hand, Cat wrote *Oliver* in tiny crimson letters. By the time Rebecca had given her bear snowy paws and black claws and added a green scarf to make her cookie look a little better next to Cat's, Cat had already decorated another stocking with a similarly intricate design for Liam.

Rebecca plucked her phone from her back pocket, snapped a photo of Cat's designs, and texted them to Megan. She turned her Christmas bear towards Cat and shrugged. 'I didn't get the artistic gene. You share that with Elizabeth and Megan.'

Cat smiled. 'It's cute.'

'Why don't you go over and give the boys their cookies?'

Cat picked up her mat and wandered around to the other side of the table. 'I made you both a little something.' She passed the boys their decorated cookies.

'That's so cool,' said Liam.

'Thank you, Auntie Cat,' said Oliver. 'I like the green and yellow stripes the best. Yellow is my favourite colour.'

'No, it's not,' said Liam. 'Your favourite colour is blue.'

Oliver folded his arms across his body. 'Is not.'

'It was last week.'

'Well, it's yellow now.'

Rebecca watched Jeremy lean between his sons to defuse the brewing tension. She sighed happily as she took in the smiling faces of her children. Their dad, having mustered more Christmas cheer than he had ever shown before, distracted them further from their squabble by asking them why Rudolph didn't go to school. The punchline of Rudolph being elf-taught took a few seconds to elicit giggles from the boys. Cat looked on with a pink glow on her cheeks and a glisten in her eyes. Rebecca was glad Jeremy had forced her to come, and a little irritated at herself that she'd had to be forced.

Rebecca picked up another teddy bear biscuit and listened in as Jeremy told Cat about his family adventure park idea. She seemed delighted by the idea. Jeremy and Rebecca hadn't discussed it again since she had advised him to sleep on it. They hadn't needed to. Rebecca could read Jeremy and he had been excited. Somehow, using the land to build a worm farm with his children had caused him to have some kind of epiphany. His eyes had danced across the landscape and a smile had spread across his face. His vision for his business had become clear and the fire inside of him had been lit.

After two more dodgily decorated teddy bears, Rebecca had reached her limit of festive fun. She moved to the other end of the table and was glad to see Jeremy and the boys had finished their pots of icing.

'What do you say, Bex? Fancy some Christmas tree shopping?'

'I told you. I have a tree in the attic.'

Jeremy shook his head. 'That scrawny white thing is not a tree.'

Rebecca clamped her hands to her hips. 'It's not a scrawny white thing. It's supposed to be snow.'

'There's no snow in your living room. A tree is supposed to be green. I'll drive out to Ashcroft Farm and pick out a real one.'

Oliver and Liam high-fived each other, and Rebecca groaned. 'Real ones leave needles everywhere. It'll probably be dead before Santa even gets here.'

Jeremy extended his hand towards her. 'I will sweep up any stray needles every day, and if it dies, I will personally bring your plastic fake monstrosity down from your attic to replace it. Deal?'

Rebecca looked down at her children's hopeful faces, and before she could look for another reason to say no, she said, 'If you bring my super-classy tree down from the attic and put it in the living room, you can get a real one for the snug in the kitchen. Deal?'

Jeremy prised her right hand off her hip. 'Deal!'

Rebecca turned to Elizabeth. 'I'm going to hate this, aren't I?'

Elizabeth grinned. 'Yes. Yes, you will.'

Rebecca sighed and scraped a hand through her hair. 'At least you're honest.'

'I am. And now I have to get back to work. Ben and I are testing chocolate infused with pomegranate.'

'Ooh, that sounds tasty,' said Cat.

'You'd think, but we can't quite get the balance of flavours working. It's so frustrating. My aim is to get it working before Christmas so we can test-run production in January.' Elizabeth waved her hand around the room. 'Leave the mess. There's no one else coming in today, so I'll sort it later.'

Elizabeth disappeared back through to the shop, and Rebecca dumped the leftover sprinkles and sugar decorations into the bin in the corner of the room. It was such a waste, but given the sticky little hands that had been all over them, they couldn't be used for anything else. Cat piled up the rubber mats they'd used for decorating and stacked the chocolate-smeared plates. Jeremy finished loading the cookies into the plastic tubs Elizabeth had left out for them and clipped the lids closed. 'Who's ready to get a Christmas tree?'

'Yes!' the boys yelled in unison.

'I want a massive tree, Daddy,' said Liam.

'One that touches the ceiling,' added Oliver.

'Remember to leave space at the top for your star,' said Cat. 'Or do you have an angel?'

The boys looked at each other blankly, then at Rebecca.

'I think it's a star,' she said.

Jeremy rolled his eyes. 'Wait until you see this thing.'

'It's not that bad,' Rebecca huffed. She turned to Cat. 'Are you up for a bit of Christmas tree shopping with us?'

Cat shook her head. 'Thanks, but I don't want to gatecrash your entire family day.'

'Nonsense. You're family, too. If you've got work to do then fine, but if you've got some time, we'd all love for you to join us.' Cat's eyes darted around the room and Rebecca hoped she wasn't thinking up an excuse not to come. 'Please,' Rebecca added.

Cat nodded. 'If you're sure you don't mind.'

Rebecca turned to her hyped-up sons. 'What do you say, boys? Should Auntie Cat come with us to buy our tree?'

The boys whooped with delight and danced around Jeremy. 'The sugar in the icing has definitely kicked in,' he said. 'I feel for you, Cat. You'll have to sit in the middle of these two in the car.'

Cat laughed and rubbed Liam on the head. 'That thought doesn't scare me one little bit.'

'Only because you haven't yet experienced it,' said Rebecca. 'I've got painkillers in my bag if a hyper-kids headache kicks in by the time we get to the farm.'

The Christmas tree farm was crowded when they arrived and Rebecca remembered the reason she'd bought her snow-covered artificial tree. Swarms of people were also the reason she shopped online in December. A weary sensation came over her as she climbed out of Jeremy's car and helped Oliver out of the back. Cat, Liam, and Jeremy rounded the front of the car and Jeremy glanced down at Rebecca's shoes.

'Hmm,' he said. 'I didn't think to tell you to wear sensible shoes.'

Rebecca looked down. 'Black leather shoes. They're about as sensible as shoes come.'

Jeremy looked at Cat's flat ballet pumps. 'You're good,' he said to her. 'They'll clean.'

Rebecca gestured to the neat rows of fir trees behind her. 'Why would we need to clean our shoes? We're only picking up a Christmas tree.'

Jeremy opened the boot of his car and dug around for something. 'We're not picking *up* a tree. We're *picking* a tree.' Rebecca turned towards Cat and was glad to see her expression was as blank as her own must have been. 'We're choosing a tree that we like, then we're cutting it down.'

Rebecca laughed. 'Why would we bother doing that when there's a pile of them over there?'

Jeremy handed Rebecca a pair of working boots. 'Change into these.'

'No.'

'You can't walk up the field in those. You'll ruin them.'

Rebecca looked down at her stiletto heels. The shoes had been an early Christmas gift to herself. She suspected Jeremy couldn't care less whether she ruined them or not, but she cared. She sighed and took the boots.

'I'll pick up the saw.'

Rebecca looked at Cat. 'I thought the trickiest part of this trip was going to be tying a tree to the roof of Jeremy's car.'

Once Rebecca had changed her shoes, Cat and the twins led the way into the farmland and along rows of trees that were fairly uniform in size. 'It smells amazing in here,' said Cat.

'Just wait until you smell it in your living room,' said Jeremy. He elbowed Rebecca. 'It's fun, huh?'

'Stop trying to drown me with your Christmas cheer. It's like pick your own strawberries but worse,' said Rebecca as she trudged alongside him.

'I love pick your own,' said Cat. 'No strawberry tastes as good as the ones you've just plucked straight from the plant.'

Jeremy nudged Rebecca again. 'See. She knows. It's the same with trees.'

'I was planning to decorate the tree, not eat it,' huffed Rebecca.

Oliver giggled and turned towards her. 'Silly Mummy. You can't eat a Christmas tree.'

'Well, you probably could,' said Jeremy. 'But it wouldn't taste very good.'

'Yuk!' added Liam. 'If I was going to eat a Christmas tree, I would eat it with peanut butter.'

'If I had to eat it,' said Oliver, 'I think I would hide it in chilli nachos like what Mummy does with mushrooms.'

'Yucky mushrooms,' said Liam.

Cat slowed and leaned back. 'Sounds like you're not fooling anyone with the mushrooms,' she whispered over her shoulder.

Rebecca nodded. 'They've been onto me for a while now.'

'The point is,' said Jeremy, 'a fresh tree lasts longer and you won't find a fresher tree than the one you chop down yourself.' Jeremy stopped, and everyone else followed his lead. 'Are you getting one, Cat?'

'Not today, but I think I'll bring Nick here to choose one. I've never had a Christmas tree before.'

'You mean a real one?' asked Rebecca.

Cat shook her head. 'I've never had any tree. I've always lived alone, so there didn't seem any point in getting one just for me.'

Rebecca touched her hand to the sharp pain in her stomach and blinked hard. This was why she preferred talking to Cat about work. Most of what she knew about the later years of Cat's childhood had come from Ryan, and it wasn't a happy story. Rebecca had last seen Cat when she was only five years old. Rebecca was a teenager then and she could still picture the smiley, bouncy little girl Cat had been. Then when Cat's adoptive parents had died and Cat had vanished, Rebecca had persuaded herself that a loving family had adopted Cat again. It had tortured their father when they found out that Cat had been raised in the care system.

As if sensing what was on Rebecca's mind, Cat reached out and touched her sister's arm. 'Can you see a tree you like?' she asked Rebecca.

'I see one I like,' Oliver said as he dashed ahead, dragging his dad with him to inspect the branches of a tree.

Rebecca felt a flash of guilt. She should have been the one consoling Cat, not the other way around.

'Auntie Cat,' said Liam. 'If you've never had a Christmas tree, does that mean you don't have any decorations?'

Cat crouched down to Liam's eye level. 'No, I don't have any decorations.'

'My brother makes amazing Christmas decorations. I can make them, too, but mine aren't as good because I don't have enough patience.'

'Is that so?' Cat cast a smile in Rebecca's direction. 'Do you think you and Oliver could make me a few decorations for my tree?'

'We will.' Liam looked delighted to be asked and sprinted away to catch up with his brother, presumably to share his excitement.

Rebecca turned to Cat. 'This must be hard for you. I'm just so sorry that we had these family Christmases that you should have been part of. I'm sorry you never got to experience that.'

'Nothing about this situation is ideal, and it's going to take time to come to terms with what's happened. I honestly don't know what kind of relationship we'll have in three month's time or in three year's time. But I do know that everyone needs to stop apologising for things that happened when we were kids.'

'I was fifteen. That's old enough.'

'Old enough for what? You were a fifteen-year-old kid dealing with things no child should ever have to deal with. You didn't have control over what happened. None of us did. And none of us made the decisions that . . .'

Her words trailed off and Rebecca knew Cat was thinking about their father. Cat and Alan had spent hours going over what had happened, and Rebecca had seen him in his office poring over the letters Cat's adoptive parents had sent. He blamed himself for not insisting that Cat be returned to her biological family, but pressing that would have put Ryan's future in jeopardy. Rebecca shifted her gaze to her boys. How do you fight for one of your children when you know it will have dire consequences for your other child? 'He did what he thought was best in a horrible set of circumstances,' said Rebecca.

Cat turned to follow Rebecca's gaze and nodded. 'I know. And I can't say that I would have made different decisions faced with the same set of circumstances. I'm ready to put the past in the past and leave it there.'

Jeremy waved to them. 'I think we've found the one,' he called over. He instructed the boys to stand back while he readied the saw he'd collected at the entrance.

Rebecca watched from the sidelines. She had also found the one. But pursuing a relationship with Jeremy risked ruining things for her children if it didn't work out. And with her new job, there was even less chance of it working out than there had been before. This wasn't the decision her father had faced. She wasn't choosing between her children. She was choosing between her own happiness and that of her children. In those circumstances, there was only one option.

27

The following morning, Rebecca crept downstairs and followed the earthy scent to her kitchen. She had to admit that the real tree was beautiful. Its festive freshness reminded her to take a deep breath before her boys came thundering down the stairs ravenous for their breakfast. She tucked her hand behind the tree and flicked the switch to turn on the twinkling gold lights. She had drawn the line at the multi-coloured lights Jeremy had wanted and had compromised by buying two sets of warm gold lights instead of the frosted white lights she was usually drawn to.

The Christmas tree lights cast a welcome glow in the gloomy family room. It was still dark outside and the central heating hadn't yet been on long enough to warm the room as much as Rebecca would have liked. She crossed the kitchen to the programmer beside the back door and reset the heating to come on an hour earlier in the mornings.

Rebecca switched on the coffee machine and heard the satisfying click as the machine came to life, soon followed by the sound of the steaming, dark liquid that she craved pouring into her mug. Megan had tried and failed to get

Rebecca to switch from a super-strong coffee in the morning to green tea, but the caffeine in the tea was nowhere near enough for Rebecca to feel awake and ready to get started on her to-do list.

The coffee was almost too hot to drink, but she gulped it down, anyway. Lots of unsolicited parenting advice and horror stories had been thrown her way while she'd been pregnant. She'd been warned about sleepless nights, dirty nappies at the worst possible time, toddler tantrums, and the importance of stashing a change of clothes for babies and mum in her changing bag. She didn't, however, remember anyone preparing her for the years of lukewarm coffee she would drink. It was like the boys had a built-in radar that sounded a claxon every time she picked up a hot drink. Lost toys, sibling arguments, sore knees, and a hundred other non-emergencies suddenly needed urgent attention before Rebecca could take her first sip. The days where she could drink at least half of her coffee while it was still hot were good days.

There was still silence upstairs. Rebecca tipped her head back and drained her coffee with a last gulp, thanking Jeremy for tiring the boys out so much the day before. She unlocked her front door, headed upstairs, and yanked on the handle of the hatch to her attic. She pulled down the Ramsay ladder, positioning the feet onto the carpet and stomping on the first step to make sure it was stable. Climbing up the stairs, Rebecca spotted the handle on the box that held her ready-to-go Christmas tree. She hated going up into the roof space and kept her Christmas tree teetering on the edge so she didn't even have to step off the ladder. It maybe wasn't Jeremy's style of tree, but it was low maintenance and would look perfect in her formal living room. Two trees seemed excessive, but it also seemed sad and wasteful to have a tree in the attic and not put it up.

Rebecca wriggled one end of the box into the gap above her head. She leaned her body close to the ladder to keep her balance and manoeuvred the box through the hatch and down by her side. She gripped the box by the handle in its centre and descended the stairs slowly, taking care not to scrape the paintwork on the walls of her hall.

As soon as Rebecca put a foot down on the carpet, she realised her mistake. She'd missed a step. She hadn't been on the last step at all. One foot thudded onto the floor and the other, still two rungs up on the ladder, twisted as she stumbled backwards and fought to keep herself upright. The long narrow box bashed to the floor, sending twelve months of dust into the air. Rebecca cracked her elbow off the wall and yelped at the sting in her ankle as she straightened up.

'Great,' she mumbled. She raised her ankle off the floor and rubbed her hand around her hot skin, already feeling the swelling that was on the way.

'Mummy,' a sleepy voice called from the other end of the hallway. Liam, carrying his favourite stuffed robot, appeared in the doorframe of the bedroom he shared with Oliver. 'I heard a noise.'

'Yes, sorry about that, darling. Mummy just dropped a box. Can you wake your brother up, please?'

Liam retreated inside the dark bedroom and Rebecca suspected he would climb straight back into bed and she would have to wake them both up once she'd vacuumed up the layer of dust now sprinkled on her jasmine-white carpet.

With the attic hatch firmly closed, the mess cleared away, and the boys busy changing into their school uniforms, Rebecca hobbled downstairs, dragging the Christmas tree box behind her.

'Hey.' Jeremy popped his head around the wall at the foot of the stairs. 'It's quiet in here.' He stepped up, grabbed the box, and carried it down the last few stairs and into the family room at the back of the house. Rebecca hobbled behind.

'The boys are just getting up. They shouldn't be long.'

'Are you limping?' Jeremy took her arm and helped her over to the sofa.

'It's nothing. I tripped getting that box out of the attic and my ankle hurts a little. It'll be fine.'

Jeremy grabbed a cushion from the sofa, clasped his hands around her lower leg, and raised it gently onto the cushion.

Just having her weight off her leg made a difference. 'That already feels better, thanks. What's that box cluttering up my hallway?'

'It's a box of Christmas decorations for the house.' Jeremy fetched the box and unloaded festive cushions, ornaments, and boxes of what looked to be icicle lights onto the chair. Everything was garish and far too big to be hung on a tree.

'I usually keep my Christmas decorations restricted to the tree. I don't like to allow them to bleed into the rest of the house. This is a bit . . .'

'Different,' Jeremy added.

'You shouldn't have spent your money on this.'

'I didn't. I got it all from your dad's attic when I was borrowing his power-drill battery charger. Mine died. He's accumulated so much over the years, I figured he wouldn't mind losing a box of it. Besides, I saw your neighbour at Mystic's. I need to put up some outdoor lighting to stop him from trying to install that inflatable reindeer on your lawn.'

Icicle lights were preferable to an inflatable Rudolph.

Jeremy abandoned the decorations, strode towards the freezer, and pulled out a bag of peas and a bag of sweetcorn. 'Are you remembering the camping cabins come today so I can't pick the boys up from school?'

'Yes. They're going to afterschool club for a couple of hours.'

Jeremy snatched the tea towel off the counter and dumped the bags of frozen vegetables inside.

'I don't need that,' said Rebecca.

'You do. Your ankle is already swollen. Why didn't you just wait for me to get here?' He flicked his head towards the box on the floor. 'We had a deal. I was supposed to take that monstrosity out of the attic for you.'

'Will you stop calling it a monstrosity. That's not very festive.'

Jeremy smirked. 'Neither is that tree.' He placed the makeshift icepack on the top of her ankle and tucked it around the sides, manoeuvring the peas down the sides of her ankle. 'I've got time to take the boys to school. You need to stay here.'

'You can take the boys to school if you like, but it's really fine. I need to get into the office, anyway.'

'Work from home.'

'I enjoy being in the office.' When the office was open during the day, Rebecca preferred to be there. It wasn't just that she wanted to be a visible boss, she also appreciated the change of scenery. She worked enough at home in the evenings and on the weekends.

'I know you like being in the office, but sometimes you shouldn't be.'

'I'm in town all day, so I can sit at my desk and rest my ankle if that makes you feel any better.'

'Will you take the peas?'

'They'll melt. It's a waste.'

'Exactly my point. Stay here, and when the peas start to thaw, you can switch them out for frozen cherries or blueberries. I even saw bags of chopped onions and peppers in there.'

Rebecca shrugged. 'Don't judge. I like shortcuts when I cook.'

'Hey, I'm not judging. I've spent weeks at a time eating what I can only describe as chemically enhanced baby food in foil sachets.' Jeremy patted the peas tighter around her ankle and took off his coat. 'I'll get you a coffee.'

'Daddy!' the boys yelled as they bounded into the room. They had changed and Liam had somehow soaked his hair and his red school jumper and now looked as though he'd been caught in the rain without his coat on.

'Why are you wet?' Jeremy asked. 'Arms up.' Liam held his arms straight up in the air. Jeremy tugged the boy's jumper off and hung it on the radiator to dry off.

'I combed my hair and I couldn't get a bumpy bit to go away, so I wet it,' said Liam.

'Mummy, what's that?' asked Oliver, pointing towards her raised leg and the tea towel.

'I twisted my ankle a little bit, so Daddy has put some ice on it to make it better.'

'Is it ice or peas?' asked Liam. He turned to his father. 'When I hurt my shoulder playing football, Mummy made my lie on the floor with peas on my sore bit.'

'It's peas,' said Jeremy. 'Cold is very good for helping sore bits to get better. Who's ready for breakfast?'

The boys threw both arms in the air and climbed up onto the stools at the breakfast bar.

'Daddy, can you make us porridge?' asked Liam. 'It'll warm Mummy up. When I had peas on my back, I was so cold. Oliver got me a blanket to heat me up.'

'That was kind of your brother. Well done, buddy.'

Oliver turned his head towards Rebecca. Her son's eyes sparkled at the praise doled out by his dad. Rebecca smiled back and watched Jeremy fetch the oats from the cupboard. He pulled a pan from the cupboard next to the cooker and fished a wooden spoon out of her ceramic utensils holder. He navigated his way around her kitchen with ease, such was his familiarity with her home. Rebecca picked up the coffee Jeremy had placed near her peas, grabbed a stack of papers from her bag, and sank down on the sofa in front of her laptop with a sigh.

28

Jeremy donned a heavy parka coat and a woollen hat and drove up to the farm. Winter had settled in. The trees were stripped bare, the grass had stopped growing, and the gates to his land glistened with ice that he expected would stay there for most of the morning. He left the gates open behind him and parked his car as close to the farmhouse as he could get to leave plenty of space for the lorries. By the end of the week, there would be nothing stopping him from launching his business and opening his farm for paying customers.

He exited his vehicle to the sound of clanging metal reverberating around the site. He set out towards the noise, but didn't get far before he spotted the problem. The gate to the sheep enclosure was swinging in the breeze and clanging against the metal post with each gust of wind powerful enough to slam it shut. The two sheep were just a few feet from the gate as he approached the enclosure.

'Stay where you are,' he called out. The headstrong sheep – Rump, of course – bolted towards the unlatched gate and, using that hard-as-nails head of hers, shoved the metal gate open all the way and ran through. Jeremy sighed as he reached the gate. 'What is wrong with her? It's like she wants to go back to Mitch's farm.' The other sheep tilted her head like a dog, then averted her gaze to the open gate. She took a step forwards and Jeremy spread his arms and legs to block her path. 'Can you please just stay here? One escapee is enough for today.'

Unnerved, the sheep retreated to the safety of the shelter. Jeremy secured the gate and then took off in pursuit of Rump.

He found his escaped sheep attempting to chomp on the icy turf in the field that would shortly become home to his camping cabins. Rump glanced up at him with a *What's your problem?* kind of expression, then returned to her grazing. 'That's not for eating,' said Jeremy. 'Come back to your own field and I'll give you some extra hay.'

Perhaps unsurprisingly, the sheep completely ignored him and carried on eating. Jeremy huffed out a breath. 'Fine. Have it your way.' He stomped towards the sheep. Rump pulled back, leaning onto her hind legs as though getting ready to pounce on Jeremy. 'Don't you dare!'

Jeremy stepped to the side and clapped his hands. 'Come on. Get moving.' All six feet two inches of Jeremy and the noise he made had at least made the sheep reconsider head-butting him. She was not, however, heading back towards her field as he had hoped. Instead, she had turned away from him and was trotting towards the farmhouse.

Jeremy jogged alongside her, trying to get in front and force her to turn in the opposite direction. Each time he moved in front of her she bucked towards him, forcing him to shift course out of the reach of her hard head. Colliding with that head at speed was an experience he was keen to avoid. 'You've sealed your fate, missy. I can't be chasing you around the farm when I've got guests onsite.'

The sheep finally slowed just before she reached the stony driveway. Jeremy's phone rang in his back pocket. 'Saved by the bell,' he snarled towards Rump. 'Bex, hi,' he said.

'Did I catch you at a bad time?'

'Kind of. I'm currently chasing a sheep around the fields trying to get her back into her enclosure.'

Rebecca snorted. 'Don't tell me the Marine is being outsmarted by a farmyard animal.'

'I'm glad my misery is amusing you.' He looked at the sheep now attempting to eat another patch of his grass. 'It's like she's oblivious to my presence, or, more likely, has a complete disregard for my presence and my position as *land owner*.' He emphasised the words and glared towards the unflinching animal.

'She's probably picking up on your grumpy vibes. Try talking to her the way the boys do. They always seem really calm around the kids.'

'Thanks for your unhelpful advice,' Jeremy huffed. 'Anyway, how's the ankle? Were you just checking in or can I do something for you?'

'You mean something other than providing me with some light-hearted comedy on a Monday morning? My ankle is much better. I'm going to head into the office. I'll take it easy, I promise.'

Jeremy checked the time on his phone. It wasn't even ten in the morning. 'You did well, Bex. You sat still for over a hundred minutes.'

'Hilarious. I'm just letting you know in case you were looking for me later. And while I remember, have you set a date for meeting your mum's boyfriend yet?'

Jeremy shook his head. 'Can we not call him that?'

'What else should we call him?'

'Lennox will do.'

'OK. Have you set a date for meeting Lennox yet? You told Ivy you would do it after Dad's birthday bash.'

'I'll add it to the list.'

'Just make sure it's near the top. You should invite him to your launch party, and it would be better for everyone if you'd at least met each other properly before then.'

'I'll sort something out.'

Rebecca wished him luck with his sheep-wrangling efforts, and he hung up. Jeremy kept a safe distance from the grumpy sheep but still within her eyeline. He dropped onto the crunchy grass, grateful for the barrier provided by his waterproof coat. 'Look, Rump. I know we haven't got off to the best start.' The sheep was on edge and Jeremy placed his hands on the ground beside him, ready to spring up and out of her way if she charged towards him. She relaxed again. 'Maybe Oliver is right and you don't like your name. Anyway, we can deal with that later. Will you please go back to your field? I can't leave you here. Two big trucks are going to be driving into this field any minute.'

The sheep turned her head and stared at him.

Jeremy rested his forehead on his knees and closed his eyes. Sheep were exhausting. 'If you go back to your field, I'll let you stay.' He covered his head with his hands in case Rump attacked him while his defences were down. He sucked in what he hoped would be a calming breath and reopened his eyes. Rump was gone. He scanned the driveway and, seeing no sign, turned to see her strutting back towards her enclosure. If he didn't know better, he would have said she had a victory canter going on.

After triple-checking that the gate to the sheep enclosure was secure, Jeremy arrived back up at the house just in time to see Serena in her vehicle, leading the lorries from Cosy Cabins up his driveway. The wooden structures that were to become his camping cabins were in pieces on their sides, waiting for someone who knew what they were doing to unload them and fit them together. Serena parked her Ford Ranger alongside Jeremy's Land Rover while he signalled to the first lorry driver where to stop. He stood back until both lorry drivers had stopped and turned off their ignitions.

Serena appeared alongside him wearing a hi-vis coat and a white hard hat. 'Right. The lorries will need to drive across this first field to get close enough to the site to unload. You OK with that, Jeremy?'

Straight to business. He liked that. 'Yeah, no problem.' The freezing temperatures had created a hard frost, which might at least save his grass from too much damage.

Jeremy let Serena take charge, and he whipped out his phone to take some photos. The long arm of the crane rose into the air, and Serena and one of the installations crew attached thick yellow straps to the edges of the load. Seconds later and the first sections of his camping cabins were being hoisted into the air and a shiver of excitement rippled through his body.

By midday, Jeremy was at a loose end. The install crew were busy working away with a speed and precision that the military would have been proud of, and there wasn't much he could do up at the house because the electrician had the power off to finish the last of the rewiring job. Figuring the greatest contribution he could make was getting the coffees in, he jumped in his car and headed into town.

He reached Mystic's just as Cat Radcliffe had packed up to leave. 'Hey, Jeremy. How's it going? It's the big install day, right?'

'It is. And you'll be pleased to know I've taken some photos for you, so you'll have in-progress shots and the before ones that Nick took.'

Jeremy handed Cat his phone, and she flicked through the photos he'd taken that morning. She lingered over a shot of the crane high in the air with the front panel of a cabin dangling from it. He'd captured a glimpse of the town through the spaces for the windows and door. 'This one is exceptional.'

Jeremy smiled and nodded. 'I had a feeling you'd like that one.'

'I do. Very much. Can I send it to myself? I'll get Nick to edit it alongside the other shots he's taken.'

'Go ahead.'

Cat fiddled with his phone for a few seconds before handing it back to him. 'Then we'll just need photos from your launch party and we'll have all of the images we need to make your new website look stunning.'

'That reminds me, you don't have a phone number for Lennox, do you?'

'Lennox? The guy your mum is seeing?'

'That's the one.'

'I don't, sorry. Can't you just ask your mum?'

'I could, but I don't want her to know I'm calling him.'

Cat raised her eyebrows and tilted her chin down. 'Hmm. You're not going to cause trouble, are you?'

Jeremy laughed and shook his head. 'No. I'm going to bond with him, or whatever.'

Cat straightened up. 'Well, glad to hear it. I don't have his number, but Josef will have it. I'm heading down to the gallery, so I can stop off at Josef's food stall with you if you like.'

'Yes, please.'

Jeremy and Cat lingered by the side of Josef's food stall. The red wooden frame of the stall sparkled with a sheen of ice, and Jeremy hoped that the man had a heater behind the counter. The scent of Josef's freshly baked pastries mingled with the salty sea air. When he'd finished serving a group of tourists, he beckoned them forward.

'Are you back for another one of my cherry twists already?' Josef asked.

'Don't tempt me,' said Cat. 'Have you met Jeremy? He's Oliver and Liam's dad.'

'Good to meet you, Jeremy. Those boys look like you. Although from what I can see, they have their mother's determined personality. Especially one of them. You'll have to forgive me. I get them muddled up.'

'Happens to me sometimes, too. Then they open their mouths and I know exactly which one is which. Liam is probably the one you're thinking of.'

'Liam. That'll be him. He's a little firecracker. You bought Archie's land, didn't you?' Jeremy nodded. He'd forgotten that everyone knew everything in Thistle Bay. 'He told me all about your campsite plans in the pub last week. It sounds just marvellous. When I was a boy, I once went pony trekking across your fields. Archie's father owned the land then, I'm told.'

Jeremy furrowed his brow, thrown by Josef's German

accent. 'You lived here when you were a boy? I'm sorry, I thought you were a newcomer.'

'A bit of both. I spent the first half of my childhood here, then the rest of my life in Germany. Until, like yourself, one of life's events brought me back.' Josef produced a cloth and wiped down his already spotless counter. 'It wasn't a birth, though; it was that other inevitable event.'

'I'm so sorry to hear that.'

Cat stretched across Josef's counter and placed her hand on his shoulder. Josef patted her hand and gave her a warm smile.

'You should come up to the farm and have a look around sometime,' said Jeremy to steer the conversation back to less intense territory.

'I'll do that. Just don't expect me to climb on the back of a pony.'

Jeremy laughed. 'You're fine there. There are no ponies anymore. Just a couple of sheep. But you'll have heard all about them.'

'I have indeed. Have you decided what to do with them yet?'

Jeremy shrugged. 'Let's just say they've grown on me somewhat, but honestly, I'm not even sure I'm allowed to keep animals on the land.'

'That's easy enough to figure out,' said Josef. 'There's a woman at the town hall council offices called Patsy. She knows everything about permissions and permits.' He gestured around his stall. 'She helped to get all of this set up for me. If you decide to look into it, stop by here first and I'll give you some pastries to take to her. Just tell her I sent you and she'll help you out.'

Cat grinned, bounced up and down, and rubbed her hands together like a kid on Christmas morning deciding which present to open first. 'Those sheep are famous. If Permits Patsy is a local, she'll have no hesitation in helping you to keep those sheep right where they are.'

'Sounds like I'm going to need a box of pastries.'

'Patsy liked my cinnamon swirls. I'll make them tomorrow if you can hold off seeing her for a day.'

'Sounds perfect. Can you box me up half a dozen of your cherry twists while I'm here, Josef? I've got a crew of hard-working lads on my farm who could use a break.' Josef grabbed a set of tongs and packed pastries into a box. 'I'll also take two of your iced buns. Can you put them in a separate bag, though?'

'Of course.'

'Oh, I almost forgot why we're here,' said Cat. 'Do you have Lennox's phone number, and if so, can we please have it?'

Josef passed Cat his phone. 'It's in there.'

Cat typed in the passcode to unlock Josef's phone and scrolled through his contacts. Within seconds Cat's phone pinged. She placed Josef's phone on the counter and took out her own. 'I'll forward you the number.'

'Thanks,' said Jeremy.

Josef handed over a white cardboard box, the warmth from the sweet treats inside seeping through the cardboard and onto Jeremy's palm. 'And here's your iced raspberry swirls.'

Jeremy took the paper bag and balanced it on top of the box. 'Thank you, Josef. While I remember, I'm having a party up at the farm on the Sunday before Christmas. It's just a few friends and family members to help me celebrate my new campsite being ready for business. I'd love it if you could join us.'

Josef's face lit up, his gaze flitting between Jeremy and Cat. 'I'll be there. Thank you.'

Jeremy walked Cat to Thistle Bay Art Gallery. Cat glanced behind them. 'That was nice of you to invite Josef.'

'You knew the password for his phone. I figured that made him more than just the guy who serves you pretzels.'

Cat smiled and nodded.

'Now, wish me luck with Permits Patsy tomorrow.'

Cat held up her hand and crossed her fingers. 'Let the cinnamon swirls do the talking.'

29

Rebecca stretched across her desk to straighten the folders containing her work tasks for the day. It had been two hours since she'd first lined them up along the edge of the table. Her landline rang, distracting her from a fizzle of frustration at how little she'd accomplished in that time. She glanced at the display. It was the internal shop number. She hit the speakerphone button. 'Morning.'

'Oh good,' said Elizabeth. 'Just checking you were in your office. Jeremy is here to see you. I'll send him back.'

'Great, thanks,' said Rebecca.

Jeremy nudged her office door open with his foot and strolled in carrying two takeaway coffees from Mystic's and a small white paper bag. 'Caffeine?'

She grinned. 'Would love some, thanks. How's it going?' She took a cup and downed a welcome gulp.

Jeremy sat on one of the chairs on the other side of her desk. 'Good. I'm on my way back up to the farm, but wanted to check a few dates and times with you. I want to take the boys to an early dinner at Mum's on Friday night. Does that work for you? You're invited, too, but I thought you might appreciate a few hours to yourself.'

Rebecca shook her head. 'They've got a party on Friday.'

'And football on Thursday.' Jeremy took a cake from the paper bag, bit into it, and slid the bag across the desk to Rebecca. She peered inside and caught a whiff of sweet pastry and raspberry jam. Digging in, she plucked the iced bun from the bag, her fingers already sticky from the white sugar glazing.

'How about Wednesday night, then?' he asked.

She nodded, took a bite of her cake, and swallowed. 'This is amazing,' she said, gesturing to the bun. 'Wednesday works. Can it be an early dinner, though? They've got school in the morning.'

'Of course. Plus, I know they're ravenous if they don't eat by six. I thought I'd pick them up from school, then drop them home again by seven thirty at the latest.'

'Sounds good.'

'I'm inviting Lennox, too,' he said, shoving the last quarter of his cake into his mouth.

'Oh no,' said Rebecca, shaking her head. Jeremy smirked, and she waited until he'd finished chewing. 'You're not using your children as a buffer so you don't have to talk things out with your mum and her boyfriend,' she added.

'That thought crossed my mind, but I knew you wouldn't go for it. I've texted Lennox and invited myself to a game of golf with him at lunchtime tomorrow. I figured if there had to be this formal introduction, I'd rather do it without Mum being all jittery in the corner.'

'That's a good idea,' she said. 'Just one problem – you can't play golf.'

'Hey, I've hit a few balls in my time.'

'Footballs, rugby balls, and baseballs,' she reminded him. 'It's not quite the same thing.'

'Anyway, do you want to come?'

'To the golf?'

'No. To dinner?'

Rebecca took another drink of her coffee and glanced down at her desk. 'Probably not. You're right, I could do with an extra few hours.'

Jeremy leaned across her desk and stretched his arm across the folders. 'Try not to work for the entire time the boys are away.'

She clasped a hand around his forearm. He enclosed her hand in his and she stiffened.

He moved his hand away. 'Now, what do you think about me keeping the sheep?'

Rebecca released her grip on Jeremy and wrapped her arms around herself, embarrassed by the momentary crack in her façade. 'Do you want to keep the sheep?'

'The thought of it doesn't horrify me as much as it did. And the boys will be crushed if we don't keep them. I just can't see how to do it.'

He thrust a tube of paper towards her, and Rebecca unrolled a set of plans for the land. Jeremy had already pencilled in his new family-friendly activities. He wasn't short of land. He just had to figure out how to better use it now that his plans had evolved. 'The sheep have to stay where they are because their barn is there and you wouldn't want to relocate it.'

'Technically, they don't need a barn, they just need shelter of some sort, so I could move them if I had to.'

'Still, I think their position is fine. They're as far away from the house as is physically possible. That seems like a suitable location to me.'

Jeremy laughed. 'Agreed.'

'The camping cabins have to stay where they are because they're being installed as we speak.'

'And the utilities are there, so we can't move them even if we wanted to.'

She pointed to a picture along the far edge of the plans. 'What's that?'

'It's the outdoor tap. It's for cleaning muddy boots in the winter, and in the summer, I figured we could attach a sprinkler system to it for the kids to play with.'

Rebecca opened the top drawer of her desk and grabbed a pencil. 'OK. Move the playpark. Put it in the field next to the sheep, and make that bottom field a dog-free zone. No one wants other people's dogs running around the park their kids are playing in, anyway.' She thought for a moment and tried to visualise what that would look like. 'You'd have to move the archery, and the bike shed you've ordered, but that's portable, right?'

'It is. I'd have to run a fence around the entire bottom perimeter to separate the running route from the park and sheep. I'm thinking people like to run with their dogs.'

Rebecca nodded and drew dotted lines on Jeremy's plans to rejig the activity boundaries he'd drawn on. 'You'll need extra fencing whatever you do. It's easier to keep it dog free if you fence it off completely.'

Jeremy sighed. 'Who knows how much that'll cost me? All to accommodate these blasted sheep.' Rebecca gave him a look. 'Fine. The little blighters are growing on me. I had no idea sheep had such distinct personalities. They remind me of the boys.'

'Did you just compare our children to a couple of sheep?'

'Spend a day with those sheep and you'll see what I

mean. They look almost identical to each other, but their personalities are wildly different.'

'If you're set on keeping them, can you come up with better names for them than Chop and Rump? I really don't want to explain that to the kids.'

'I was thinking I'd let the boys name them.'

Rebecca shook her head. 'You'll end up with names that are equally ridiculous.'

'I'll retain the right to veto.'

'When have you ever been able to say no to those doe eyes?'

Jeremy was a tough-guy Marine to some people, but to his children, he was the pushover parent. He liked to think it was because he was gone for such long periods of time that he wanted to give his children everything he could during the brief spells of time he spent with them. Rebecca knew better. Their children had already learned how to manipulate their father. They were masters of the innocent yet hopeful eyes, the slight downturn of the lips, and, her personal favourite, slipping their small hands into Jeremy's sizable palms as if reminding him of their irresistible cuteness.

'I actually quite like the names they came up with at your dad's party. Olive and Marmalade. Maybe we should just go with those names and tell the boys it's a done deal so they don't change their minds.'

'Better than Chop and Rump.'

Jeremy rolled the plans back up. 'Thanks, Bex. That really helped.'

'Did it? Because I'm fairly sure you could have figured all of that out yourself. What's going on?'

He grinned. 'Maybe I just wanted to see you. Catch you later. I need to stop off at Mystic's again to pick up a box of pastries I left there and a takeaway coffee order. Serena and the guys will be waiting for me.'

He closed her office door on his way out. Rebecca dropped the pencil back into her drawer and slammed it shut. She hated the way he just threw her name in there. Serena. She had no right to be annoyed. Jeremy had offered himself to her completely, but she had said no and orchestrated her own unhappiness.

Besides, it wasn't that she could see Jeremy with Serena, it was that she'd envisioned Jeremy with someone who wasn't her and she hadn't liked it. But she was doing the right thing.

After work, Rebecca pulled out of the junction and onto Main Street. The glow from the streetlight bounced off a head of long blonde hair. Even from behind, Rebecca recognised the curves of Serena's body, this time wrapped in a knee-length grey jacket and high-heeled boots that still left her a full head shorter than her companion. Jeremy. Serena's hand swung up from her side and found Jeremy's shoulder. A feeling of dread washed over Rebecca. She couldn't watch. She indicated and turned into a side street, taking the long route to afterschool club.

A rare silence hung in the back of her car as she drove the boys home. The automatic light on her house came on just as she swung her car into the driveway.

When everyone was out of the car, she unlocked the front door and pushed it open, her hand easily finding the light switch inside. The hallway went from dark to less dark and she cursed herself for forgetting to change the light bulb again. The current bulb was one of those annoying ones that took forever to brighten up. It hadn't been a problem in the autumn, but it was well and truly winter now, which meant she and the boys came home to darkness every weekday.

'Shoes off,' she instructed. Liam had already slipped off his school shoes and tossed them in the wicker basket she'd placed under the glass-topped console table in the hallway. 'Are you managing, Ol?'

Oliver shook his head. 'I have a knot in my laces.' Rebecca knelt down and untied Oliver's left shoe while he wiggled his foot out of the other one. 'Is Daddy coming to dinner?'

'Not tonight, darling.'

The boys ate leftovers for dinner and were showered and in bed within an hour of them arriving home. They were so shattered they didn't even notice Rebecca corralling them into bed a half hour earlier than usual.

She popped the cork on a bottle of Cabernet Sauvignon, prepared a platter of cheese and biscuits, and washed a handful of grapes.

A reminder flashed on her phone. She swiped to clear it away and was left with her screensaver. Her stomach churned as she pored over the image of her and Jeremy at the beach with the boys. Jeremy's outstretched arm filled the edge of the screen as he held out his phone to snap the photo.

She shivered. The house was cold, the silence felt isolating, and her plate of food became suddenly unappetising.

Love isn't practical. With running a company and raising two young children, she needed practical. Rebecca poured a glass of wine, took several large slurps, and collapsed in on herself on the sofa in her snug. She didn't want Jeremy to be with someone else, but if she didn't open herself up to being with him, that was exactly what would happen. He would meet someone and fall in love with them, if he hadn't already. The image of Jeremy and Serena walking up Main Street seemed to be seared into her mind.

Maybe Serena had come to Thistle Bay to oversee the installation of the camping cabins and she wouldn't ever leave. Rebecca would have to watch Serena beginning her exciting new life with the father of her children. The boys would have a stepmother, and every time Rebecca dropped them off at their dad's, the life she could have had would greet her with her artificially white teeth and silky blonde hair.

Rebecca leaned forward and topped up her wine, cursing when the deep-red liquid sloshed over the rim of the glass. She was self-aware enough to know that she was freaking out, but her freak-out was being caused by an entirely plausible situation. Serena was beautiful and Jeremy was everything someone could want in a partner.

She got up, snatched her phone and a square of kitchen roll from the worktop and dialled Elizabeth's number.

'Hi, Rebecca. Everything OK?'

Rebecca was mildly miffed that her sister's first thought was that she had a problem. She could have just been calling to say hi or to share good news. 'Yes, it's fine. I just . . . erm. . . just wondered if you're around.' She folded the kitchen roll over and dabbed at her spilled drink.

'I'm having a glass of wine at Seashell Cottage with Cat. Do you want to come along? . . . Rebecca? You still there?'

'I can't. The boys are upstairs asleep.'

'We'll come to you.'

Rebecca opened her mouth to protest, but all that came out was, 'OK.'

Rebecca's footsteps echoed off the walls of the hallway as

she paced back and forth, counting the steps, until she heard the soft murmur of voices outside. She opened the door to find Elizabeth and Cat squeezing themselves past her car. 'What's wrong?' asked Elizabeth.

'Nothing.' Rebecca led Elizabeth and Cat through to her kitchen. Rebecca slumped onto the sofa, Cat perched on the grey-velvet cube stool, and Elizabeth headed straight for the cupboard that held the glasses.

'Out with it,' said Elizabeth as she handed one glass to Cat and placed the other beside Rebecca's. She sat on the sofa and patted the space next to her for Cat.

Cat moved to the sofa, and Rebecca held the wine bottle out to fill her glass. Her hand trembled and Elizabeth took the bottle from her to finish the task.

'It's Jeremy, isn't it?' Elizabeth said.

'Actually, it's Cabernet Sauvignon.'

'Stop changing the subject.'

'It's not Jeremy.'

'Well, it can't be business, or you would have called Ryan. And it can't be Dad or the boys because you'd be completely clear-headed about that. That only leaves Jeremy.'

'God, my life sounds so empty.'

'There's one thing your life isn't, and that's empty.'

'Everything is just so . . .' Rebecca was as shocked as her sisters when a tear rolled down her cheek. 'I don't even know where to start.'

Cat leaned forward and pressed a hand to Rebecca's knee. 'We're on your side.'

'I'm not,' said Elizabeth. 'I'm Team Jeremy all the way.'

'You can't be Team Jeremy,' Cat said. 'You're her sister.'

'We're not talking about some guy who's screwed her over here. If we were, of course I'd be Team Rebecca. This is

Jeremy. He's been in love with her since high school. They locked themselves away like lovesick teenagers every time he was on leave, and one of those lock-ins led to the birth of our two fabulously spirited nephews. And as if that weren't enough, our big sister here is completely and utterly in love with Jeremy, too.'

In fact, it wasn't one of their many lock-ins that had led to her pregnancy. It had been a last-minute get-together in London, but that was beside the point.

Rebecca felt Cat's gaze on her.

'Is that true?' Cat asked. 'Are you in love with Jeremy?'

Rebecca hesitated, her heart pounding in her ears. If she said it out loud, she couldn't ever take it back. 'I am.'

'Well, hell, I'm switching to Team Jeremy.' Cat looped her arm through Elizabeth's.

Cat's willingness to share her thoughts on Rebecca's relationship gave Rebecca a glimmer of hope that at least one precarious relationship in her life was seeing progress.

'I've left it too late. Jeremy now wants to be on Team Serena.'

Elizabeth shook her head. 'No way. Why do you think that?'

'I saw them together and they looked pretty cosy. They were heading down Main Street when I went to pick up the boys. They were probably heading to Gloria's. And before you say it, Serena is not staying there. I checked.'

'They were probably heading to Mystic's for some food,' said Elizabeth.

'How is that better?'

'Because it's innocent. You're worrying over nothing.' That was why Rebecca had asked Elizabeth to come over. She needed some rational thinking, and despite her sister's rosy-romanced view of the world, her thoughts were clearly more rational than Rebecca's right now. 'The man came back here to build the family he never had but always wanted. He's spent the last five years planning for this, and he's not about to let a pretty blonde distract him from that.'

Rebecca felt Elizabeth's stare. 'If something was meant to happen between us, wouldn't it have happened by now?'

Cat picked up a photograph of Oliver and Liam as toddlers from the coffee table. 'I thought something had already happened between you two. And it sounds to me like it happened a lot.'

Elizabeth glanced at the photograph and shook her head. 'The only reason Jeremy isn't here right now is because you told him you wanted to take things slowly.'

Rebecca took another gulp of her wine and looked down into her glass. 'I actually told him I didn't have space in my life for a relationship, and us getting together would be too confusing for Oliver and Liam, and devastating for them if it didn't work. I told him it would never happen between us.'

'Well, that was stupid,' said Cat.

'And stubborn,' Elizabeth added, releasing an exasperated sigh.

Rebecca had glimpsed a life without Jeremy and it wasn't as comfortable a place as she had expected it to be. 'How do I fix it?'

'You go to the mattresses,' said Elizabeth.

Rebecca and Cat both wrinkled their foreheads. 'From *The Godfather*?' Cat asked.

'No. From *You've Got Mail*,' said Elizabeth.

Rebecca shook her head and looked between the two of them. 'What does that even mean?'

'It means you fight for him,' said Cat.

Elizabeth nodded her agreement. 'And you start by being honest with him.'

'I've never lied to him. Not proper lying anyway.'

'But have you been open with him? Have you told him how you truly feel about him?' Cat asked.

'Exactly.' Elizabeth thumped her wine glass on the table triumphantly.

Rebecca suspected the glass of wine her sister had been having with Cat when she called wasn't the first one she'd had that evening. 'I think you've had enough for a Monday night?'

'Hey, I work Saturdays, so this is technically my weekend. What's your excuse?'

'I'm having an emotional crisis.'

'Fair enough.' Elizabeth reached forward and topped up Rebecca's glass.

Rebecca tipped her head back and stared up at the ceiling. She hadn't told Jeremy how she really felt about him. Not even when he'd declared his love for her. All it would have taken was for her to say, *I love you, too*. But saying it would only have made things more difficult for them. She didn't want to give up all hope of them ever being together, but nothing had changed, meaning their chances of making a go of it hadn't changed either.

For them to be together, change was needed, and it had to come from her.

30

Jeremy's conversation with Permits Patsy hadn't been as straightforward as he had hoped. She had rather sternly informed him it was a bit late in the day for rethinking his entire business model. His attempts to argue that it was only a modest deviation from his original plan and that he'd only just found out about the sheep had been swiftly disregarded. The cinnamon swirls had won her round in the end and Jeremy was now sitting in his car with a pile of forms to complete, most of which he was certain weren't necessary and were just Patsy's way of testing his resolve to keep the animals. And because his morning hadn't been awkward enough, here he was sitting in the clubhouse car park waiting for Lennox to arrive so Jeremy could embarrass himself by demonstrating his complete lack of skill on the golf course.

A sporty metallic-blue Audi pulled into the car park. Lennox gave Jeremy a wave, then reversed into the space alongside Jeremy's mud-splashed Land Rover. Jeremy blew out a breath and climbed out of his car.

Lennox was already at the back of the Audi wrestling a

golf club bag free from the boot. 'It's a good day for a game. I was glad to get your text,' said Lennox.

Jeremy followed Lennox's gaze up to the cloudless sky. 'I'm going to level with you, Lennox. I've never played a round of golf.'

'Ah. I wondered. I'd asked Ivy before you came home if you play and she said she didn't think so.'

Jeremy bristled at the mention of his mother's name on Lennox's lips and ran a hand across the back of his head. 'Shall we get this over with?'

Lennox unfolded a metal contraption on wheels, hooked his golf bag onto it, and strode towards the clubhouse. 'Let's warm up on the driving range first.'

They signed in and collected two buckets of golf balls. Lennox selected two bays at the far end of the range. Jeremy looked out at the manicured lawn, still bright green despite the frosty weather. It was littered with golf balls that had been launched far up the range, with only a handful of stragglers seemingly accidentally chipped this side of the first distance marker. If his mum was serious about this man, Jeremy would have to spend some time at the range to hold his own on the course. But first, he had to find out if Lennox was serious about his mum.

'What's going on with you and my mum?' he asked, cutting right to the key question.

'Well,' said Lennox, not appearing in any way flustered by Jeremy, 'we love each other and plan to spend a lot more time together. I want her to move in with me. She's hesitating because she's not sure how you'll feel about that.'

Jeremy's mouth gaped open. He wasn't expecting that. It seemed like Lennox was also a man who got right to the point.

'How long have you been seeing each other?' Jeremy asked.

'A little over a year. When you get to our age, things move faster.'

'Have you ever been married?' Jeremy asked.

Lennox nodded. 'Once. My wife passed away far too young. Ten years ago.'

'I'm sorry to hear that. Do you have children?'

'Two girls. My eldest, Samantha, has just turned thirty and my youngest, Charlotte, is twenty-eight.'

Jeremy knew that. He'd researched, or cyber-stalked, as some people might call it, Lennox. The man didn't do social media, but his youngest daughter, Charlotte, or Lottie, as she seemed to call herself, was very active online. She posted everything from beautifully presented breakfasts to post-gym selfies and family get-togethers. His mum even featured in some photos.

It was a photo taken at a summer barbecue that confirmed to Jeremy he was looking in the right place. His mother had been sitting in the centre of the image, cheeks flushed, with a broad smile on her face. Lennox had been sitting beside her, his arm draped across her shoulders. They'd both been holding full champagne flutes, toasting something that Jeremy didn't know about. Ivy had slotted nicely into Lennox's family. It was like his mum had this entire other life that not only was he not a part of but he hadn't even known existed. All the months he spent away from home, he'd only ever thought about how much of the boys' lives he was missing. It hadn't occurred to him to wonder what else he was missing.

'Your mum wanted to wait until you were home for good before telling you about us. She didn't want you worrying about her when you were away.'

That sounded like something his mum would do. She always put everyone else before herself. Not unlike Rebecca.

'My marriage was everything you could ever hope for. Lots of love and laughter. A life spent together. When I met your mother, I was immediately smitten. But I doubted my feelings. I thought I couldn't be so lucky twice in one lifetime. Then my daughter Lottie told me that the Empire State Building gets struck by lightning twenty-five times a year and something clicked for me. I love Ivy very much. When you are my age, and with my life experience, what's important looks a little simpler, like the way her cheeks still blush when I buy her tulips. I love the excitement I see in her when we talk about travelling together. Your mother has been through a lot in her life.' Lennox looked away. 'You both have.' He turned his gaze back to Jeremy. 'I want family barbecues and birthday parties with her by my side and me by hers. I want Christmas dinner and a massive table where our two families can come together and share some festive joy. Ivy has become very important to me. I care deeply about your mother. Now that you're home, I hope you'll give me a chance to prove that to you.'

Jeremy gaped at Lennox. The man had taken every concern Jeremy had had and quashed them all with one speech.

Lennox handed Jeremy a golf club. 'Do you want to show me what you've got?'

Jeremy took the club, lined up the ball, and whacked it as hard as he could. It flew through the air and bounced a couple of times before rolling to a stop just beyond the two-hundred-yard marker.

'Not bad at all,' said Lennox. 'You sure you've never played before?'

Jeremy laughed. 'Nope. I fear that one was a fluke and the next forty-nine won't go quite as well.'

Lennox grabbed a ball from the bucket at the edge of Jeremy's bay and handed it to him. 'Only one way to find out.'

The golf balls disappeared fast as they whacked a few in between pauses for further interrogation from Jeremy, which Ivy would not have approved of, and some technique suggestions from Lennox. Jeremy found the man to be friendly and open. He handled himself with ease, and gave Jeremy no reason to doubt his sincerity. Jeremy even found himself relaxing in the man's company. Neither of them mentioned the shower incident, and they probably shared the view that it was a conversation best avoided until they were both ready to joke about it.

'Ivy is planning a dinner for us this week, I believe,' said Lennox.

'Tomorrow night. It's last minute because we were trying to schedule it around the boys' football practice.'

'The active social lives of five-year-olds.' There was no judgement in Lennox's tone. 'I told Ivy I would pick up takeaway, but she said she'd rather cook. She'll be nervous, I expect, so cooking will keep her mind from overthinking it all day.'

Jeremy laughed. It seemed Lennox had got to know his mother rather well in the year they'd been together. If she wasn't nervous-cleaning, she was nervous-cooking. The woman couldn't sit still and giving her hands something to do was how she dealt with life's challenges.

'Is your lad still a vegetarian?'

'He is,' said Jeremy. 'We've not figured out how to deal with that yet.'

'I wouldn't worry about it,' said Lennox. 'One of my

daughters has been a vegetarian since she was a teenager and she's very healthy.'

Jeremy suspected he knew which daughter that was. He hadn't seen any greasy cheeseburgers or roast dinners in Lottie's posts. It was all avocado toast, green juices, smoothies randomly decorated with purple flowers, and something called Buddha bowls, which seemed to just be a trendy name for a bowl of salad.

'He's just too young to make that kind of decision. Five-year-olds have a lot of growing left to do.'

'At least he seems to understand that being a vegetarian means eating a vegetable-based diet.'

'Have you spent much time with the boys?' Jeremy asked. Rebecca said they'd met Lennox, but he got the impression it was just in passing. Now he was wondering how much time his children had spent with their grandma's boyfriend.

'Not a lot,' said Lennox as he smacked a few balls with much-practised precision. 'Ivy didn't think it was right until she'd spoken to you about it. They're good boys, from what I've seen. Keep that lovely mother of theirs busy.'

'They do.'

Just how busy they kept Rebecca had been a constant source of guilt over the last five years. One child was hard work. Twins was even harder, and he hadn't been around for very much of it. Rebecca had told him so many times that a present dad isn't necessarily a good dad. He knew that first hand. This was his opportunity to be present. He could see his children every day. Take them to football, or drama, or music classes, or whatever else interested them as they grew up. He would take them to the park for an hour to give Rebecca a break; he'd take his turn cooking dinner and doing homework.

He'd spent over twenty years seeing the rest of the world and experiencing things only a fraction of the population would ever see, or even hear about. Simplifying life was a goal right up there with seeing his children grow up. It felt good to be home, and thanks to a couple of errant sheep and a box of worms, he was excited about launching his business. The only prickle of doubt left was Rebecca. Life was fragile and there were no guarantees. Her need for certainty and to be in control of everything wouldn't allow her to give them a chance.

He swallowed hard as the possibility that they might never be together settled in his gut.

31

Rebecca arrived at Ivy's house clutching a fragrant bouquet of dusky-pink roses that she'd picked up on the way home that evening. She knocked on the door and let herself in, feeling confident that any possible unclothed house guests would be her sons, who were still at that age where they considered running around naked to be hilarious.

Jeremy rushed to greet her before she'd even closed the front door. He grazed his lips across her cheek. 'Thanks for coming. You didn't have to.'

'I'm not here for you. After your boys' bonding session with Lennox, I figured it wasn't fair on your mum if it was four against one.'

Jeremy laughed. 'The two of you can definitely take the four of us.'

'No question.' Rebecca followed Jeremy to the kitchen, where Ivy was standing at the cooker stirring a sauce on the hob.

'Hi, love,' Ivy said. 'The boys are in the garden with Lennox.'

Rebecca peered out of the kitchen window. Liam was bouncing around in his makeshift goals between two conifers and Oliver was lining up the football to take his shot. Lennox was talking, and whatever he was saying, Liam was listening to every word, his little forehead lined with rare concentration. 'It looks like there's some very serious football practice going on out there.'

'They've been at it for an hour already,' said Jeremy. 'I've just come in because it's freezing.'

Rebecca arched her eyebrows. 'The Marine can't handle the cold?'

'I don't have to handle it anymore,' said Jeremy with a satisfied grin.

Rebecca had once asked Jeremy what it was like to go to war. He'd replied with only one word. Unimaginable. When his military career had shifted from combat zones to drug patrol, she had been relieved. Sleep had become easier and she no longer dreaded calls from unknown numbers. But the last year, once Jeremy had set a date for leaving the military for good, had almost been more stressful than the previous twenty years. The dread had returned. A fear that something would happen to ruin Jeremy's plans for the future had become deep-set. Only in that moment, standing side by side with Jeremy and watching their boys enjoying themselves, did she realise she could finally release that fear.

Now she had to decide if she was brave enough to tackle another major fear. After her meltdown the other night, she was now certain that she wanted to give herself and Jeremy a chance. Jeremy draped his arm around her shoulders and she snuggled close. His lips skimmed her hair with a kiss, and for a few seconds she imagined what it would be like to have this every day. She leaned her head closer to his for another few seconds, then prised herself away from his gentle hold. Tonight was all about Ivy.

Rebecca opened the cupboard next to the fridge and produced a glass vase. She filled it with water and grabbed scissors from a drawer. 'Has Oliver mentioned what he's planning to eat tonight?'

'I'm making tapas, so lots of veggie options, and a chilli, meatballs, and chorizo potatoes,' said Ivy.

'Sounds delicious. If that doesn't tempt him back to meat, nothing will.' Rebecca unwrapped the flowers, snipped the ends off the stems, and plunged them into the water.

'Jeremy, get Rebecca a drink,' Ivy instructed.

Rebecca arranged the bouquet in the vase and moved the flowers into the dining room, placing them beside a vase of purple tulips on the console table near the door. The warm mocha walls had been repainted a subtle ivory and Ivy's glass-fronted sideboard had been removed, giving the compact room a new sense of space. She returned to the kitchen. 'Can I give you a hand with the food?' she asked.

'No, thank you, love. You should take a seat and get the weight off your ankle.'

'Jeremy told you, huh? It's fine, really. It feels much better already.'

Ivy pressed her hands onto the edge of the worktop and swivelled her head to look at Rebecca. 'There was a time in my life when I, too, felt as though I had the world on my shoulders.'

As perceptive as ever, Ivy wasn't referring to her swollen ankle any longer. Rebecca clasped Ivy's hand and cut in. 'I would never compare my situation to what you had to endure.'

Ivy smiled. 'The solution is the same, love. Things

changed for me when I asked for help. When I realised I didn't have to deal with everything on my own. One little word and people rallied round.'

Jeremy appeared behind Rebecca and handed her a glass of red wine. She took the glass and breathed in the warming aroma. 'Thanks.'

'Now that you're OK with Lennox, will you come home?' Ivy asked. 'I feel terrible that my only son is back in town and he's sleeping in a bed and breakfast.'

Jeremy laughed. 'It's Gloria's bed and breakfast. The woman is practically family. Besides, I wouldn't want to cramp your style. Having your grown-up son kicking about isn't the best way to start a relationship.'

Ivy hesitated. 'We're not exactly at the start of our relationship,' she said, eyes glued to Jeremy, awaiting his reaction.

Jeremy placed an arm around his mother's shoulders and pulled her towards him. 'I know that. But it sounds as though you're at the start of a new stage in your relationship and I don't want to get in the way of that. Besides, Gloria's room has this incredible view over the water. That little patch of grass and shrubs you call a garden just can't compete.'

Ivy snatched the dishtowel from the worktop and flicked it in his direction. 'Have it your way. Let me give the boys a shout.'

Rebecca waited until Ivy had disappeared out of the back door. 'How are you really feeling?'

'I thought you weren't here for me,' said Jeremy.

'I'm not.' She took a sip of her wine.

'It's weird. And I feel weird saying that since we're all grown-ups.'

'I think a parent meeting a new partner is weird, whatever your age.' She meant Ivy, of course, but an image of Serena with her luscious blonde hair flashed into her mind, and Rebecca took another gulp of her wine. 'Did you notice the paintwork in the dining room?'

'I did.'

'Are you thinking what I'm thinking?'

Jeremy nodded. 'That Lennox has been decorating. It's good that she has someone to help her out.'

'That's not what I was thinking.'

'Mummy!' squealed Oliver, running towards her and stretching his arms around her waist. 'I scored sixteen goals.'

'Sixteen! Oh my goodness. That's a lot of goals,' said Rebecca.

'Well done, buddy,' said Jeremy, ruffling up Oliver's hair.

A forlorn-looking Liam slouched through the door and Rebecca knew from the look on his face that he was disappointed by his goalkeeping skills.

'What's with the face?' Jeremy asked.

'I let in sixteen goals,' said Liam.

'And how many did you save?' asked Rebecca.

'It doesn't matter how many you save,' said Liam. 'It only matters how many you let in.'

'That's true for match day,' said Lennox, carrying two bowls, steam rising from the food inside. He herded everyone through to the dining room. 'But when you're practising, the goals you save are just as important as the ones you let in. Those are the goals you learn from, and it's that practice that makes you better on match day.'

'Really?' Liam asked, turning to Rebecca to double-check Lennox's statement.

'That's right,' she confirmed. Liam brightened and gave his brother a high-five.

'Has everyone washed their hands?' Ivy asked, appearing with another two bowls of food.

Oliver and Liam dashed out of the room, and Rebecca sent Jeremy after them to make sure they scrubbed their hands properly while she helped Ivy to bring through the rest of the food.

Once everyone was seated and had filled their plates, Jeremy cleared his throat. 'Boys, I have some exciting news.' The boys rested their elbows on the table and leaned forward, mirroring each other's actions. 'I went to see a lady at the council today and she told me we're allowed to keep Olive and Marmalade on our farm.'

'Forever?' asked Liam.

'Yes, forever,' said Jeremy.

Rebecca made a mental note to look up the life expectancy of a sheep.

Oliver smiled. 'I think that's going to make Olive very happy.'

'I think so, too,' said Jeremy. 'And hopefully that means she'll stop trying to head-butt me,' he mumbled to Rebecca.

'It sounds like you boys are going to be very busy helping Daddy on the farm,' said Ivy.

The boys nodded enthusiastically, and Rebecca hoped their interest in the animals didn't wane as quickly as Liam's interest in guitar lessons had.

Oliver turned to Lennox. 'Are you going to marry Grandma?'

Rebecca put her hand under the table and rested it on Jeremy's thigh.

Lennox laughed and exchanged an amused look with Ivy. 'Maybe one day,' he said.

The muscles in Jeremy's leg tensed. 'Are you retired,

Lennox?' Rebecca asked, not so subtly steering the conversation away from marriage.

'Mostly,' said Lennox. 'I'm an architect. My business was successful enough for me to put my girls through university and for me to spend a ridiculous amount of time on the golf course. I still take on the occasional project when I'm in the mood, but nothing too taxing.'

Rebecca froze, feeling Jeremy's eyes on her. Oliver was wolfing down a bowl of chilli, having not even asked if it was vegetarian. She heard Jeremy take a breath, and she turned to glare at him, an unspoken instruction to not make a big deal out of it. 'That sounds like a good place to be,' Rebecca said to Lennox. Jeremy's gaze flitted around the room, looking everywhere except at Oliver.

'It is. It sounds like your farmhouse is a bit of a project,' Lennox said to Jeremy. 'You doing the work yourself?'

Jeremy picked up a bowl of paprika-spiced potatoes and handed it to Rebecca. 'My focus so far has been ripping the inside to pieces. I've just had it rewired, but it needs a new roof and every wall needs plastered before I can touch it. The camping cabins are being installed this week. You should come up for a look around.'

'I'd like that,' said Lennox.

Ivy smiled and the tension lines at the corners of her eyes smoothed out at seeing her son making an effort with Lennox. Rebecca added another spoon of potatoes to her plate. Lennox seemed like a decent man, and if Ivy had found someone she liked enough to introduce to her family, then Rebecca was delighted for her. The woman was long overdue for some luck in the love department.

With the boys having conspired with Ivy for a rare sleepover on a school night, Rebecca unlocked her front door and entered her cottage alone. Once she'd removed her coat and shoes, she paused, struck by the oppressive silence. Usually, she treasured an empty house. It meant she had an entire evening to get caught up with work, eat a meal that required little in the way of cooking, and have a glass of wine without having to put it down every few seconds to deal with the never-ending list of parenting duties. Tonight felt different, and it wasn't because she'd already had the food and wine. She'd made a decision that she wanted to be with Jeremy and she hadn't taken the only logical step to making it happen. It was time to make her decision real. In the dim light of her kitchen, Rebecca flicked the switch on the kettle and turned on her laptop. Boiling water bubbled in the background as she drafted the press release – *Ryan Knight becomes Thistle Bay Chocolate Company's new CEO*.

Tomorrow, everything would change.

32

By the weekend, nothing had changed. Ryan was making the most of the first snow in Glenshee and had gone off skiing for a few days. That's why Rebecca hadn't yet talked to Jeremy. He didn't need to know until the plans were in place. He'd only worry and question her decision and she didn't need that. She wanted to give their relationship the best chance of working and that meant something else in her life had to go.

The week had gone by fast, though. Jeremy had worked all hours on the farm. The camping cabins were fully installed, a replacement road had been laid, and the place was losing its building site appearance. Plus, Rebecca had watched Serena say her goodbyes to Jeremy with nothing more than a warm smile and a handshake.

On Sunday morning, Rebecca arranged to meet Cat and Elizabeth at Mystic's for coffee and cake, challenging herself to chat about anything except work. For once, that was going to be easy. Until she could speak to Ryan, work was a topic she was happy to avoid.

She got Oliver and Liam their own table in the corner

and left them to sit by themselves colouring a homemade congratulations banner for their dad and feeling very grown-up.

Elizabeth had arrived and ordered first. She loaded three mugs of coffee onto a tray and joined Rebecca at the table in front of the fire.

Rebecca chose the sofa facing the back of the coffee shop. 'I'll sit this side so I can keep my eye on those two.'

Elizabeth flopped down on the opposite sofa. 'Here she comes. How's the hangover?' Elizabeth asked Cat as she neared their table.

'Non-existent. I slept it off until about,' Cat made a show of looking at her watch, 'half an hour ago.'

'Heavy night?' Rebecca asked.

'Yeah.' Cat removed her coat, flung it over the back of the sofa, and sat down next to Elizabeth. 'Rachel came through for a supposedly quiet night in. We somehow ended up in The Smugglers Inn and didn't leave until Christos made us.'

Rebecca really needed to invite Rachel Barnes to their next family get-together. As Cat's best friend since they were two ten-year-olds in foster care, she was as much family to Cat as any of the Knights were. Probably more so.

Mystic swept past their table carrying two mugs of hot chocolate with a topping of whipped cream and mini marshmallows. Shaved flakes of mint chocolate peppered the snowy top. 'Your order is up, Rebecca. I'll deliver it to the two customers in the corner, shall I?'

'Yes, thank you.' The boys dived into their drinks. Their giggling and slurping was on the verge of becoming too raucous, and Rebecca cleared her throat loudly to catch their attention. She put her finger to her lips, indicating for them to quieten down a bit.

A phone buzzed somewhere nearby and all three sisters reached out to check their mobiles.

'It's me,' said Rebecca. She plucked the phone from her handbag on the sofa beside her. 'Hey, Ryan.'

'Hi. You busy?' her brother asked.

'Just having a drink with Cat and Elizabeth.'

'Non-alcoholic, I hope.'

'Of course. It's not even lunchtime and we're saving ourselves for later.' Rebecca took a drink of her coffee and glanced towards the boys. Their heads were still down, their hands busy.

'About that,' said Ryan. 'I won't make it through for Jeremy's launch party tonight. Harry Mitchell just called. They're heading to Edinburgh as we speak, ready for our meeting tomorrow, but he's asked if there's any way we can do it tonight instead?'

'Tonight? But it's Sunday.'

'I know. Apparently, the rail strikes planned for tomorrow are going ahead and they want to get home again tonight if they can.'

Rebecca sighed. 'Can't they just do it over email like everyone else does these days? Or hire a car for the journey back tomorrow? And before you tell me again that he's old-fashioned, can I just remind you it's Sunday? He can't be that old-fashioned if he's working on a Sunday.'

'What's going on?' asked Elizabeth.

'The conference centre folks want to meet to conclude the deal tonight. Could you keep the boys this afternoon and take them up to Jeremy's with you? He's installing new fencing today, so I don't want to drop them off too early.'

Elizabeth nodded. 'Will you be back in time for the party?'

Rebecca pursed her lips. 'Probably not.'

'You should go to Jeremy's,' said Cat. 'I can head through to Edinburgh and take the meeting with Ryan.'

'Thanks, but Jeremy wants you there to see the place in action since you'll have to write about it for his website.'

'Rebecca, go to Jeremy's party,' Ryan insisted. 'I was just calling to let you know what was happening. I'm on my way back to Edinburgh now. I don't need you there. The meeting is just a formality. I can do it myself.'

Ryan could take the meeting by himself. The detail had been worked out and final contracts drawn up. This was just a handshake before signing on the dotted line, as far as she knew. But they'd never had a meeting yet when Harry Mitchell hadn't asked to change something. Rebecca pressed her fingers into her temples. She could take the meeting, then talk to Ryan face to face. 'I'll see you at five.'

Ryan was already in the boardroom when Rebecca arrived at their offices in Edinburgh. This was his territory. When they had outgrown their production capacity in Thistle Bay, Ryan had proposed opening a new facility in Edinburgh rather than trying to find other premises locally. She and their father had liked the idea, and Ryan had taken on the responsibility of sourcing both the location and the machinery needed to expand their production. Ryan had moved from Thistle Bay and was now a permanent resident in Edinburgh, spending most of his week in the city.

'You're early,' said Ryan, glancing at his smart watch. 'I wasn't expecting you for another half hour at least. Jane gave me a quiet call and has assured me the deal is done as far as she's concerned.'

'Let's just see if her dad agrees.' Rebecca removed her

scarf, stuffed it into her handbag, and hung her coat on the coat stand in the corner.

'Fingers crossed, then we can get you back on the road and up to Jeremy's, where you should be. Is he ready for the big launch?'

'I think so. He's still got a few things to finish up before he'll open for paying guests, but it's incredible what he's been able to pull off in just a few short weeks. You won't recognise the place next time you're up.'

'And how are things going with you two now Jeremy's back?'

Rebecca shrugged. 'He's been back before.'

'Not wanting to talk about it. Understood.'

Rebecca shot him a look. 'There's just nothing to talk about.' There *was* something to talk about, but she thought that conversation was best kept until after their meeting. 'What's our plan for just getting this contract signed?'

'We ran the first test of the personalised bags last week. The samples are in there.' Ryan pointed to a cardboard box at the other end of the table. 'I'm hoping when Harry sees them, he'll be keen to get started.'

Rebecca peered into the box. 'I'll lay these out,' she said. 'They look impressive. Are you happy with them?'

'I am now. It took me so long to get the labelling right, but we worked it out and I think it looks perfect. If we get the contract, I've sourced another machine that will make it easier to do smaller production runs. To do that, we had to stop production on Line Three and change the packaging and labels to run these through. It's doable. It would just be more efficient to have a dedicated line for smaller production runs. We can turn the machines on and off when needed rather than re-planning our main lines.'

Rebecca nodded. 'Makes sense. Hopefully, this meeting

is just a formality as you say. But before we commit to anything, are you still keen on the idea?'

Ryan thought for a moment. She liked that about him. He wasn't impulsive, and he didn't chase shiny new things if he didn't see how they fitted into their longer-term business goals. 'I am. Diversifying our income is always a good idea, and I think this allows us to dip our toes into the corporate world without it detracting from our core business.'

'I just wish Cat had been prepared to help. It was her idea and I think it would have been good for her to see it through.' Cat had agreed to a contract to maintain Thistle Bay Chocolate Company's website, but otherwise had sidestepped every other attempt Rebecca had made to involve her more in the business. Getting to know Cat outside of work was going well, but Rebecca still had to make sure Cat knew there was a place for her in the business if she ever wanted it.

'Cat helped me with the label design, actually,' said Ryan, getting up to pour them coffee from an urn at the back of the room.

'I thought we had a design company do that for us?'

'We did. Cat came with me to brief them and helped me refine the early design concepts. What you saw was the final three.'

Rebecca chewed the end of her nail and took the mug of coffee Ryan offered her.

'What's with the face?' Ryan asked.

'What face?'

'Are you miffed about Cat being involved?'

'Of course not. I want her to get involved. I've been asking for her help for weeks.'

Ryan pushed her hand holding her coffee towards her, and she took a gulp. 'You haven't been asking her for her help. You've been asking her to give up her business and come and work in ours.'

'Is that so terrible? It's a family business and I just want to make sure she knows there's space in the family for her.' Rebecca scanned the new artwork on the walls and the mocha-coloured feature wall. 'By the way, what happened in here?'

'Good, isn't it? Another one of Cat's suggestions. She thought the room was boring. That's not the word she used, but it's what she meant. Arthur painted it, and Cat got Nick to frame some of the factory shots he'd taken when he was photographing for the website.'

Ryan's watch buzzed and the screen lit up. 'That's Jane. They're outside. I've got rolls from the coffee shop near me in the kitchen. I'll get the rolls. You get the visitors?'

'Sure,' said Rebecca. She took another look around the room. It appeared Cat was still making her mark on the business despite resisting all of Rebecca's attempts to include her. She glanced at her phone. If they could get the meeting concluded in the next hour, that would give her time to speak to Ryan and get back to Thistle Bay and make it to at least a bit of Jeremy's launch party. She'd messaged him. She should have called him and told him herself that she might not be there, but she didn't want to hear the disappointment in his voice. Not when she was so close to being able to give him the happily ever after he'd come home for. Rebecca stashed the used coffee cups in one of the low cupboards along the back wall and followed Ryan out of the boardroom.

33

With the newly named Olive and Marmalade watching his every move, Jeremy had worked all day to sink his new fence posts into the ground. Grateful that yesterday's rain had thawed the ground, he swung his sledgehammer in the air and whacked it down on the top of the last post, settling it into its designated hole.

He tossed his hammer onto the grass and glugged down half of his bottle of water. 'Do you see the extra work you two are causing me?'

Olive offered a loud bleat, her reply sounding less aggressive than usual. They'd reached somewhat of a truce in the last few days, which meant Olive had stopped trying to attack him every time she saw him. Jeremy sauntered to the fence enclosing the sheep in their field. Marmalade came over and allowed him to scratch the top of her head as she leaned against the fence.

'The place is looking pretty good, don't you think?'

Jeremy surveyed the view in front of him. He had transformed Archie Henderson's farm into his vision. The kids' play park was still an open space, but the archery field was up and running. Colourful targets lined the enclosure, standing out against the green landscape and ready for a row of kids gripping their bows and releasing their arrows towards their golden centres. Jeremy had created designated spaces for bike storage, den building, and bush craft workshops.

Each of the four camping cabins had its own outdoor dining space. He'd only completed the decking around one cabin so far, but he'd finish the others in time. The hexagonal barbecue cabin in the middle of the accommodation field was everything Jeremy had hoped it would be. With its Nordic spruce timber structure and grey felt roof, it was deceptively large inside without dominating the space. Up to twenty people could gather to cook family meals or lounge on the benches around the open grill. Today, he would fire it up and see it in action as he prepared a feast for his friends and family.

Elizabeth was bringing the boys, so all he had left to do was pop to Gloria's for a shower and collect his mother, who had insisted on helping him to set up the food and drinks before the guests were due to arrive. He was trying not to read too much into Rebecca bailing and telling him by text as casually as if she was running late for lunch.

Jeremy gathered up his tools and picked up the shovel he'd been using to dig the fence posts in.

'It seems like someone is enjoying the outdoor life.'

Jeremy turned to see Nick Bell standing behind him with his camera bag strapped across his body and carrying two stacked cardboard boxes. 'Always have. One of the reasons I enjoyed being a Marine. A cosy office job was never for me.'

'Same here.' Nick cast a glance towards the shovel in Jeremy's hand. 'You seem to enjoy the farming life, too.'

'If Mystic has sent you here to convince me to keep those sheep, you can tell her they're staying.' As if on cue, one of the sheep gave a loud bleat, and from the cranky nature of the noise, Jeremy was sure it was Olive.

'Nah. Cat sent me.' Nick dropped the boxes onto the grass. 'She wants some photos before the party kicks off. Sounds like I should take some portraits of these famous sheep, too.'

'Only if you want to be head-butted by a farm animal.'

Nick patted the bag slung across his body. 'That's what the big lenses are for. Close-ups from a distance. Do they really head-butt you?'

'One of them has. Although she only seemed to do it to me. She literally eats food out of Oliver's hands and lies down at Susie's feet.'

Nick laughed. 'You must be giving off an *I'm going to sell you for someone to make burgers from you* vibe.'

Jeremy rubbed a sweaty hand across the back of his neck. 'Well, not anymore. And as weird as it sounds, it's like they know. What's all this?'

Nick opened the flap of one of the boxes. 'Cat thought you probably wouldn't have much onsite yet, so she pulled together some props to decorate a cabin.'

Jeremy crouched down and rummaged through a collection of crisp white bed linen, towels, candles in green glass jars, an artificial aloe vera plant, and other knickknacks to turn the only furnished cabin from a bare box of wood into a cosy holiday home.

'Where did she get all of this?'

'She borrowed it from Gloria. This is the daytime box, apparently. She'll be here shortly with an evening box including fairy lights, blankets, and red wine for a few photos that will appeal directly to stressed-out parents.'

Jeremy yanked up a box. 'I'd better get decorating then.'

Nick picked up the other box and scanned Jeremy's filthy clothes. 'I think you'd best just leave everything in the box until Cat gets here.'

Ivy was at her front door waiting for Jeremy when he arrived. Lennox stood just behind her. She had a broad grin, pink on her cheeks, and a glisten in her eyes that reminded Jeremy of how far they had both come.

He walked up the short path to her door. The new welcome mat caught his eye first, with its crisp lettering yet to be blurred by muddy shoes. 'So, when were you going to tell me you've been decorating the house to sell it?'

His mother's cheeks flushed to the tips of her ears. Rebecca's hunch had been right.

'I'm not in a hurry. The house will be here until your farmhouse is ready. I know you don't want to move back home, but it's here for you if you need it.'

Jeremy nodded. There was no point trying to persuade her he wouldn't need to move back home. He'd show her instead. 'Ready to go?'

'Yes. Can't wait.' Ivy bounced off the step, leaving Lennox to close the door and lock it behind them.

Jeremy opened the car door, and Ivy climbed into the passenger seat. 'Thank you for asking Lennox to come along,' she said in a hushed tone.

Jeremy leaned into the car. 'Of course. This is a friends and family event and it seems like he's now a bit of both.'

His mother grinned at him as Lennox took a seat in the back and closed the door. Jeremy liked to see her happy, and if Lennox added to that happiness, then that was just fine by him.

They drove up the newly tarmacked entrance to the farm. It wasn't the most rustic of entrances, but it provided easy access and egress and he didn't fancy having to help his customers push their cars out of muddy holes and off grass verges.

'What on earth? Why is everyone here so early?' asked Jeremy.

The space he'd allocated for guest parking was already full, with vehicles spilling over onto the white gravel driveway he'd installed for reasons of security and proper drainage. With strangers sleeping on his land, he wanted to hear guests arriving or intruders skulking around his property. He figured the latter was unlikely, but training and experience made planning for that possibility second nature.

Jeremy parked in front of the house. He opened the car door, exiting to a sea of faces and a round of applause from the friends and family who had helped him on his journey over the last year, and the last few weeks in particular. Well, almost everyone.

Oliver and Liam had centre stage as usual, each holding one end of a banner that read *Congratulations Daddy* with what looked like a splodge of dried hot chocolate on a crinkled corner. They whooped with delight at the excitement of it all.

Cat stepped forwards, and the crowd quietened. 'I know you weren't expecting us for another hour, but we thought you'd worked so hard you deserved a little surprise, too. The floor is yours.'

Jeremy grinned at the children and cleared his throat. 'Most of you know I'm not big on speeches,' he said, 'so I'll keep this short. This is the beginning of a new chapter for me. The house is still a building site inside, but my dream of using the land to create a business that allowed me to stay here with my family, my boys, has been realised. Rugged Retreats officially opens for business in January, and thank you to each and every one of you who has helped me to do that. Now, let's fire up the barbecue.'

Jeremy followed the crowd down the winding monoblocked path built for guests to travel from the main entrance to the camping cabins without having to stomp across the grass with their luggage. Someone had switched on the green lights that shone up from the path's edges. With the winter daylight fading fast, the farm had a whimsical vibe that helped to hide the handful of unfinished jobs.

Oliver and Liam ran around the grass giggling and playing fetch with Skye, Nick's dog, and a squeaky squirrel. Nick followed them around with his camera, snapping pictures as they shot past him. Jeremy watched the boys scurry across the grass to the food that had mysteriously made its way out of his makeshift kitchen and been unboxed onto trays and plates he'd never seen before. It seemed Cat had taken it upon herself to set up his party before he got back with his mum, and she'd done better than he would have.

Oliver and Liam snuck handfuls of the roasted peanuts someone had placed in a bowl at the far end of the table. When they scampered away with not-so-subtle giggles, thinking they'd evaded detection, Jeremy lifted the bowl of nuts. Given that the boys had been rolling around the ground and playing with Nick's dog, he'd save that bowl just for them. The little dog trailed at their heels, seemingly sensing they were the most likely source of food.

Cat had taken on the role of hostess and was making

sure everyone had a drink from the copious quantities of alcohol that he'd laid out earlier on one of the wooden picnic benches. His mother mingled with a glass of red wine in one hand and a silver platter of savoury pastry canapés that he assumed Josef had made in the other. Josef had declared his intention to bake for the event despite Jeremy insisting he was to attend as a guest, not a supplier. It was only supposed to be Cat and Nick who were pulling double duty as working guests, Cat to experience the park in action and get some inspiration for the new website's copy and Nick to take some website-worthy photographs.

Alan Knight, Josef, Lennox, and Archie Henderson were holed up around the fire inside the barbecue hut. The tang of seared meat and burning wood hung in the air.

'It must be strange for you to see this,' Alan said to Archie.

Archie shook his head. 'Not at all. It's good to see new life breathed into the space.'

Jeremy left them to the cooking, took his mother's hand, and led her to the camping cabin he'd kitted out for him and the boys to sleep in that night. He adored the curved walls and the clean look of light wood and crisp white bedding, thanks to Cat and Gloria. With their sloped design and compact size, it was impossible to imagine that the inside was big enough to house a seating area, beds, a kitchenette, and a shower room. 'What do you think?' he asked.

Ivy smiled and clasped her hands together in front of her mouth. 'I've never seen anything like it. They're really beautiful.'

Jeremy wrapped his arm around his mother's shoulders and looked down at her. 'I think it's time for you to put your house on the market.'

Her grin widened, and a single tear slipped down her cheek. 'I'm so proud of you, Jeremy.'

'I'm proud of you, too, Mum.'

The pop from another bottle of wine being opened caught Ivy's attention. 'Time for a top-up.'

Cat was now manning the drinks table and had opened a bottle of Merlot.

'Cat!' called Josef as he left the barbecue hut and shuffled towards them. 'Before you pour that wine, I've got something here for Jeremy. In that blue bag there.'

Jeremy strolled to the table and followed Josef's gaze to a large reusable shopping bag tucked underneath. He hefted the bag up and deposited it on the bench. 'What do we have here?'

'It's a mulled wine urn,' said Josef. 'A little gift to wish you luck with your new venture. It's the same one I use when I sell mulled wine on the stall.'

'Are you allowed to sell mulled wine on the stall?' Cat asked.

Josef frowned. 'Why would I not be allowed to sell it?'

Cat shrugged. 'Wouldn't you need an alcohol licence for that?'

Josef gave a hearty laugh and smoothed his hand across his grey hair. 'I never gave that any thought. You're probably right, Cat.' He glanced around him, then leaned between her and Jeremy. 'Let's pretend you didn't just tell me that.'

Cat shook her head disapprovingly, and Jeremy smiled. 'I have a feeling you'd be able to talk your way out of that one if anyone official ever questioned it. I, on the other hand, am definitely allowed to serve alcohol, so let's have a proper look at this.'

'You don't already have one, do you?' asked Josef.

'No.' The tape on the box had already been sliced through. Jeremy opened the boxed and peeked inside.

'That's good because I've already opened it up and given it a good scrub, so I'm not sure I could take it back.'

'A gift was unnecessary,' said Jeremy. He put his hands down the sides of the urn and yanked it free from the box. Cat moved the cardboard away, and Jeremy slid the urn onto the table.

Josef unlatched the top of the stainless steel urn, allowing the festive scent of cinnamon, cloves, and orange peel to escape. 'I've used these little bags.' He stuck his hand into the urn and produced a ball of spices wrapped in a muslin cloth. 'Pour the wine in and set the temperature with that dial there, and the urn will warm it up for you. And it'll keep it warm. Although in my experience, seven litres of wine disappears fast in this town.' Josef chuckled, stooped under the table, and brought out another bag that he must have stashed under there earlier. He presented three glass jars and unclipped the lids. 'Flaked almonds, raisins, and orange slices.'

Jeremy leaned over the urn and breathed in the warming spices and the fruity notes in the wine he poured in. He picked up another bottle of red and Cat handed him the bottle opener. 'This is the perfect gift, Josef. Thank you.'

'You're welcome. A cold night, good company, meat sizzling on the fire, and a little *glühwein* to warm the soul – with a combination like that, your business will thrive.'

Jeremy put his arm around Josef's shoulders. 'I think it will.'

Josef ambled back to the barbecue hut with Cat. Nick had moved on from chasing the boys around and was now photographing Susie's outstretched arm as she stood facing a cabin and clutching a glass of red wine.

Jeremy sidled up to Gloria. 'When the bookings come in, I'm going to need someone to help me out. Susie Jacobs would be perfect. She has great customer service skills and is fantastic with the sheep. What are my chances of being able to entice her away from the coffee shop without Mystic falling out with me?'

Gloria grinned and patted him on the arm. 'I might have a solution for you.'

'Really?'

Gloria nodded. 'Do nothing for a few days and I'll get back to you. Now be an angel and top up my glass, will you?'

With Gloria's glass refilled, Jeremy stood for a moment to take in his surroundings.

The swelling inside his chest was the feeling he wanted to create for his guests. Rugged Retreats wasn't about lads challenging themselves and getting dirty on obstacle courses. That was part of his old life. It was about families having a precious few days of fun together. He looked at Oliver and Liam rolling around on the grass with a never-tiring Skye. Rugged Retreats was about playing together, eating together, and making memories together that would last a lifetime. It was perfect. He was happy. Mostly. Rebecca being here to share his opening night was the only thing he would change.

Cat reappeared and caught his eye. 'You OK?'

Jeremy poured a glass of the now warmed wine and handed it to her. 'Did you organise all of this for me?'

Cat shook her head. 'Nope. It was Rebecca. She got everyone here early so they could surprise you. She gave each of us jobs; I was on decoration, Nick did the lighting, and Elizabeth plated up the food.'

He couldn't believe Rebecca had done all of this and

then hadn't bothered to show up to see it. Her head was all over the place and it wasn't good for either of them.

Gloria tucked napkins into the front of Oliver and Liam's coats. Alan handed them each a burger in a roll, and Liam dropped his on the grass before he could take a bite. Skye pounced on the beef in a heartbeat and scurried away, her little jaw bulging, before anyone could intervene. Jeremy smiled, trying to hang on to a fading feeling of happiness. There was no chance of anything more happening between him and Rebecca. Maybe it was time he accepted that and moved on.

34

Two hours and one agreement in principle later, Rebecca shoved the main door of their Edinburgh offices open and shivered as a rush of cold air barrelled into her. If she had a clear run back to Thistle Bay, she would make it to Jeremy's in time to show her face at his party. The conversation with Ryan had been rushed, but at least they'd had a chance to talk face to face. He had just said that the consequences of her decision were something they both needed to think about carefully. She'd thought of little else for the last week, analysing every pro and con she could think of, and each time she had come to the same conclusion. Ryan taking over the business changed everything. But that was the point.

She strode towards her car, slipping her hand into the zipped pocket of her handbag for her car keys. Her fingers touched nothing but the smooth satin lining. She opened her bag wide and dug through every pocket. She yanked out the scarf she'd stashed earlier and shook it, hoping her keys would drop to the ground.

'Damn it!' She pulled the office door open again,

slinging her bag back over her shoulder, and stomped towards Ryan's office.

Ryan was unplugging his laptop and stowing it in its case when Rebecca appeared in his doorway. 'You haven't seen my car keys, have you?' she asked.

'No.' Ryan zipped up his laptop case. 'Have you checked the boardroom in case they've fallen out in there?'

Rebecca nudged the chairs in front of Ryan's desk out of the way to check underneath them. There was nothing but a dropped pen. She scooped it up and chucked it towards Ryan.

Ryan opened his desk drawer and swiped the pen in. 'Come on, I'll help you look.'

The boardroom was frustratingly clean with no sign of her missing keys. Rebecca kicked the bin, hoping to hear metal jangling inside, but there was nothing but paper.

Ryan was on his knees, rummaging inside the low cupboards. 'They won't be in there,' said Rebecca.

'Keys have a habit of showing up in the unlikeliest of places.' He sighed and stood up. 'But just not in these cupboards.'

Rebecca blew out a breath and paced around the room.

'What time do you need to pick up the boys?'

She shook her head. 'It doesn't matter. They're staying with Jeremy tonight. Their first night in the camping cabins.'

Ryan dug his hand into his pocket and produced his car keys. 'Take my car and hopefully you can still make it to Jeremy's before the party ends.'

Rebecca pulled her phone from her pocket and looked at the time. 'I need my car. I'll have to stay here and call out the recovery company.'

Ryan steered her towards the door and tossed his car

keys at her. 'Go. I'll sort out your car and drive it up tomorrow.'

Rebecca fought his grasp. 'I can't let you do that.'

'You can. Vehicle recovery is a corporate contract, so I don't need you here. Right now, it's Jeremy who needs you.'

She held out Ryan's car keys, but he closed her hand around them. 'Thanks,' she said.

Rebecca climbed into Ryan's car. Her brother thought he was doing her a favour, but her missing car keys seemed to her like a sign that she shouldn't go. She connected her phone to the vehicle's Bluetooth. She put the car in gear, dialled Megan's number, and drove out of the car park, listening to the international dialling tone.

'Hey, Rebecca,' said Megan, answering. 'What's happened?'

Rebecca sighed. 'Nothing's happened. Why does everyone think something's wrong when I call them?'

'That's a question for you, not me,' her sister replied.

'Whatever. In your bedroom at Dad's house, there's a painting of a black spaniel. Is that Nick's dog?'

'That's right, it's Skye. I painted it last summer after one of Dad's barbecues.'

'I was thinking Cat might like it.'

'Oh yes. Tell her it's there. She's welcome to have it if she wants.'

'I think she'd love it, but I think she'd love it even more if you gave it to her. It's an ideal gift for one sister to give another sister.' Rebecca waited for Megan's thoughts, and after what seemed like too long a pause, she asked, 'Are you still there?'

'Under all that armour,' said Megan, 'you're a pretty amazing big sister, Rebecca. Now, why did you really call?'

Rebecca steeled herself for a bit of light mocking from

her sister. 'You believe in the universe sending you signs, right?'

'Yes,' Megan said without hesitation or judgement.

'Hypothetically, say you're going to an event that some people think is important.' Rebecca hesitated. 'Actually, it *is* important, but you lose your keys just before you go. That's a sign that you shouldn't go, right?'

'What event?' Megan asked.

'It doesn't matter what it is, does it?'

'Not really. I'm just curious.'

'Jeremy is opening his adventure park for friends and family tonight. I had to go to a meeting in Edinburgh, so I was always going to be late. But then just as I was leaving, I realised I've lost my car keys. Now I'm thinking it might be some kind of sign that I shouldn't go.'

'You sound like you're in the car. You found your keys then?'

'Ryan lent me his car.'

'I thought you didn't believe in signs from the universe?'

'I don't,' said Rebecca.

'There you go then,' said Megan. 'It's not a sign.'

Rebecca navigated the roundabout and increased her speed to join the dual carriageway. 'But you believe in stuff like that. You think it's a sign, right?' Rebecca had raked through the boxes of books her yoga-loving sister had left at their father's house before she'd jetted off to Majorca. She had an entire box of books, journals, and tarot cards on signs from the universe and activating the law of attraction. She even had a book on the spiritual meaning of animals. When Rebecca had once almost run over a fox, Megan had given Rebecca a lecture on the importance of spirit animals and being open to guidance from a higher power. Rebecca had insisted it was just a young fox with no road sense.

'To me, it's a sign,' said Megan.

'That I shouldn't go?' asked Rebecca.

'Actually, no.'

Rebecca gripped the steering wheel tighter. Her sister was infuriating sometimes and now Rebecca's mood was as dark as the early-evening winter sky. 'Can you stop talking in riddles and just tell me what you think?'

'You don't want to hear it.'

'I do want to hear it. That's why I called you.'

'OK, fine,' said Megan. 'Losing your keys is thought to represent feelings of insecurity. You don't feel in control and it's making you feel vulnerable. It can also be a symbol of a missed opportunity.'

Rebecca drove onto the Queensferry Crossing in silence.

'Does any of that resonate with you?' Megan asked.

'Yes. It tells me my first instinct was right. Signs from the universe are a lot of rubbish.'

'Then you have nothing to worry about,' said Megan cheerily. 'It's just missing keys. They'll turn up or you'll order a new set.'

'So how's Majorca?'

'I've started teaching this early-morning art class on the beach. It's all these retired ex-pats looking to do something creative before the sun gets too hot for them to go out.'

'How hot does it get in winter?'

'It was fourteen today, but that's tropical for them. They're a pasty bunch.'

Rebecca laughed, grateful to her sister for distracting her on her journey back to Thistle Bay. She wasn't feeling insecure and vulnerable. Yes, she liked to be in control of things, but it was literally her job, and her role as a parent. And she was in control.

By the time Rebecca arrived back in town, she'd been

fully updated on Megan's travels and she'd decided to drive to Jeremy's and show her face at the party.

In the darkness, Rebecca nearly missed the driveway. Jeremy hadn't yet erected a sign, and the gates were closed, which threw her off. She stopped Ryan's car in the gap in front of the gates and peered up the track. Everything was in darkness. She couldn't see any other cars in front of the farmhouse. The cabins were either also in darkness or too far away from the road for her to see any glow in their windows. Her shoulders slumped. She'd missed the entire thing.

Megan's words flitted into her mind. This wasn't her missed opportunity. This was Jeremy's event, not hers. The only missed opportunity for Rebecca tonight would have been if she hadn't gone to the meeting and the business had missed out on the conference centres contract. Besides, the meeting had been the perfect opportunity for her to talk to Ryan face to face. She'd owed him that much.

She left the warmth of Ryan's car and stepped towards the heavy metal gates. Her hand pressed against the icy bolt holding the gate in place as she studied her options. She looked up the dark track again. There wasn't any point in going in now. Her appearance would only wind the boys up if they were still awake. She dug her hands into her coat pocket and her fingers wrapped around a set of car keys. Her keys.

'Damn it!' She got back in her car and placed a call to Ryan.

35

THE FOLLOWING MORNING, WITH NO CHILDREN TO SLOW HER down, Rebecca showered and dressed quickly. She lingered in the kitchen, watching the time. When the clock struck quarter to nine, she grabbed a folder from her bag and headed to the bed and breakfast. There was a good chance Jeremy had swung by there after the school drop-off to pack up his limited possessions ready to move into the cabin.

Gloria stood behind her reception desk, huffing at the beeps coming from her laptop. 'You OK there, Gloria?'

'Update your software, it said. So I did. And then it just stopped allowing me to click on things.' She thudded her fingers on the keyboard. 'That's the last time I listen to you.'

'Do you want me to look?'

'No, thank you. I've just restarted it. That'll sort it. What can I do for you?'

'I was looking for Jeremy.'

'You just missed him.' Gloria gestured to the folder Rebecca held. 'I'd offer to take that from you, but he's taken everything with him so I'm guessing you'll see him before I do.'

Rebecca slid the folder across the reception desk. 'This is for you, actually.'

Gloria picked it up and looked inside. 'My boiler maintenance contract.' She smiled and came out from behind her desk. She reached her hand towards Rebecca's fringe and paused. 'Thank you.' She moved her hand away and squeezed the top of Rebecca's arm.

Rebecca pulled her closer, wrapped her arms around Gloria, and took comfort from their embrace. 'Oh, come on through, boys,' said Gloria, pulling back. 'I've laid out coffee for you in the dining room.'

Two workmen had appeared in the hallway. They nodded to Rebecca and disappeared into the other room. 'Who are they?' she asked.

'The contractors. They're fixing that downstairs room.'

'I thought you weren't going to fix it until Megan was back.'

Gloria shook her head. 'No, no. Megan is just doing the mural. I'll have everything else sorted before then. New plastering, painting, and a new carpet.'

'I can help you with that. Have you already agreed a price with the contractors?'

'Rebecca, it may have been quite some time since you needed me to look after you, but it's still quite some time away before I need you to look after me. It's all in hand. There's nothing for you to do.'

Another beep from the laptop sounded. Gloria glanced back at her screen and smiled. 'It looks like everything is going to be just fine.'

Rebecca left the bed and breakfast and was diverted to Josef's stall by his wave. 'You look like a girl in need of a pastry.' Josef picked up his metal tongs and scooped up a horseshoe-shaped pastry sprinkled with almonds, its ends

Snowfall and Second Chances

dipped in chocolate. He held it out for her. 'This will put colour back in your cheeks in no time.'

Rebecca rummaged in her handbag for her purse, but Josef waved her away. 'On the house,' he said.

'Thanks. I'm actually famished.'

'Oh yes, I can imagine those little boys of yours keep you pretty busy in the mornings. Being a baker, I was always up and out of the house well before the school run started.' Josef reached to his right-hand side and touched something. Some kind of memento of his wife perhaps, given the faraway look in his eyes. 'Eat something and have Mystic make you a coffee before you go to work. Sometimes putting yourself first is what's best for everyone. They tell you that every time you take a flight.'

'A flight?' Rebecca bit into her cake, not sure what detour this conversation had just taken.

Josef nodded and rearranged his pastries to cover the gaps. 'Yes. Put on your own oxygen mask before you help someone else. You can't help anyone if you're unconscious. It's a good life lesson, I always think.'

'Unconscious?'

Josef guffawed at her confusion. 'You can't make others truly happy if you're not happy yourself. It's as simple as that. I said the same thing to your sister the other week.'

'Cat?'

Josef shook his head. 'No, the other one. The one who's just broken up with her boyfriend.'

'Megan?'

'That's her,' Josef said, glancing behind Rebecca.

Rebecca turned to see a queue had formed. 'I'd best let you get back to work. Thank you for this.'

She took Josef's advice and grabbed a couple of coffees from Mystic's before heading up to Jeremy's farm, all while resisting the urge to phone Megan and find out why she hadn't mentioned her relationship was over. If Megan had wanted to talk about it, she would have.

Rebecca arrived at the farm and looked out over what had been nothing but a crumbling old farmhouse and half a dozen green fields. Jeremy had transformed it into a welcoming and social space for friends and families to gather. She followed the path to the barbecue hut, led by the scent of burning wood. The door was ajar, giving a glimpse of the flickering orange flames inside.

A flutter of excitement filled her stomach at the sight of Jeremy standing beside the fire and, for once, going nowhere. And neither was she. Jeremy came out to meet her, and she handed him a coffee as somewhat of a pathetic peace offering. 'I'm sorry I missed last night.'

Jeremy stepped in front of her, took both drinks, and placed them on the floor just inside the wooden cabin. He took her hands in his. 'Close your eyes,' he said. She arched an eyebrow at him and he laughed. 'Nothing bad is going to happen. I promise.'

'That doesn't reassure me any.'

Jeremy took a deep breath and closed his eyes. 'Come on, Bex. It's worth it.'

She closed her eyes, but peeked at him every couple of seconds, almost expecting to be shoved into a mound of mud or for a sheep to appear at her side and try to eat her coat. Jeremy's breathing was steady and his eyelids didn't so much as twitch.

Deciding her scepticism was unwarranted, she took a deep breath and closed her eyes. She matched her breathing to Jeremy's and clutched his hands a little tighter. The to-do list permanently etched in her mind seemed to clear with each intake of cool air. Her shoulders relaxed down. She hadn't even been aware they were tense. The only sound was their breathing and gentle rustling from nearby bushes. She imagined hedge sparrows flitting in and out of the branches, rummaging around for food.

With two five-year-old children, silence was rare, and she never took the opportunity to really notice it. Her house was only quiet when the boys were in bed and the first thing she usually did then was grab her laptop and fill that silence with furious typing.

The air was calm and fresh. She felt anchored to the spot and anchored to the man who held her hands.

She opened her eyes, blinking a few times at the bright sky. Jeremy watched her. The brown of his eyes picked up flecks of green from the surrounding landscape.

'I love you, Jeremy,' she said. 'And not just because of the boys. I'm in love with you, and I can't see you every day and not be with you. When I think about . . .' She stopped and swallowed hard, trying to clear the emotion that ached in her throat.

He grinned, giddy with joy, and pulled her into him. Her arms slid around his waist. 'I love you, too,' he said. 'But you know that. It's always been you, Bex.'

Rebecca laughed and swiped at her watery eyes. She rose on her tiptoes, coming face to face with him, and planted a kiss on his lips. He glided his fingers through her hair at the nape of her neck and kissed her back. She was right where she belonged. She snuggled closer to him and felt a swelling in her chest. Her fear had almost prevented her from having this.

Jeremy pulled back, his hands settling on her hips. 'Are we really doing this?'

She couldn't blame him for his hesitation. For weeks she'd done nothing but tell him it wouldn't work between them. Her body trembled and she closed her hands around his forearms to steady herself. 'We're really doing this. Here is where I want to be.'

'What happened to *nothing lasts forever*?'

Rebecca shook her head. 'We don't need it to last forever. Just another fifty years or so.'

Jeremy laughed, wrapped his arms around her waist, and tucked her head under his chin. 'I think we can manage that.'

His lips skimmed her hair, then moved to her cheek and down to her neck before finally finding her mouth. Their kiss was full of hunger and desire. He held her gaze as he led her to his cabin. She was in love with this man, and he felt the same. A shiver of excitement rushed through her body. She felt herself unravelling under his touch, and for once, losing control didn't scare her.

36

Jeremy emptied the cold coffee into the sink and tossed the takeaway cups Rebecca had brought into the recycling. It was all finally happening. He was home with his boys, his business was in good shape for its launch, and Rebecca was ready to take the next step with him. He'd never seen her so emotionally exposed, so vulnerable. After tiptoeing around their emotions for so long, they'd finally said they loved each other, and it had been electrifying.

She was still anxious about it all. She'd hesitated before she left, probably fighting the urge to remind him they were still taking things slowly, but she stayed quiet. He was grateful she'd chosen not to kill the mood by talk of practicalities. It wouldn't be smooth from here on in, nothing between them ever had been, but he was looking forward to figuring it all out. Together.

His stomach grumbled for a late lunch. He stepped outside, and the crisp country air filled his lungs as he locked the cabin door. He headed straight for Mystic Coffee and ordered two bacon rolls.

'Have a seat. I'll bring them over when they're ready,'

said Mystic.

Cat and Nick were sitting in front of the fireplace, and Jeremy walked over. 'Mind if I join you?'

'Of course. Have a seat,' said Nick. 'We were just talking about you.'

'About my good looks and charming nature, I presume.' Jeremy tossed another log on the fire and a shower of sparks erupted inside the hearth, sending a fresh wave of heat in his direction. He took a seat on the sofa opposite the couple.

'About the good looks and charming nature of your new business.' Cat swivelled the laptop in front of her around to show Jeremy the screen.

Jeremy flicked through a folder of photos taken the day before. 'Thank you. To both of you. You've made the place look amazing.'

Cat turned her laptop around and snapped its lid closed. 'No. You've made the place look amazing. I have everything you need to get your website live and set up your booking software. Rugged Retreats is going to be sold out before you know it.'

'And great name, by the way,' said Nick.

'Thanks,' said Jeremy. 'I thought it had a bit of a ring to it.'

'Oh hi,' Cat said, looking behind him.

Jeremy spun around to see who she was talking to just as Ryan Knight sat on the sofa beside him. 'Have you seen Rebecca today?' Ryan asked.

Jeremy grinned. 'I have.'

'Then I'm sorry, but I think I'm about to wipe that smile off your face.'

Ryan handed him a sheet of paper. Jeremy looked down for just a second, then his gaze immediately shifted back to Ryan. He didn't need to read the full press release. The headline alone was enough. *Ryan Knight becomes Thistle Bay Chocolate Company's new CEO.*

'Is this public?'

Ryan shook his head. 'No. It's Rebecca's draft. She gave it to me last night.'

'And what did you say?'

'What could I say? There's no way I can talk her out of this. You know what she's like. And you and I both know why she's doing this.'

'Because of me.'

Ryan put a hand on Jeremy's shoulder. 'Sorry, mate.'

'What's going on?' Nick asked.

Ryan handed over the press release, and Cat and Nick scanned the document. Cat covered her mouth with her hand.

Mystic delivered Jeremy's bacon rolls, and he took a bite, the salty flavour of the bacon exploding in his mouth. He always thought better on a full stomach.

'Can I get you something, honey?' Mystic asked Ryan.

'Just a coffee,' said Ryan. 'I'll come and grab it.'

Jeremy had polished off one of his bacon rolls and had started on the other by the time Ryan came back. In between bites, he filled Cat, Nick, and Ryan in on his conversation with Rebecca that morning. Until Ryan had walked in the door, everything in Jeremy's plan had clicked into place. Only Rebecca had been keeping a hell of a secret from him because she'd known he would be livid about it. And he was. But venting his frustration wasn't the way to solve this particular problem. Jeremy took the last bite of his roll.

'Does Alan know about this?' asked Cat.

Ryan shook his head. 'No. I'm hoping we can fix it before he finds out.'

'What are you going to do?' Nick asked Jeremy.

Jeremy wiped his hands on a napkin. 'Nothing. Rebecca doesn't listen to reason. I'm going to pretend that I don't know and give her tonight to think about this.' He touched his hand to the press release. 'Can I have this?'

'Sure,' said Ryan. 'She told me she's been thinking about it for a while and her mind is made up.'

'Oh, I'm sure that's true. No one will persuade her she's made the wrong decision. She has to come to that conclusion on her own.'

Elizabeth bustled her way into Mystic's and appeared at their table clutching her phone, a small teal-coloured bag, and a hairbrush. Jeremy slid the press release towards her, but Elizabeth waved him away. 'I've seen it. I need a photo,' she said to Cat, tossing the bag towards her. 'Use whatever you want in there.'

Cat unzipped the bag and pulled out a stash of makeup. 'What's going on?'

Elizabeth beamed. 'I have an idea.'

'I'm not sure this concerns us,' Jeremy said to Ryan, rising to leave.

Elizabeth held her phone out on the palm of her hand. 'Actually, it does. Who wants to take the photo?'

Jeremy had no clue what Elizabeth was up to. Cat seemed to be on board as though some secret sister chat had been telepathically exchanged between the girls. Cat dabbed lip gloss on her lips, rubbed her hands together, then dragged the brush through her hair. 'Ready,' she announced.

The three men looked at each other. Jeremy shrugged and pointed to Nick. 'He's the photographer.'

Elizabeth flicked her phone to camera mode and thrust the device towards Nick. 'I'm making Rebecca a photo album.'

Cat grinned. 'Perfect,' she said.

Jeremy looked to Ryan, who held his hands up in an *I don't know what they're doing either* gesture.

Elizabeth sat beside Cat and they both flashed wide smiles while Nick snapped a dozen pictures. 'Rebecca has depressing photos everywhere. Oliver and Liam are practically babies in the photo on her coffee table. Ryan is an actual baby in the only photo she has of him, and poor Cat isn't anywhere. Neither are you, Jeremy. Sorry.'

'Hey, I'm on her screensaver,' Jeremy added in a huff.

'My point is,' Elizabeth continued, 'we've all grown up to be decent, kind, and capable individuals. That's in no small part because of Rebecca. But it's time for her to take a step back and let us take care of ourselves.'

'I think she realises that,' said Ryan. 'That's why she wants me to take the job.'

Cat and Elizabeth both shook their heads emphatically. 'She doesn't realise that at all,' said Elizabeth. 'She's not *giving you* the job. She's not *taking it* herself.'

'Ergo, giving it to me,' said Ryan, drawing out his words. 'That's the same thing.'

'No, it's not,' said Jeremy, catching up with Elizabeth's thought process. 'Rebecca thinks she can't look after her family, be a mother, be with me, *and* take the big job. You want to show her that none of you need looking after. She can lighten her load without sacrificing her career.'

'Exactly.' Elizabeth stood up. 'Now if you'll excuse me, I've got some photos to print.'

Cat jumped up. 'We can do that at Nick's gallery.' She turned to Nick. 'Can't we?'

'Help yourselves,' said Nick. Cat and Elizabeth bolted away. 'I think I'll get another coffee and keep out of the way. Anyone want anything?'

'No, thanks,' said Jeremy.

'You still think we should do nothing?' asked Ryan.

Jeremy stood up. 'Yeah, I do. She needs you to do your job and me to do mine.' He glanced at the time on his phone. 'And right now, my job is co-parenting and demonstrating I'm capable of taking our relationship as slowly as Rebecca needs it to go.'

By the time eight o'clock came, Jeremy was sprawling out on Rebecca's sofa and propping his feet up on the table. 'I think looking after two five-year-olds is more exhausting than trekking through the snow in Arctic Norway.'

Rebecca closed her laptop and hopped off the seat at the kitchen counter. 'Coffee, wine, or beer?'

'Wine. Red to warm me up, please.'

'Fancy some food?' she asked.

'Always. I'll cook. What do you have?' Jeremy had fed the boys leftover curry from the freezer while Rebecca had finished up some work.

'I was thinking a takeaway.'

'Excellent idea.' Jeremy jumped up and ran his hand across his stubbled jaw. He really needed a shave. Just because he was no longer in the military didn't mean he should let his standards fall away completely. 'If you call it in, I'll go and pick it up.'

'What do you fancy?' Rebecca asked him.

'Whatever you want is good with me.'

Rebecca fiddled with a few buttons on her phone, then looked back at him. 'Done.'

'What was that?'

'I ordered on the app.' She glanced away from him and

her cheeks flushed a little pink. 'My favourites are saved.'

Jeremy nodded and dropped back onto the sofa. He knew cooking wasn't one of Rebecca's favourite activities. She was strict about having family dinners with the children on weekends. Weekday evenings were a bit less planned, and having a takeaway on standby was probably pretty helpful.

'Did you get your work finished?'

Rebecca uncorked a bottle of red wine and left it on the counter to breathe. She pulled two glasses from a cupboard and joined him in the living room. 'The conference venue suppliers have officially signed the deal.'

'Brilliant. You need to celebrate.' He had a few ideas about how they could celebrate, but they all involved being upstairs and wearing very little clothing. Probably not the best way to show her he could take things at her pace.

She hadn't told him about her decision not to take the job and he didn't want her to. Not tonight. It was better for Rebecca to sit with her decision for another day. To try it on and see how it felt. He was certain she'd made the wrong decision. What he wasn't certain about was what it would mean for their relationship when she figured that out. He needed them to mark the start of their new relationship somehow, in a way that didn't freak her out. He pictured the antique diamond engagement ring he'd bought from Fred Cromarty when he'd dropped the creepy pictures off, its platinum band twisted gracefully around sparkling twin diamonds. She wasn't anywhere near ready for that. But he was, and he was happy to wait as long as it took for her to get there, too.

'Why are you smiling?' she asked.

'Was I?' He shrugged. 'Just happy, I guess. Hey, did I show you the kitchen I was thinking about?' he asked, to keep her away from work chat. He leaned forward, plucked a brochure off the coffee table, and flicked to a page with a bright white kitchen and a sleek marble top with light-grey veining.

'I don't think it's right,' Rebecca said, giving the page only a passing glance.

'Really? I thought you would love this.'

'Oh, I do. I just don't think it's right for the farmhouse. You need something more rustic. This is too new. It would just feel out of place.'

She turned a few pages and paused on a sage-green kitchen. Jeremy was antsy beside her. 'I'm not sure about that one,' he said.

'Ignore the kitchen. Look at this countertop.'

'I thought you would have gone for a lighter worktop.'

'I'm thinking lighter units. The room has two sources of natural light, but it's only from that small window at the front and the door at the back. If you go too dark, the room will feel dingy. I like the idea of a butcher-block style of worktop, a lighter counter for the island, then that wooden table you love in the dining space. The textures and colours are nice and balanced. It's modern meets rustic.'

'Sounds like us. You're sleek and fancy, and I'm a bit more rugged around the edges.'

Rebecca raised her eyebrows and tossed the kitchen brochure back towards him. She stood up. 'I'll get the wine. You get the food.'

The doorbell rang, and Jeremy jumped up to answer it. 'How did you know they were here?'

'I had a feeling,' said Rebecca.

'How very Megan of you.'

Rebecca laughed. 'The app vibrated.'

'Yeah, that sounds more like it.'

37

Jeremy had gone back to his camping cabin home after they'd eaten last night. Rebecca had asked him to stay, but he'd whispered in her ear, 'Taking it slowly, remember?' and she couldn't argue with that. Besides, she hadn't told him about her decision not to take the chief executive job. He would have tried to talk her out of it and it would have ended in an argument. She hadn't wanted to sour what had been a pretty perfect day.

An overnight snowfall had closed the school and kicked off the Christmas holidays a couple of days earlier than scheduled. Rebecca had no desire to power up her laptop. If someone needed her, they'd call. She got the boys dressed and headed outdoors. The town was a wintery wonderland. A single set of dainty footprints from a cat or maybe a fox created the only dents in the otherwise pristine landscape leading from Rebecca's cottage. That soon changed as Oliver and Liam raced across the street towards the park, the snow from the soles of their boots flying behind them.

When they reached the play park, Liam climbed the metal steps up to the top of the slide. He launched himself arms first down the slide, ploughing a mound of snow as he went.

Rebecca breathed in the crisp air and pressed her gloved hands to her cheeks for a moment of relief from the icy bite of December weather. Football was cancelled for the week, swimming lessons were finished until the New Year, and she didn't plan to pick up her laptop until at least after lunch today. She fished her phone out of her coat pocket, opened her camera, and snapped a picture of the boys rolling a giant snowball as the base for their snowman. She sent it to Jeremy and her family group chat, with an invitation for anyone who was around to join them.

Within minutes, Cat arrived carrying a silver faux-leather photo album and a carrot. 'I heard someone needed a nose,' she said. The boys giggled, snatched the carrot, and disappeared to the other end of the park in search of stones that could serve as buttons.

Cat handed Rebecca the photo album. 'I saw your message and thought it might be a good time to bring this round.'

Rebecca swiped away snow from the bench on the edge of the park and sat down. 'What is it?' She gestured for Cat to sit with her.

'A project Elizabeth has been working on. She said you needed some up-to-date photos. I thought it might be nice to give you an album full of choices. I enjoy flicking through my old photos.'

Rebecca opened the album and looked through the prints. The first one was the family photo Nick had taken at their dad's birthday party. There were shots of the boys on their first day of school, her brothers and sisters in various combinations, and the one of Rebecca, Jeremy, and the boys that was currently Rebecca's screensaver.

The only photograph not taken in the last year was the final one. It was an image of a young Rebecca cuddled up with her mother. They were reading an Agatha Christie novel together. Rebecca grinned at the memory. It wasn't just the mystery Rebecca had loved. It was the uninterrupted time with her mum, with none of her younger siblings in tow. Plus, her dad's objections to their choice of reading material stoked a tiny rebellious streak in Rebecca that she rarely indulged. 'How have I never seen this photo before?'

'I don't know. Dad gave us it.'

Rebecca didn't miss Cat's use of the title *Dad*. She'd only ever heard Cat calling him Alan. It represented a considerable step forward in putting the past behind them.

'Elizabeth put sticky notes on the prints she thinks should replace the ones in your living room.'

Rebecca touched the vibrant yellow note attached to the photo of her and their mother. 'I see that. That's such a . . . me thing to do. Thanks for bringing it round. I truly love it. And I guess my photos do need updating.'

'Elizabeth thought I'd see you before she would, so she asked me to pass it on to you.'

'Interesting seeing as Elizabeth and I literally work in the same building.'

Cat scooped up a handful of snow and rolled it between her gloved palms. 'Yeah, I figured I'd just play along with whatever Elizabeth's plan was.'

'Well, I'm glad you did. It's good to see you. I've enjoyed spending time with you these last couple of weeks. About non-work stuff.'

'Does that mean you're going to stop asking me to join the business?'

Rebecca tensed her shoulders. She could tell Cat she

would stop, but she knew herself. It would be hard. Thistle Bay Chocolate Company was a family business and she wanted everyone in her family to feel part of it. She had to be open about her own feelings, even if it wasn't what someone wanted to hear. 'Honestly, I can't guarantee that. I want everyone in the family to feel as though they have a place in the business. But I know that what that looks like is different for each of us. If you're happy maintaining our website and don't want to be involved in anything else then I'll do my best to respect that.'

Cat smiled. 'That's fair.'

The muscles in Rebecca's shoulders relaxed. 'I'm the same with Megan. Call it a big-sister duty or something.'

Cat placed the ball of snow she'd been working on between them on the bench. She scooped up another handful of snow. 'I like having a big sister.'

'How do you feel about three big sisters and a brother?'

Cat picked up the snowball between them. 'I'm learning to love it. I liked seeing Megan again. Do you think she'll ever come home for good?'

Rebecca nodded. 'I think so. Did you hear she's broken up with her boyfriend?'

Cat shook her head. 'No. Was it serious?'

'They'd been together about a year, but I never heard her planning for anything long term with him, so I think she's OK. Apparently, those matchmaking twins have a grandson they'd like to introduce her to, though.'

A laugh escaped Cat's lips. 'Thank goodness they're gone. They were so determined to set Nick up with their granddaughter.'

At the risk of ruining a great conversation, Rebecca broached a subject she wouldn't have hesitated to raise had it been Elizabeth or Megan. 'I couldn't help noticing that you flinched a little when the baby chat came up at the kids' Christmas fair.'

'Wouldn't you? Nick and I haven't been together that long. It's far too soon for that chat.'

Rebecca nodded to concede the point.

'Nick noticed, too. He questioned me on it later that night.'

'Yikes, how did that go?'

Cat laughed. 'Surprisingly well. I'm nowhere near ready for kids, I realised, but we both agreed we'd like to have them in the future.'

A warmth spread through Rebecca's body despite the cold. Cat sharing intimate details of her relationship felt like another sign that their own relationship was thawing. They were truly becoming sisters. 'That's good.'

'I thought so. It's a conversation I've never had with a guy before. It certainly wasn't one I was planning to have so soon with Nick, but it's good to know we're heading in the same direction, even if that direction is still a long way off. Do you know what I mean?'

'I do, actually.' It was what Jeremy had said when he'd first come home. All he had needed to know was that she wanted them to be together, and if she did, he didn't care how slowly she wanted to take things. They were together now. She was in love with him. That meant that if things didn't work out between them, it wasn't going to be easy to deal with regardless of how fast or slow their relationship moved. All she could do was lean in to their love for each other and trust that it was strong enough to see them through whatever challenges they faced.

Cat nudged Rebecca's arm. 'How do you feel about me attacking your children with snowballs?'

Rebecca removed her gloves, reached forward, and gathered a snowball of her own. The ice was sharp against her bare skin, but her gloves were cream cashmere and not snowball friendly. 'Girls against boys?'

Cat and Rebecca unleashed a blast of snowballs. Joyful giggles filled the air as Oliver and Liam retaliated with a hastily formed cluster of their own snowballs.

With Cat gone and the rest of her family missing in action, Rebecca got up to persuade the boys it was time to head back inside. Her phone vibrated in her pocket with a message from Jeremy offering to take the boys to let Rebecca work. She called out to the boys. The icy wind whipped around her. Her cheeks stung, and she dabbed away water from the corners of her eyes. Snowflakes landed on her coat and dissolved into the thick fabric like sugar melting on warm porridge. The morning light was fading already, as if the sky was ready to decant another few inches of snowfall.

'Mummy, I can't feel my fingers,' complained Oliver.

'I know, darling. Let me hurry on your brother and I'll take you both to see Daddy.'

Oliver immediately brightened. 'Will he have hot chocolate?'

Rebecca waved to Liam and gave him her hurry-up glare. 'I don't know, but he will definitely have cake. We'll pack a bag of goodies and take it with us.' The promise of cake was enough to send Oliver hurtling towards his brother, who was hanging by his legs on the monkey bars. A few words from Oliver and Liam hauled himself upright and dropped to the ground. Both boys turned and sprinted towards her.

Back at the cottage, Rebecca packed a bag of food,

swapped her cashmere for ski gloves, and bundled the boys into the car for the short drive to Jeremy's farm. Although he had officially named his business Rugged Retreats, she had yet to move on from calling it the farm. The bleating from Olive and Marmalade every time she visited didn't help.

They drove cautiously through the deserted snowy roads and arrived at Jeremy's, finding him wrapped up and waiting for them in front of the house. The house was essentially a shell inside, but Jeremy had decorated it outside with icicle lights and half a dozen Christmas trees in red pots spaced evenly along the façade.

He took the bag of food Rebecca had packed. 'Let's head to the cabins. We can pack away this food, then play in the snow.'

Jeremy strode ahead along the winding path. He bundled Oliver and Liam into the barbecue hut, dumped the shopping bag on the floor, and shut the door on them. 'They'll be fine in there. The fire isn't on.'

Rebecca took her hands out of her gloves and moved towards the door. 'Jeremy, I can smell the smoke.'

'OK, fine, there's a babysitter in there.'

'Who?'

'It doesn't matter. What matters is that we have five minutes for us to talk.'

Rebecca shoved her gloves into her coat pocket. 'About what?' she asked, although she knew exactly what he wanted to talk about.

'I saw Ryan.'

'Look, Jeremy, it's for the best. It's what I want.'

Jeremy took her hand and clasped it between his warm palms. 'What chance do you think we have if you give up on your dreams to be with me?'

'I'm not giving up my dreams. I'm just asking for the opportunity to make a different decision.'

'You're not, though. You're making a compromise, a massive one, that doesn't need to be made.'

'But if I take the job, then nothing has changed. Our chances of making this work are . . .' She couldn't even bring herself to say the words. To acknowledge that failure was likely. 'If I take the job, then nothing has changed.'

Jeremy grinned with a certainty that Rebecca just couldn't share. 'Bex, everything has changed. We're finally being honest with each other about how we feel. And you being willing to step away from the top job is because you realise it doesn't have to be you. And you're right – it doesn't have to be you.'

'But it *can* be me. Is that where you're going?'

'The only place I'm going is inside that barbecue hut. I've got a bit of a snow day party going on in there. If you want to, we're going to go in together and celebrate our new love. Nothing more. The rest is up to you.'

Rebecca eyed Jeremy with a tinge of doubt. Was that it? She'd expected an argument, or at the very least, for him to attempt to talk her out of it. He gripped her hand tighter, put his other hand on the door handle, and waited.

'Is that really all you're going to say?'

Jeremy nodded. 'The decision is yours. Your career – the business, the job – that's just one part of you. I love all of you. Whatever you decide is good with me.'

'About this snow day party and celebrating our new love . . .'

He raised their arms and kissed the back of her hand. 'I know, I know. You want to take things slowly. I, on the other hand, want to make this official before you change your mind again.'

She smiled and nodded. 'That's fair. Let's do it.'

Jeremy yanked open the door. A roaring fire in the centre of the cabin and a cheer from their families greeted the couple. Alan and Gloria beamed with pride. Alan was one step closer to getting one of his children married off. Gloria was no doubt happy to give her matchmaking skills a rest, at least as far as Rebecca was concerned. Ryan should probably stay vigilant. Ivy dabbed at tears in her eyes and Lennox wrapped a comforting arm around her. Elizabeth had taken on responsibility for keeping Oliver and Liam in their place and had a protective hand on each boy's shoulder, which Rebecca was grateful for, given the flames flickering in the fire pit behind them. Ryan, Cat, and Nick grinned from benches on the far side of the open fire. Even Skye the dog had her eyes trained on the happy new couple, and thanks to her dad's phone, Megan was making an appearance via video call from what looked to be a sunny balcony in Majorca. The only hint of it being winter in Majorca was the shawl Megan had draped across her shoulders.

'Sorry I can't be there to witness your embarrassment, Rebecca,' said Megan, 'but congratulations. You didn't half take the scenic route, but you got there in the end.'

Rebecca laughed and gave Jeremy a peck on the cheek. She was far from embarrassed. She no longer felt the need to keep her private life quite so private. 'I'm going to let Dad put his arm down again. I'm thrilled for you guys. See you in February.' Megan waved from the screen of their dad's phone, then cut the call off.

'What's happening in February?' asked Rebecca.

'Megan is coming home. She's taking over from Susie at Gloria's, then we'll see,' said Alan, as relaxed as ever about Megan's comings and goings.

Rebecca looked around the room at the sea of faces, none of which looked as confused as she felt. 'What have I missed?'

Jeremy turned towards her to explain. 'I need *help* running this place, so Susie has agreed to work with me part-time. Gloria needs *help* running her bed and breakfast. Megan was going to be at a loose end until she figured out what she wants to do next, so she's going to *help* Gloria.'

'And just in case you missed Jeremy's sledgehammer of a point there,' said Elizabeth, rolling her eyes at Jeremy, 'whatever you decide, Cat, Ryan, and I are all here to help you.'

Alan cleared his throat. 'And I'm not going anywhere until April, so you've got time. Figure out what you really want and we'll take it from there. Everything is an option.'

When she saw her family's beaming faces, she could feel their happiness radiating. They had no expectations beyond showing their joy at Rebecca and Jeremy's good news and keeping warm on a wintery morning. Jeremy was right. Nothing had really changed, yet everything had changed. She'd shackled herself with obligations that only she had imposed on herself. Those shackles had somehow melted away and what she wanted, what she truly wanted, was obvious. She squeezed Jeremy's hand tighter and grinned, certain that she was making the right decision for the right reason. 'I want the job,' she announced.

'Really?' asked Ryan, already grinning.

'Don't feel pressured into it,' Jeremy cut in. 'You don't need to decide today.'

Rebecca smiled. 'I know. But it was never the job that had to change. It was always me. People don't need me as much as I think they do. That was a burden I placed on myself. I need to trust that the people I care about will ask me for help when they need it. And I need to allow people to help me, too.' She turned to Jeremy. 'I want you, and I want the job, as complicated and messy as that might be. I think we can handle it.'

Jeremy's face lit up with a wide grin. He wrapped his arms securely around her and lifted her from the floor. She threw her head back in laughter, and when her feet touched the floor, she pressed a soft kiss to his lips.

Elizabeth made a show of clearing her throat, catching everyone's attention. 'Over to you, boys,' she said.

Oliver and Liam unrolled the banner they had made for Jeremy and shouted, 'Congratulations, Mummy!' The word *Daddy* had been scored through in thick felt-tip pen and *Mummy* had been scrawled in the white space above. Her family's applause echoed around the wooden hut.

Rebecca gave the boys a hug before Elizabeth guided them away to watch the sausages sizzle. Ryan and Nick seemed to have put themselves in charge of cooking food over the open fire. Her family busied themselves with whatever they'd been doing before her entrance and Rebecca turned to Jeremy. 'This was a risky move,' she said.

'What do you mean?' he asked.

'I might have said no to the job.'

'Hey, we were only here to celebrate our new love. That's the only bit I was sure of. Everything else is on you.'

'Oh really? And the boys just happened to have their modified banner ready to brandish? It says *Congratulations, Mummy*, not *Congratulations, Mummy and Daddy*.'

Jeremy shrugged. 'That was nothing to do with me.'

Flames from both the fire and desire danced in Jeremy's eyes. He kissed her and tears sprang to her eyes. What she felt for him had never gone away. It hadn't even dulled with the passage of time and the thousands of miles often between them. She'd missed the moment that their teenage lust had transformed into love, but it didn't matter. She saw it now. Their love was real, and she wanted more of it.

'This is where I want to be,' she said.

He smiled. 'Me, too.'

'I'm sorry I made you take the scenic route.'

Jeremy pulled her towards him and wrapped his arms around her again. 'I'm pretty sure it was me who started us on that path.'

Rebecca ran her hand down Jeremy's back. 'Everything that happened led us here. And I wouldn't change a thing.'

Liam interrupted their embrace. 'Auntie Elizabeth said you two lovebirds need to eat.' He was gripping a plate holding two bacon rolls and two sausages in hot dog buns, his knuckles white as he held the plate still.

Jeremy took the plate, much to Liam's obvious relief. 'Auntie Elizabeth is right. Help yourselves, boys.'

Oliver and Liam snatched the sausage buns and shovelled the ends into their mouths. Oliver's days of wanting to be a stegosaurus seemed to be over.

'Are we sleeping over in the cabin again?' Liam asked between bites.

'Yes, I think we will,' said Rebecca.

'Are you staying, too, Mummy?' he asked.

'I am. I want to see what it's like to be a guest here.'

'It's so fun,' mumbled Oliver through his mouthful of food.

Rebecca slipped her arm around Jeremy's waist. 'I was actually thinking that Daddy should come and live with us. Then, when the farmhouse is ready, we should all come and live here. Together. What do you think, boys?'

'I'm going to go and tell Olive and Marmalade,' screeched Oliver, running for the door.

'Wait for me.' Liam darted after his brother, leaving the

barbecue hut door swinging on its hinges and a flurry of snow blowing inside.

'I think that was a yes.'

'Are you sure about this? You love your cottage. I never expected you to move up here.'

Rebecca snuggled closer to Jeremy. 'I told you. This is where I want to be.'

THE END

ACKNOWLEDGMENTS

It's been lovely to return to Thistle Bay and write Snowfall and Second Chances. My goal with my contemporary fiction is to write the kind of feel-good fiction I enjoy reading. I love small towns, cosy coffee shops, and unashamedly optimistic stories. I hope you have enjoyed reading Rebecca and Jeremy's story as much as I enjoyed writing it.

I'd like to thank Charlie Wilson for her editorial expertise.

Thank you to the team at MiblArt for my gorgeous cover design.

And, as always, thank you to Gavin, Evie, and Stuart.

ABOUT THE AUTHOR

Claire Anders was born and raised in a seaside town in Scotland. She now lives in Edinburgh with her husband and daughter. When she's not writing, you can usually find her walking her dog in the nearby woods or with a book in one hand and chocolate in the other.

Between Moons was Claire's first historical fiction novel. Claire also writes contemporary feel-good fiction with a touch of romance. All of her books feature strong friendships and supportive communities with a secret or two thrown into the mix.

facebook.com/claireandersauthor

ALSO BY CLAIRE ANDERS

Historical Fiction

Between Moons - A gripping WWII historical novel

Contemporary Fiction

Sunrise in Thistle Bay - An uplifting small-town romance

New Beginnings - A Thistle Bay short story

Snowfall and Second Chances - A festive feel-good romance

www.ingramcontent.com/pod-product-compliance
Lightning Source LLC
Chambersburg PA
CBHW021052080526
44587CB00010B/227